II Acts

Leading a 21st Century
New Testament Church

by Terry Broadwater

I believe we desperately need to come back to the truth about the Church and the truth about the roles and responsibility of leadership in the local church. We must rediscover the pattern, purpose, and power for ministry that the New Testament, especially the book of Acts, reveals! (Page 22)

As leaders, we must never become so caught up in "our" programs or "our" ministries that we fail to see the greater purpose to which we have been called. We are in the people-building business, not the program-building business. Our job is that of Christ-bearers. We are to bear the life of Christ within us, pouring it forth to touch and to build into the lives of those who have been entrusted to our care in the Lord. (Pages 49–50)

Leaders will face personal challenges. It simply won't work to ask others to change while we ourselves remain entrenched where we have always been. Leaders must first deal with their own personal issues before they can with integrity ask others to change....Leaders who are changing personally can in turn lead others to change. Personal change will always precede corporate change. (Page 57)

God has created His Church to function beautifully, all parts working together. Every part is crucial. When each part is doing what God formed it to do, a healthy church is the result. And a healthy church will be a growing church. There are so many seminars about church growth. But do you know what? We don't need them. I'll let you in on a secret: God is not concerned about growth; He's concerned about health. (Page 133)

Passion is an intense emotion. It compels us to action, and it brings with it a strong devotion. Passion is the energy of our souls. God created us to be passionate people – passionate about Him. The first place to focus our passion is in God. A passion for God will give you a purpose for life. (Page 139)

The church in which I serve as pastor is not "my" church; the ministry is not "my" ministry; and the people are not "my" people, either. Rather, it is Christ's church; it is His ministry through me, and it is His people to whom I'm ministering. The moment we seek to control these things, we lose the point. The Lord is not concerned with my taking ownership of my ministry; He is concerned with His taking ownership of me. (Page 151)

Leaders are to help people to make the most of their parts in the body. There must be room for each ministry and each gift to serve in some capacity. Every believer should have an outlet for ministry. This is true even for those who are very young in the Lord. If we follow Christ, we give, we serve; we don't simply take ministry into ourselves week after week, month after month. (Page 153)

Notice how Jesus spent three years investing His time into the lives of His disciples. Then they could invest into others' lives, who could in turn invest into others' lives. This is how the Kingdom is designed to grow. Each one reach one and teach one! (Page 188)

...the local church also has to make commitments. First, there is the commitment to instruct. It is not enough for people to show up; we must have something substantial to feed them. If they are willing to set aside the time to come, we must make certain that what we have to offer is worth the sacrifice they are making....they are sacrificing time that could be used elsewhere. (Page 205)

The case can be made that the Church must recover its New Testament identity and become the people of God pursuing the New Testament pattern and proclaiming the Good News through the power of the Holy Spirit. As this comes to pass, we shall see that "all that Jesus began to do and teach" will again be multiplied, mobilized, and manifested through the Church in every corner of the world. (Page 220)

The reason so many see making converts as the climax to their efforts is because it isn't that difficult to lead someone to Jesus. Having that same person become a follower of Jesus is much more difficult.... Evangelism leads people to Jesus, but discipleship is teaching, training, transitioning, and transforming people into followers of Jesus! (Page 223)

The mindset of the Church is changing from a maintenance mentality to a "mobilized for ministry" mentality. The "sheep" are becoming "soldiers." God's anointed and appointed leaders are emerging and leading the Church in a reformation as they get people in formation to go forth and make disciples of all nations. (Page 239)

Dedication

To my Lord Jesus Christ...
Be my Focus.
Be the Center of all I am and of everything I do.
Consume me, so that only You remain.
Burn away my flesh and pride.
Take my life; be the Lord of everything.
In the shadow of Your Glory
I will hide!

To my wonderful wife, Jo Ann...
You are my partner in LIFE.
You've stood by me when others retreated.
You've spoken faith in me when others remained silent.
You've run with me with the revelation.
Thank you for dreaming with me!
There are no adequate words to express how much I love you.
Imagine that!

To my amazing children, Casey, Corey and Cayla...
Three C's—creative, compassionate, and cool (sorry!).
You are far more than all I could have ever hoped for.
I count it a privilege to be your father.
Love, Dad

To my parents...
Mom, I hope all the "talks" paid off.
You've taught me how to persevere and never quit.
Dad, you never missed a game.
You've taught me that family is my first priority in ministry.
I love you both!

Acknowledgments

There are several key people whom I must credit with contributing signifi-cantly to my life as a leader in ministry. Without them, this book would not have been possible. They, and many others that I could mention, have taught me three simple, yet profound lessons for LIFE: (1) You can learn something every day from anyone; (2) Ministry is not an opportunity — it's a re-sponsibility; (3) Leadership is often leading people where they don't think they can go, to become what they don't think they can be, and to do what they don't think they can!

The church at Leesburg, The Worship Center...*Thank you for believing in a young couple and growing with us in the ministry. Look what the Lord has done!*

The church at Hagerstown, Bethel Assembly...*Thank you for releasing me to come alongside others in expanding the Kingdom locally, regionally, and globally. We are a family of families, and Jo Ann and I love you deeply!*

The Bethel Pastoral Leadership Team and Support Staff...*Curt, Missy, Alvin, Keith, Kevin, Bob, Kim, Adina, and "gang," thank you for taking min-istry seriously and for being willing to go to new levels of excellence and effec-tiveness. Remember, "P's" have power, acrostics are anointed, and HBO is just "Humble Broadwater Opinion"!*

The Bethel Eldership...*Doug, Denny, Jeremy, Dave, Les, Monty, Curt, Henry, Jeff, Alvin, Clarence, and Cris, you are an extension of the pastoral leadership, commanders in the camp, and I greatly appreciate your commit-ment to fulfilling your roles and responsibilities. Thank you for your trust, friendship, accountability, and spiritual support!*

Clarence Horst...*Your ability to manage so many things at the same time with such excellence is truly a gift! Your administrative assistance and taking care of all the details is invaluable. No eggshells and no stress. You make me look better than I really am! Thank you!*

Michelle Henson...*Jo Ann and I appreciate your integrity and selfless service. You've made all the changes to all the documents without complaining. Thank you!*

Ron Johnson...*You are a great man of God! Thank you for imparting into my life and sharing your vision of foundational pillars and making converts, planting churches, and impacting cultures. You poured gasoline on the flame in my soul!*

David Cartledge...*Well, David, the first fruitful bough has budded! Your prophetic words over my life and the church have been like a script that only God could have written. Thank you for being obedient and bold, and a catalyst for change!*

Bob Rhoden...*You've been a true "change-agent" in the Potomac District, and an inspiration to me in the ministry. Thank you for leading change and believing in my leadership. New levels require renewed leaders!*

Diane McDougal...*You are a woman of faith, whose faithfulness will be richly rewarded. I commend you for taking up the cause and fighting the good fight of faith. Thank you for believing that this book can make a difference!*

Ben Vattelana...*Thank you for believing in the vision and for being a man of faith. You've got a pastor's heart.*

Joel Cortes...*Thank you for supporting the ministry of expanding the Kingdom and being willing to go to the ends of the earth!*

Gary Cote...*Thank you for sharing your knowledge of God's Word and for encouraging me in the writing of this book.*

Cris Snyder...*Thank you for the prayer support and for modeling true sacrifice and servanthood!*

I pray that God will use this book to instruct, influence, and inspire leaders and churches everywhere to be the twenty-first century New Testament Church and to contribute to continuing the book of Acts in our day.

2nd Acts Ministries, Inc., is dedicated to helping found, form, and facilitate twenty-first century New Testament churches and leaders through church consultations, leadership conferences, and evangelistic crusades. *2nd Acts Ministries* has also developed a variety of resources for use in these areas. For more information:

Please visit our Web site at: www.2ndacts.org

Or write us at: 2nd Acts Ministries, Inc.
                    P.O. Box 2976
                    Hagerstown, MD 21741-2976

Contents

"Terry Broadwater not only points out the necessity for significant change in the way we do church, but clearly shows how to achieve it. His personal leadership experiences give validity and relevance to the ideas and principles he writes about. This is a book that will be valued by all those who dare to 'lead'. I have seen the transforming power of this kind of leadership in Australia over the past twenty five years. There is no substitute for it in the modern church."

David Cartledge
Executive Presbyter
Assemblies of God Australia

"Here Terry Broadwater shares his heart and his passion. This book will challenge the status quo of pastors and churches and will inspire those who are captivated by vision."

Dr. H. Robert Rhoden
Executive Presbyter
Assemblies of God
Potomac District Council Superintendent

Introduction

Many books have been written by the experts on the subject of the Church. While I may not count myself as one of these, my experience has grown out of leading churches that could be described as "turn-around" situations. These churches had become somewhat isolated from the community, inwardly focused, and internally structured on programs. They had seemingly found a level of ministry that was convenient, comfortable, and not too costly. Although good things were being accomplished, nothing that could be marked as "great" was taking place. I am of the opinion that gifted people can do good things; but great things require God, because He alone is great.

There are many good churches with good people in them doing good things; that is exactly what the problem seems to be! Unfortunately, many good churches and good denominations are not doing so well in attendance and membership. Again, many experts could produce all kinds of reasons for this reality, based on research and studies. But I would suggest that much of the Church today is mired in mediocrity with a maintenance mentality rather than a Kingdom expansion mindset. Many local churches have little or no impact on their communities, and few people are being brought to Christ. Local churches are closing their doors more often than new ones are being opened because God's great purpose, pattern, and power for the Church has long been lost amid the programs and religious rituals.

There is a desperate need for a second Reformation, as far-reaching and life-changing as in the days of Martin Luther. There is a desperate need for the restoration of the true purpose for the House of God as it was in the days of King Josiah (Second Kings 22-23). There is a desperate need for the raising up of a generation of Joshua leaders to take possession of the promises of God for this moment in history. There is a desperate need for a return to the biblical foundation, formation, and facilitation of the Church. There is a desperate need for the New Testament Church in this twenty-first century!

A New Testament church is God's partner in accomplishing His purposes on this planet. There is exciting evidence today that God is doing a very old, yet "new," thing. It's happening in the church that I am leading, and it's happening in many others as well. God's anointed and appointed leaders are leading the Church in a revival of the renewal of God's purpose, pattern, and power for the Church! Once again, God is establishing apostolic churches today according to the archetype of the church at Antioch (Acts 11-13).

New Testament churches like the one at Antioch were the necessary and dynamic ministry centers that were responsible for penetrating and changing cultures with the message of Jesus Christ in the first century. What about our world in this century? I believe that the world of the twenty-first century, with its myriad people and problems, desperately needs to encounter the Person of Jesus Christ ministering in and through Christians just as powerfully as they did in the first century. When that encounter is experienced, what will ensue will be just as world-changing as what we read about in the book of Acts!

I used to watch *Pinky and the Brain*[1], a cartoon about two lab mice. (I confess that I still watch it from time to time!) As the theme song states, "one is a genius, the other's insane." Not-so-bright Pinky is tall and slender, while the "genius" Brain has a short body with a very oversized head. However, we soon realize that the crazy one is not so crazy and the smart one is not so smart. We see the two mice as small and insignificant in the world. Herein lies the plot. As episode after episode unfolds, Brain is consumed with his overwhelming passion and desire to: "Try to take over the world!" Pinky, meanwhile, never seems to quite grasp what day it is, let alone what his purpose is. Every episode contains this exchange:

Pinky: "What are we going to do today, Brain?"
Brain: "The same thing we do every day, Pinky. Try to take over the world!"

May I suggest to you that, as silly as it may sound, this is fairly representative of much of the leadership in the Church today? While we may not be as smart as we think we are, nor perhaps as crazy as others think we are, someone does need to echo Pinky's query: "What are we [the Church] going to do today?" And someone needs to lay hold of Brain's response: "The same thing we do every day. Try to take over the world!" In Jesus' Name! The first-century New Testament Church did just that in a very real sense, and so can we. And that's what this book is all about:

- Rediscovering the purpose of the New Testament Church.
- Restoring the pattern of the New Testament Church.
- Recovering the power of the New Testament Church.
- Renewing the passion of the New Testament Church.
- Reforming the people of the New Testament Church.

It is my hope that this book will help identify the ministry *foundation, formation,* and *facilitation* of the first century New Testament Church. It is only as we conform to the New Testament pattern for ministry, purpose of ministry, and power to do ministry that we can become the twenty-first century New Testament Church.

Let the second Church of Acts change the world!

1. *Pinky and the Brain,* created by Amblin Entertainment in association with Warner Brothers Animation, copyright 1995.

Part One

A Challenge to the
21st Century Leader

[Chapter One]
The Process of Change

I had been leading a church in Virginia for about eight years when we decided to make some changes to its basic platform and organization. My wife, Jo Ann, and I had come to the church in 1989 with our sons, Casey and Corey; our daughter, Cayla, was born in 1991. During those eight years, the church had grown from a group of about thirty people to around two hundred fifty members.

Those eight years had been a challenge, to say the least. However, despite the difficulties, we had come to the place where we were finally beginning to see the fruit of our labor. And we had labored! We painted walls, plowed snow, prayed, preached, and printed bulletins. During those early years we did what we thought we were supposed to do. It was, for the most part, incredibly frustrating.

Although I have always thrived when confronted with a challenge, I was challenged in ways I never imagined. Jo Ann struggled with deep depression for over a year before finally emerging from that darkness. I experienced a burnout and survived only by God's grace. The church experienced some major spiritual warfare because of some deep-rooted problems, but came through it victoriously.

In all of these things, and through many other trials, we learned to depend on God, to determine to *"run with perseverance the race marked out for us,"* and to *"fix our eyes on Jesus, the author and perfecter of faith"* (see Hebrews 12:1-2).

Looking back, the experience of overcoming those problems and trials was the best thing that could have happened. Why? Because it changed me. It changed our family. It changed the church. God, in a way that only He could, was turning our problems into a process of change! Change was exactly what had been happening to us and to the church. What was the catalyst? The realization that there had to be more to leading the church than simply showing up on Sundays and helping people to wade through another week.

The breakthrough for me came when I read Rick Warren's book *The Purpose-Driven Church.*[1] Warren's message inspired me to begin challenging our church to think about what we were doing and why we were doing it. Was it on purpose? What was our purpose? Were we simply doing what we had always done, while expecting to see different results? As we examined our purpose, suddenly there was an entirely new level of excitement and expectation among the people of the church.

Although at the time I couldn't fully comprehend what God was doing in my life, I now know I was *conceiving* the Spirit-breathed purpose for my life as a leader in the church. Interestingly, the past nine years had been a gestation period of carrying this purpose for my life so that it could be fully formed. Now, through all of the dynamics of delivery, this purpose is free to come forth at God's appointed time!

For most of those first eight years as a young pastor in Virginia, I had no idea what to do. I had ministry experience as the result of being in church most of my life and serving in several leadership roles. I had my education. I had a piece of paper in my wallet that stated I was an official minister with the Assemblies of God. I subscribed to magazines on ministry, and I attended conferences and seminars. I administrated the office, oversaw the boards of deacons and trustees, organized the church ministries, and conducted business meetings right out of *Robert's Rules of Order!*

I went after people right and left: those who were always right and those who had just left the church for the umpteenth time! I read the *Minister's Manual,* although it seemed to be primarily about dedications, weddings, and funerals.

Now, I am not trying to downplay the significance of these things, but I am saying that they can soon become our focus of ministry without our even realizing it. When they do, they can rob us of our true passion and purpose.

Sadly, too many church leaders end up out of the ministry, out of their marriages, and out of their minds because they're following a formula that often results in broken-down dreams and broken-down lives!

Startling Statistics

The handwriting is on the wall; we must wake up to what is wrong with the Church and what is going to make it right. The data is alarming! Statistics reveal that 1,500 pastors are leaving the ministry each month in the United States. Eighty percent of pastors and eighty-four percent of their spouses are discouraged or are dealing with depression. Seventy percent have no one they can call a close friend and confidant. Eighty percent of Bible school graduates who enter full-time ministry are no longer in ministry within five years. And ninety-five percent of pastors do not pray with their wives.[2]

Jack and Trisha Frost of Shiloh Place Ministries state, "From what we are hearing from senior pastors and from staff members, there seems to also be a major increase in staff and leadership team members who are dissatisfied with their positions, the church, the pastor, or the pastor's vision. It seems that many staff and team members are focusing on the personality flaws of the senior pastor, especially the flaws that have nothing to do with Paul's list of qualifications for a pastor. Others are trying to see their own vision and personal preferences for ministry styles implemented within the church or ministry. If they are not getting a favorable response to this, then many are responding with hurt feelings and offense. Apparently, they are not willing to let this be an opportunity for their own hidden darkness and impure motives to be exposed so that there may be greater intimacy with the Father and with family."[3]

Another alarm sounded in 1998, when LifeWay Publishers researched forced resignations in Baptist churches. Their survey looked for the primary reasons why pastors were fired from their pastorates. Out of the number of pastors forced to resign, surveys revealed the following five reasons for termination: 447 left because of control issues over who was to lead the church; 298 left because of poor people skills on the part of the pastor; 222 left because of the church's resistance to change; 212 left because the pastor's leadership style was perceived as being too strong; and 181 left because of conflicts already present when the pastor arrived at the church.[4]

According to the Rocky Mountain Family Council in their Fact Sheet "Pastors at Risk,"[5] Focus on the Family did a survey of nearly 5,000 pastors, and the results reflect serious data that should alarm the Body of Christ. Forty percent of pastors who responded to the survey said that in the preceding three months they had considered stepping down from their pastorates. Pastors reported that their principal problem was keeping their personal and family lives in balance with their ministry responsibilities. Their second greatest difficulty was in motivating their congregation members to live consistent lives of faith and to help the church fulfill the Great Commission. The survey goes on to show that it isn't only pastors who are struggling; pastors' wives are struggling as well. More than half of the pastors' wives who responded to the Focus survey indicated that they were fighting severe depression.

The Hazards of Leadership

In his book *Pastors at Risk,*[6] H.B. London, Jr., identified several hazards faced by pastors today, the first being the "walk on water" syndrome. This is the assumption on the part of church members that their pastor is somehow superhuman. Unfortunately, some pastors begin to buy into this mindset as well. They begin acting as if they are superhuman and as a result start to resist walking in accountability.

The second hazard pastors face is monumental personal problems. London cites a *Leadership* magazine survey that reveals what pastors think about work, home, and lifestyles. Ninety-four percent of the pastors who responded to the survey felt pressured to have an ideal family. Twenty-four percent had received marital counseling. Twenty-two percent needed and sought a supplemental income to meet their family's expenses, and twenty-eight percent felt their current compensation was insufficient. The survey also indicated that sixty-nine percent of pastors' wives work outside the home to make ends meet. The most frequently cited problems in clergy marriages were insufficient time with family, handling of money, income level, communication difficulties, and congregational expectations.

Frankly, a pastor's family is no different from any other in the church; they have financial difficulties, problems with time pressures, and intimacy problems between husband and wife. But the added pressures of "living in a fishbowl" and being under the scrutinizing eyes of many "judges" forces many pastors to the brink of failure.

The third hazard that London notes in his book is church migration. His information sources estimate that eighty percent of church growth in recent years is a direct result of people relocating from one local church to another. This migration can work to the benefit of large churches and to the disadvantage of average or smaller congregations. It can also produce jaded believers who drift from place to place. When things are not working out according to their desires or preferences in one church, they simply move on to another.

Another hazard for pastors today is that electronic technology shapes the preferences of people. Many question why they should trudge to church to hear an average sermon when they can tune in a fantastic pastor on TV. Why go to the effort of attending a Bible study at church when they can study in an on-line group? In fact, why even bother to try to form and maintain time-consuming, self-sacrificing relationships in the church when there are so many people they can befriend at their own convenience via the Internet? This mindset keeps people out of the physical church.

The fifth difficulty is that people are busier, more distracted, and live more hectic lives. Therefore, church is reduced to becoming just another meeting — another item on the agenda. It becomes much less than the predominant influence in our lives that it's meant to be.

Other hazards and difficulties cited by London include the consumer mentality that saturates the American way of life; suffocating expectations of the congregation; the loss of moral absolutes in our society; financial struggles; dwindling public confidence; dysfunctional people within the congregation; and marital infidelity.

With the leadership of churches under siege by overwhelming difficulties, it should come as no great surprise that the Church has become ineffective in its God-given mission.

The Challenge of Change

To suggest that something needs to change should be unnecessary. But what isn't as obvious is that real change is not occurring! *Change* is defined by Webster this way: "to make the form, nature, content, etc., of (something) different from what it is or from what it would be if left alone."[7] The Bible defines change another way:

> *And do not be conformed to this world, but be transformed by the renewing of your mind, that you may prove what the will of God is, that which is good and acceptable and perfect.*
> *...Therefore if anyone is in Christ, he is a new creature; the old things passed away; behold, new things have come....Be renewed in the spirit of your mind, and put on the new self, which in the likeness of God has been created in righteousness and holiness of the truth.*
> Romans 12:2, Second Corinthians 5:17, Ephesians 4:23-24

If we can identify the problem, we must be willing to set forth changes that will bring about solutions. We simply cannot afford to let the leadership and the church alone. Certainly God, by His Spirit, is confronting us in an effort to cause us to change! At this point, it is crucial that we follow Paul's instructions to the Romans:

> *For through the grace given to me I say to everyone among you not to think more highly of himself than he ought to think; but to think so as to have sound judgment, as God has allotted to each a measure of faith.*
> Romans 12:3

We must be brutally honest in our estimate of ourselves as leaders, measuring our value by the faith the Lord God has given us. As we continue in the Word of God, we become disciples who know the truth — and it is that truth which will set us free (see John 8:31-32).

I believe we desperately need to come back to the truth about the Church and the truth about the roles and responsibility of leadership in the local church. We must rediscover the pattern, purpose, and power for ministry that the New Testament, especially the book of Acts, reveals!

So what happened to that church in Virginia? Well, finally, after eight long and eventful years, I was beginning to sense that the church and I were "getting it"! What were we "getting"? We were entering into an understanding that the book of Acts contained some important information about what the local church is supposed to be and what it is meant to do. We were beginning to identify and prioritize some of the key elements of the New Testament Church as seen in Acts 2:42-47. The church in Virginia began growing as a result. I personally was being renewed and refreshed as I set about prioritizing my life and leadership. I began to focus more upon those areas in which the Lord had specifically gifted me to serve, the areas where I was most passionate about what God was doing.

This was a wonderful time of discovery for all of us. But it was only a beginning. In retrospect, I can't even say we were taking baby steps yet — it was more like the first time a baby rolls over! People were excited; the church was growing; I was growing as a leader. We were even ready to expand the platform up front to accommodate our growing worship ministry of musicians and singers.

And so we did. One week, beginning on Monday, we ripped out our old traditional platform with its old traditional design and structure. I had stood on that platform for eight years, preaching and proclaiming the changes that God can make in our lives. We were obviously experiencing many of those changes, individually and corporately. How symbolic that we were also changing the physical building where we met to worship! But the response was not what I had expected.

By the following Sunday, the old structure had been removed and the new structure had taken its place. As I stood on that much more suitable stage, expecting the church to be more excited than it had ever been before, I looked out upon a group of people sitting in stunned silence. They were clearly sulking! What was even more startling was the fact that this went on for weeks and months afterward.

I learned something powerful that day. Most people are excited about change — as long as it stays on the surface. If you sing some new songs, start a few new ministries, and even share a new vision of what the future can look like, almost everyone will agree with you. But as soon as you start to dismantle the old, out-of-date structures and set up a new framework to facilitate the ministry of the church, suddenly everyone gets really cranky and uncomfortable.

I experienced it then for the first time; I've subsequently experienced it many more times as I've had to change and as I've led others in changing. It isn't the things on the surface that need to change most of all; it is the deeper areas, the structure that holds our lives in ministry and the life of the church that must be transformed and renewed. We cannot be so distracted by the superficial changes that need to be made that we neglect to change the very structures themselves!

A summary of George Barna's book *Turnaround Churches*[8] indicates this very thing. Some churches attempt to change by ignoring changes in the ministry context. Others gravitate to one end of the spectrum and essentially reinvent themselves, creating a new ministry while attempting to adapt to the change. Most churches reside between these two extremes. They are aware of changes taking place around them, tinkering here and there with policies, programs, perspectives, and personnel just enough to get by without having to radically revisit their philosophy of ministry or their processes for ministry.

Interestingly, Barna has also concluded that if churches are to change to become more effective, they will need to have the right kind of leader — one who can turn a church around. Unfortunately, Barna's data seems to indicate that such pastors are rare in today's churches. Furthermore, he states that the demise of a church can usually be avoided, but that most of today's church leaders lack the ministry mindset that it takes to successfully implement change.

If we are to go forth, we must proceed with courage. All of the changes I've experienced in my life personally and in the lives of the churches with which I have been involved have been born out of the courage to change — to change mindsets, to change methods, and to change ministers.

According to Romans 12:2, change in any capacity really begins by changing the way we think. Much of what so many leaders and laity think about the Church today isn't exactly biblical, which has certainly contributed to the postmodernist, self-consumed view now held by so many in our society.

If we were thinking in terms of absolute truth regarding how the Church should be founded, formed, and facilitated, we would certainly see a Church that is committed to fulfilling the biblical mandate of "making disciples," which is the intentional process of infusing people's minds with the mind of Christ.

How can we change mindsets in our churches? We can align our thinking with the Word of God as we encounter and embrace the truth of God. His Word must again become the standard that is raised in our churches; it must be that upon which we meditate all day long (Psalm 119:97, Joshua 1:8).

This will result in a change of method, which is a change in the basic organization of the church and in the way we minister; the organization of the church is changed when we have encountered and embraced the theocracy of God. As we enter into God's pattern for church government, justice and righteousness will be established among the people of God (Isaiah 9:6-7).

Then, changing ministers needn't mean moving some people out and others in, but refers rather to the process of changing the characteristics of the people in the church as we encounter and embrace the testimony of God in Jesus Christ. Christianity must once again be focused on receiving and expressing Jesus' likeness and love in us. *By this will people know we are truly devoted followers of Christ.* (See John 13:34-35.)

A Dynamic Change

The book of Acts, which chronicles the life of the Church in the first century, begins with a bang. A dynamic explosion took place in an upper room — an explosion so powerful, so awesome, that it blew away the religious systems and structures not only of that day, but of all time! When the dust had cleared, in the place of religious ritual and routine, the Church had sprung forth.

At first there were 120 people; then 3,000 more were added; then another 5,000 came; until Luke simply records the statistics as "great numbers." Jesus had told His followers that they would receive this *dunamis* (power) and that it would change everything:

> *"But you will receive power when the Holy Spirit has come upon you; and you shall be My witnesses both in Jerusalem, and in all Judea and Samaria, and even to the remotest part of the earth."* Acts 1:8

Things happened exactly as Jesus had foretold. The result was a world that was greatly impacted and changed by the witness of the Church.

How many believers are there today? How many more could there be if the Church was operating in the same dynamic power and pattern as the first century Church? Could it be that we need to experience another explosion of God's power that will transform the world now as it did then? I'm convinced so.

Sadly, many of the religious structures and systems that were blown apart at Pentecost seem to have been reconstructed. The demonic spirits once cast out by the first century New Testament Church seem to have somehow crept back into a place of prominence while the Church was busy looking elsewhere.

We see this all around us — in the New Age movement, in secular humanism, in Islam, in Eastern mysticism, and even in the institutionalization of much of the present-day Church. Even Christian movements and fellowships have been infiltrated by these religious spirits and have systematically devolved into denominations and religious sects. Man-made rules and regulations have replaced relationship with God through Jesus Christ.

Politicians on platforms proclaiming that which is pleasing to the people have replaced preachers in pulpits proclaiming that which is pleasing to God. "Doing church" by following the newest program has replaced following the New Testament pattern. It isn't surprising that in all of this we have lost the power to change the world!

Perhaps we need another experience of the explosive *dunamis* of that first Pentecost. However, I believe that cannot and will not occur until there are those who are willing to "wait on the Lord" as did the 120 in that upper room in Jerusalem. They obeyed Jesus' instructions and did not leave Jerusalem until the Father sent what He promised. (See Acts 1:4.)

It is clear that there is a pattern we must follow if we are to receive the only power that can change the world. Unfortunately, it is also clear that we have not been following Jesus' instructions: we have not been seeking His power; we have not been telling people everywhere about Jesus; and we have not been changing the world!

Today the Christian Church is in a state of rapid flux, both in the United States and around the world. According to the American Religious Identification Survey, the percentage of American adults who identify themselves as Christians was eighty-six percent in 1990, while that figure dropped to seventy-seven percent in 2001.[9] This is an unparalleled drop. Confidence in the traditional religious institutions has hit an all-time low.

While there appears to be a major increase in interest in spirituality among North Americans, this increase has not brought about greater church involvement. At the present rates of change, Islam will become the dominant religion in the world before 2050, while a majority of Americans will be non-Christians by the year 2035. The number of unchurched people has increased rapidly in the United States. Agnosticism, atheism, and secularism are growing rapidly. Interest in alternative religious movements such as the New Age and neopaganism movements is growing rapidly. In particular, Wiccans are doubling in number about every thirty months. From 1992 through 1999, average attendance in American churches dropped by twelve percent, while the population has increased by nine percent![10]

There is also a new trend that has emerged: People who once attended church in their childhood and left in their twenties are no longer returning to the church as they grow older, as was once the case. If this trend continues, the future for organized Christianity in the United States looks grim. Churches across the nation could fail as older parishioners die off and are not replaced by younger believers.

Not coincidentally, at the same time that church attendance has dramatically dropped, there has been a significant increase in the number of religious experts who believe and proclaim that the Bible contains errors and that God's nature is not what people have been led to believe that it is.

Can we honestly say that we are telling people everywhere about Jesus? No! This is why, regardless of denominational affiliation, we must see ourselves as having been wandering in a wilderness, traveling the well-rutted path of religious ritual and in desperate need of a change of scenery! Some may sit in silence, some may be stunned, and some may even sulk; but if the structure needs to be changed, then let's get on with the process!

God has always called on His chosen leaders to guide His people into new dimensions and dynamics of His purposes and into the power necessary to carry out those purposes. Where there is God's anointed and appointed leadership, God's anointed and appointed work will get done! Leadership is the key; it always has been and it always will be. John Kotter states in his book *Leading Change* that "leadership is a set of processes that create organizations … or adapts them to significantly changing circumstances." He further states that "leadership defines what the future should look like, aligns people with that vision, and inspires them to make it happen despite the obstacles."[11]

I believe that in order for there to be a second Acts explosion and experience in this day, church leadership is going to have to do some changing! The direction of the Church is going to have to change. The vision and mission of the Church is going to have to change.

The Church must be focused on God's purpose so people can be brought into proper alignment to fulfill that purpose. The Church must be encouraged to change the world, despite the challenges. It's time to *"let God transform you into a new person by changing the way you think"* (see Romans 12:2, NLT).

We have come to that point of confrontation and into our own time of visitation (see Luke 19:41-44). Jesus once wept over Jerusalem because the people of that city were about to experience the consequences of their not recognizing how God had come to them. According to the original Greek language, a "time of visitation" is when God sets an appointed time of examination. The situation could go one way or the other.

God has come today to examine us. He has come to weigh our ways, our deeds, and our characters. Our destiny will be determined accordingly, whether joyous or sad. Is there a twinkle in God's eye or a tear? Will we experience a second Reformation, or will we see our works dismantled until one stone is not left upon another? Do we recognize Him as He moves among us? Are we ready to lead our churches out of legislation and into liberty, out of dictating rules and regulations and into defining God-appointed roles and responsibilities, out of a maintenance mentality and into a ministry mobilization mindset?

A process of change must take place in ministers, methods, and mindsets! Why? Because it is obvious that we need a new experience of God's explosive power to change us so the world can be changed. That time has come!

Revitalizing the Church

I am convinced that the key to recovering the kind of influence and impact that the early Church had on the world is fourfold. First, we need to rediscover the only real purpose of the Church. Second, we need to recover the power of the Holy Spirit to accomplish the work of the Kingdom. Third, we need to restore the five-fold leadership offices. And fourth, we need to release people into ministry according to their giftedness.

This, in simple terms, is the pattern of the New Testament Church.

It needs to be our pattern today. But that cannot happen unless we are willing to change! And that process of change must first begin in God's ministers, His leaders.

> *Do not call to mind the former things, or ponder things of the past. Behold, I will do something new, now it will spring forth; will you not be aware of it? I will even make a roadway in the wilderness, rivers in the desert.* Isaiah 43:18-19

God is doing a new thing in our day. He is changing the way we think about things; He is changing the way we do things; He is changing the way we see things. He is changing us! As God is moving in a new dimension, we have the opportunity to partner with Him in fulfilling His purposes. What an awe-inspiring idea!

In fact, God is not just doing some new little thing in this church or that local body. There is a wave of the Spirit moving in the Church today. People are being caught up in it, often without recognizing its significance.

I believe that the current move of the Spirit is bringing about a second Reformation within the Church, reforming the Church *by the Spirit*. The first Reformation, which reformed the Church *by the Word*, brought about the end of the Dark Ages. That one foundational, profound truth of the first Reformation had an impact then that is still ringing forth today.

Today, again, there is a move of God on such a sweeping scale that old patterns of thought and action no longer apply. God is ready for a new reformation, a new restoration of His Divine Spirit and Truth that will change our world. God is ready. Are you?

The Lord is bringing us into a process of change. He invites us to partner with Him in fulfilling His purposes, but that cannot be done while we stay where we are. We cannot help to build a cathedral if we are sitting in a chair across the street. We have to adjust our position, our activity, our mindset. We have to change!

A New Day Dawns

Isaiah spoke of three important things we can do if we are to begin to be the leaders God is calling us to be. First, we are to forget the former things. Old forms of ministry, lifeless traditions, ways we have been doing things that were fruitless — forget all these as God brings new life into the Church.

Second, don't ponder the things of the past. Has someone hurt you by his words, actions, or attitudes? Has anyone wronged you? Do not allow your mind to dwell on these things. Don't simply ignore them, either. Take them to the Lord, seek to bring about reconciliation and restitution, then allow the Holy Spirit to do His work. Do not dwell on how you were wronged or allow yourself to be bound in bitterness or unforgiveness. Move forward in God.

We need to move on beyond past glory, past moves of God, as well. Those experiences may have been wonderful, life-changing, mind-shattering — but they were what God was doing in the past. Do not hold tightly to the things that used to work — the programs, the songs, the ministries. These are simply the structures that may need to be replaced as the Lord God continues to move on. Allow Him to remove the old where He desires, so that He can make way for the new.

Finally, live in expectancy. The Lord is doing a new thing — expect it! Look for it! Fix your eyes upon Him to see what He is doing in and through His people. Look for the Lord's work daily; you won't be disappointed.

God is raising up His Church, His apostolic New Testament people. He is also raising up a new kind of leader for this Church. We can no longer walk as we once walked, but we must move forward in God's plan and purpose for His people.

1. Rick Warren, *The Purpose-Driven Church*, (Grand Rapids, MI: Zondervan, 1995).
2. Statistics are quoted from Maranatha Life's *Life-Line for Pastors*, on their Internet site at www.maranathalife.com/lifeline/badnews.htm.
3. Jack and Trisha Frost, *Shepherd's Song* newsletter, "Crisis in Leadership: A Season of Chagrin in the Church," www.shilohplace.org/crisisin.htm, (Conway, SC: Shiloh Place Ministries, 2001).
4. Charles Willis, "Forced Terminations of Pastors, Staff Leveling Off, Survey Results Show," www.lifeway.com/about_pr0801l.asp, (Nashville, TN: Lifeway News, August 2001).
5. "Pastors at Risk,"www.rmfc.org/fs/fs0022.html, (Denver, CO: Rocky Mountain Family Council).
6. H.B. London Jr., et. al., *Pastors at Risk*, (Colorado Springs, CO: Chariot Victor, 1993).
7. Webster's Encyclopedic Unabridged Dictionary of the English Language, p. 246 (Beaverton, OR: Merriam-Webster, 1989).
8. George Barna, *Turnaround Churches*, (Ventura, CA: Regal Books, 1993).
9. "American Religious Identification Survey," www.gc.cuny.edu/studies/key_findings.htm, (New York, NY: Graduate Center of the City University of New York, 2001).
10. Statistics are taken from "Trends Among Christian Believers in America," www.religioustolerance.org/chr_tren.htm, (Kingston, ON, Canada: Ontario Consultants on Religious Tolerance).
11. John Kotter, *Leading Change*, (Boston, MA: Harvard Business School Press, 1996).

[Chapter Two]
The Pattern for Leadership Change

*Now it came about after the death of Moses the servant of the LORD,
that the LORD spoke to Joshua the son of Nun, Moses' servant, saying,
"Moses My servant is dead; now therefore arise, cross this Jordan, you
and all this people, to the land which I am giving to them, to the sons of
Israel."* Joshua 1:1-2

A twenty-first century New Testament church will require a new
kind of leader — one who is not afraid of change and who is able to
successfully initiate change within the church. Only when change is
welcomed within local church leadership can it filter down into other
areas of the local church.

The Joshua Generation

The beginning of the book of Joshua provides some helpful insights
into the principles of change. If you will recall, Israel had come out of
bondage in Egypt; the sons of Israel had been led through the wilderness by Moses, the deliverer God had chosen. What Moses had done in
leading the people was good; however, the work was not yet complete.
Now it was time for a change of leadership.

We can find two crucial insights from these verses. First, the way
things had been done in the past would not continue in the future. The
people were used to Moses. They knew how he did things; they knew
how he reacted in various situations. They had followed this man for
years. They knew him! Joshua … well, they knew Joshua, too. Joshua
was the second in command, the servant, the next best. He was important … but he wasn't Moses.

Now, suddenly, Joshua was in charge. The people had to change
their thoughts and their mindsets concerning this man. Just as impor-

tantly — perhaps more so — Joshua himself had to change his perception of who he was and of what God was calling him to do. Yes, Moses had been training him and leading by example. Moses had even placed his hands on him and commissioned him for service, but Moses was still around. All at once, the training wheels were off, and Joshua had to go forth without his mentor.

This is crucial to the times in which we live. This time in Israel's history gives us a glimpse of an understanding that we must embrace if we are to press forward into what God has for us. Just as the Jews had to allow for a change of ministers, so must we. Just as the Jews had to change their methods, so must we. And just as the Jews had to change their mindsets, so must we. The only way such change can occur is if we change the way we think (see Romans 12:2).

Our leadership, too, must move from a Moses mentality to a Joshua mentality. I believe this is what God is doing today! This is what He is speaking to us. We must cease our wandering, move forward, and occupy. We are not to continue to wander around the mountain again and again. That may have happened for a time; but God is bringing that chapter to a close. The "sheep" of the pasture now need to become the "soldiers" taking the land!

Let's look more closely at the three crucial changes God is making in His Church as we move from a Moses mentality to a Joshua mentality.

A Change in Ministers

The first change is fairly obvious: Moses must die. It will do no good for Joshua to be trained and ready to minister if Moses is still alive; for as long as Moses is alive, he is still in command.

What does it mean for Moses to die in our churches? It means that the old season is over and the new is poised and waiting to arise. It means that we are coming into a new season of leading the Church into her destiny in God and in fulfilling His purposes on the earth. There will be a major shift in the way the Church will be led. Interestingly, Moses was a shepherd, but Joshua was a soldier.

There are two ways in which God can bring about this change in leadership in the local church. The first way is by bringing about personal change in the leaders or ministers who are already there. Just as Jacob became Israel and Saul became Paul, so can God work miraculous transformation in each of us. God will be challenging you to change; He will continually call you to new areas in Him, to new levels of holiness and obedience. Unlike Moses, the existing leaders may not have to be physically moved out of the way, but they do need to allow God to have His way in them.

The second way God can bring about a change in leadership is to change the personnel involved. Samuel replaced Eli; David replaced Saul. In both cases, it was not simply a continuation of ministry or service that was involved. Rather, it was a change in era, a change in the understanding of what God was doing. God may replace some of the leaders of local churches, particularly if they are not willing to be malleable in the hand of the Lord. However, He would prefer to add to the existing leadership, building up the leaders' teams by bringing the very people and giftings that are needed to carry out His plan for a particular local body.

I have been both amazed and encouraged by the leadership changes we have seen in our church as we have committed to functioning in the New Testament pattern. As we have opened our lives to God to change each of us, He has orchestrated changes within us, as well as brought about some changes of personnel in leadership. In several cases, I've seen God very strategically move some leaders on to bless other places while moving others into the church to form a different level of leadership. Without question, God resources the responsibility He gives us!

Leadership transformation arrives neither conveniently nor without cost. As the level of responsibility rises, leadership must rise with it, as the result of either personal changes or personnel changes. In either case, the process is never an easy one. It often entails pain, frustration, and pressure. Leaders must be able to deal with the ramifications of the decisions they have made — ramifications that may include emotional fallout, financial changes, and scheduling pressures, among other things. As God told Joshua, courageous leadership is what is required. That can only come from an absolute assurance that God is with you. After all, obeying what God requires really only has two options: Do and be blessed; don't and be cursed! I have seen both sides of the issue, and obeying, even though it may entail great patience and perseverance, is far more rewarding in the end.

God changes us personally, and He will change the personnel necessary at the leadership level, and in other areas, to perform His purposes! I have not only experienced this personally with my leadership team, but I've seen it happen in other leadership teams as well.

God has a new level of ministry for you. He has a new level of passion, power, and purpose. He has something significant to do in you and through you. Has God given you a dream, a vision of ministry? Have prophetic words been spoken to you, foretelling areas of ministry or of personal growth or relationship that have not yet been realized? Have you sensed God Himself speaking to you, calling you to experience more of Him? Now is the time to pick up that vision and to blow the dust off your dreams. God has wonderful things for you ... if you are willing to change to accommodate them.

A Change in Methods

After Moses had died, leadership was passed on to Joshua. But the change of leadership was not the only change involved. There was also a change in the methodology of ministry; there was a new place, a new purpose, and a new plan. In order to attain the Promised Land, Israel first had to cross the Jordan River. There could be no moving ahead in God's purposes unless that river was crossed. The people could have sat and looked at the river for months, yet they would have been no further in God's plan. They could have held seminars on river crossings and to talk about how great the Promised Land would be, yet not entered in. They could have wandered up and down along the bank of the river, thinking they were getting somewhere, yet making no progress at all.

We have our rivers to cross, too.

All of us have barriers in our lives, those things that hinder us from entering into all God has for us. They may be emotional barriers, or spiritual, or racial, or physical, or methods of ministry. It really doesn't matter what they are, for God is saying that whatever river we face, it is time to cross over. It is time to move on, unhindered by those things that would pull us back and keep us from fulfilling the call of God in our lives and in our churches.

If you desire to be a leader who walks in the anointing God has for His Church in this day, and if you desire to lead others into that place in God, then commit to a new dimension and means of God's moving in, among, and through His people; consecrate yourself before your God to walk holy before Him and in His ways; and cross over into that new place and ministry that He has ordained for you.

Go to a new level. You may have to get in over your head! The river is at flood stage. Like Joshua, leaders today must be the first to cross into a new way of doing things.

The move God is stirring will bring no less than a renewal of the experiences recorded in the Word concerning the early Church. We will see the book of Acts from a new perspective — because we will live it! Are you ready and willing to become a leader of a second Acts church?

Then allow the old chapter of your life, of the life of the local church, to close. Turn the page and begin the new chapter!

This is the only way to grow into the next level of leadership that God has for you. You cannot read a book by reading the same page over and over, can you? Turn the page! If there are differences with others, reconcile them. If there have been offenses given or received, make it right.

Then turn the page and move forward ... and watch as the Lord makes a way for you to cross through the waters (see Joshua 3:14-17).

Just as Joshua was confronted with a change in the level of his ministry — which really meant a change in processing God's plan — so must we be willing to change and move to a new level in ours. There was no more passivity about the Promised Land; it was time to take possession. There was no more manna and no more wandering; it was time to sow and to harvest. That was a drastic change for these people who had been hiking through the wilderness their entire lives.

God desires a drastic change in our lives as well. He is moving in a new dynamic and a new dimension in this new century; the book of Acts will be revisited and relived. Moses is gone. The old way is past. There will be no more merely tending sheep, but rather training soldiers to take possession in Jesus' name (see Acts 4:23-31). Let's move forward.

A Change in Mindsets

When God lays hold of you and begins to transform you, bringing you to a new level in ministry, there are two things you will lose: your identity and your familiarity — how you think of yourself and how others think about you.

When Joshua was promoted from being Moses' aide to being the leader of the nation, he changed identity. The Paul who spent three years in the desert was not the same as the Saul who had rapidly advanced in knowledge and education among the Jews. David the king was a somewhat different identity than David the shepherd, or David the musician. You must be willing to lose your identity, your sense of who you are. You must be ready to lay down your life to take up His. *"We will be like Him...."* You must be ready to think the way He thinks!

What do I mean by losing your familiarity? I mean losing the things with which you have grown comfortable. The Israelites were used to being fed manna, they were used to not needing to make or buy new clothes, they were used to not even having to decide which way to travel.

Things weren't so bad for them. They didn't even have to think; all that they needed was provided. But in the Promised Land, they would have to conquer enemies. They would have to plant and to harvest. They had to move from the familiar into that which had to be possessed by faith. If they were to move on and come into the land God had provided for them, there was no other way. They had to think differently than the way they had been used to.

If you are a leader, then God is not merely giving you an opportunity; He is giving you a responsibility. What is the difference? Think about it. An opportunity is optional, but a responsibility is required. We look at Joshua as a leader and see what a great opportunity he had to lead God's people. But the reality is that he was given a great responsibility for those people. He was responsible to lead under God's direction. Short of turning his back on what his God was asking him to do, there was no real option involved.

I am a husband, a father, a leader in my local church. I have responsibilities in each of these roles. While there is great opportunity to bless others in these roles, there are also things that are required of me. What are we required to do as leaders in the local church? It is our responsibility to lead the church to be a second Acts church! We need to change by changing the way we think about the church and our roles and responsibilities as leaders.

Changing Our Minds

When God begins to signal change, there are several very human responses. Most people go through these stages as a progression. The first stage is the defensive, knee-jerk reaction of denial: "I don't need to change!" How often have we heard this type of response in the church? In the second stage, once we finally admit that change might conceivably be needed — even within ourselves — we reach the level of discomfort: "I'm struggling with the way things are changing!" We may see the need for change, yet still have difficulty in making the necessary change in our lives or in the life of the church.

The third stage is discovery, in which we realize just how much change is needed, and what the end goal of that change will be. This is when we are willing to say, "I'm ready to change in whatever way I have to in order to reach that goal." The final stage is that of devotion, both to the goal and to the process involved: "I am committed to continuing to be an agent of change." This is when we see that the process is clearly moving forward, and others who have been mired in the earlier stages begin to be swept along in the process of change and transformation. God is at work in such a place!

Joshua experienced it and so will you…if you really want to be an agent of change!

It is time to possess the promise of God. He is ready to take His people onto a new level. He is ready for the twenty-first century New Testament Church, the second Acts Church, to come forth in power and in glory.

Are you ready to go?

[Chapter Three]
The Pastoral Leader-shift of the Church

Now there were at Antioch, in the church that was there, prophets and teachers: Barnabas, and Simeon who was called Niger, and Lucius of Cyrene, and Manaen who had been brought up with Herod the tetrarch, and Saul. While they were ministering to [or, worshiping] the Lord and fasting, the Holy Spirit said, "Set apart for Me Barnabas and Saul for the work to which I have called them." Then, when they had fasted and prayed and laid their hands on them, they sent them away.

Acts 13:1-3

I have come to the conclusion that many churches are "roller coaster" churches. Such local bodies are marked by slow and steady climbs upward, reaching a new level — only to suddenly plummet downward at a rate that would thrill a daredevil. Some churches go through many twists and turns throughout the years, some so violent that people are thrown right out of their pews!

Unfortunately, too many churches could be described this way. Because the "ride" is so tumultuous, few people are waiting in line to get on board. After all, the people who have disembarked, or picked themselves up off the ground, have set out to warn everyone else to stay away from that ride!

Why do people get on a roller coaster in the first place? Usually it's for the thrill and the adventure. Think about that for a moment. There are feelings of anticipation and excitement as people line up for services and ministries. Some people are fearless and some are fearful; many others seem to be just going along for the ride. But at least initially, everyone is there because of the potential excitement they really are hoping to encounter. And so the line forms and people start to get on board.

Now, there are all types of roller coaster churches. There are high-speed churches that just want to take people as fast as possible up and down the track. There are some that have no track at all; instead, they suspend their riders from a top rail with their feet dangling in the air and nothing to stand on. There are monorail churches that serve to simply ease people along a single-track system, enabling everyone to settle in comfortably so they can take in the scenery.

There are the racer churches, twin-coaster churches traveling on identical courses with the sole purpose of seeing which one can outdo the other. There are the conventional churches that, despite technology, still use the old methods for taking people up and down an old-fashioned, wooden track. There are simulator churches that aren't really churches at all — they just create the illusion of traveling up and down a track.

We need to get the church on the right track! Yet what is that right track?

The Paradigm Shift in the Book of Acts

We first need to understand that the twenty-first century New Testament Church — the second Acts Church — is an apostolic Church. We are to build after the pattern set forth by the apostles of the early Church. As we walk according to that pattern, we will find ourselves also walking in the power of that Church. Our task is to look to the pattern shown in the Church in Acts to discern the will of the Lord for our time as we seek to build according to the pattern He has provided.

Fortunately, God has not only given us instructions throughout the New Testament concerning how the local church is to be established; He has even given us a case study: the church at Antioch. Let's look at the roots of this movement and then see what God was doing among the people there. Perhaps it will help us to discover the right track.

As we begin our look at this body, we find that a new move of God was breaking forth. Peter was being used by God to bring the Gospel to those who had formerly been left out: the Gentiles.

Within just a few brief years — about six to eight years after Pentecost — God was about to do something new in the earth.

Acts 10 contains the account of Cornelius, a centurion of the Italian cohort — in other words, a Gentile. The Scriptures describe him as a devout man who feared the Lord, a man of prayer who was generous to the Jews. As he was praying one day, he was shown an angelic vision. Through this vision, through Cornelius' obedience to it, and through

Peter's receiving a vision of his own, the apostle was brought to Caesarea to minister to those assembled there.

The first part of his message shows that a light had shone in upon Peter's understanding, opening a new way of thought and belief concerning the place of the Gentiles in God's plan.

> *Opening his mouth, Peter said: "I most certainly understand now that God is not one to show partiality, but in every nation the man who fears Him and does what is right is welcome to Him."*
>
> Acts 10:34-35

Peter didn't get a chance to finish his sermon, because the Holy Spirit had something else in mind. While Peter was still talking with them, *"the Holy Spirit fell upon all those who were listening to the message"* (Acts 10:44). Peter had all of these new believers baptized, then stayed on for a few days' teaching.

Now, Peter had clearly heard from the Lord before going to Cornelius. He had seen the vision of the sheet — God's video screen, if you will. And God had made it very clear to Peter that we are not to call unacceptable that which God calls acceptable (see verse 15). Just as He will do for us, God sent Peter to a place where He had already prepared the people to hear the Word. And He was waiting and ready to pour forth the new wine on the Gentiles, regardless of what Peter might have thought!

So how did the believers at Jerusalem respond? Were they so excited at this new development that they couldn't wait to go out and find a Gentile to share the Gospel with? Amazingly, the answer is no. Peter was criticized for what God Himself was doing (see Acts 11:1-3). He was placed in a position of having to defend himself and explain his actions (see verses 4-16).

After Peter had given his account and explained how the Holy Spirit had come upon the Gentiles, the leaders of the Jewish believers there glorified God and acknowledged that the Lord was granting repentance and life to the Gentiles (Acts 11:18). But in the very next verse, Luke tells us they continued to speak to the Jews only. Unbelievable! They believed this new move was of God, yet they seemingly refused to enter into it themselves, being content to allow Peter and a few others to minister to the Gentiles.

Meanwhile, "some believers" (their names were not necessary as far as Luke was concerned) went down to Antioch from Cyprus and Cyrene where large numbers of Gentiles were turning to the Lord (Acts

11:20-21). Historians estimate that as many as 500,000 new believers were birthed in Antioch; nothing of the kind was happening among the believers at Jerusalem. You would think the leaders in Jerusalem would now embrace what God was doing. But you would be wrong.

Although they did acknowledge that this new move was of God, the leaders of the church at Jerusalem sent Barnabas to Antioch rather than going themselves (Acts 11:22). Sometimes we can see that a new move is of God, yet still desire the same old thing. Sometimes we like to be comfortable with what we know rather than pressing in to the thing God is doing now. So we send someone else!

Barnabas ministered to these new converts, then went to Tarsus and brought back Saul (later he would become Paul) to help with the ministry. Together, Barnabas and Saul were discipling these believers, positioning them to fulfill God's purpose. The church at Antioch was planted. It was a church that would change the world!

The Pattern and Power of the Church at Antioch

At this point, we can see that the book of Acts falls naturally into two divisions. In the first section the focus is on Peter's work with the church at Jerusalem. In Acts 11-13 there is a shift in focus from that body to the church in Antioch, and from Peter to Paul. An astonishing thing happened: The work that was seeded from the Jerusalem church became a stronger church than its parent church.

This is part of what we will see as we walk in the power and the anointing that God has for us today. As new works are begun, we will see that they surpass the parent churches, both numerically and in the anointing and power of the Spirit.

If we desire to have strong churches that are filled with power and anointing, we must look to the pattern given us in the Word. Scriptures speak of the church in Antioch as being such a strong witness and testimony to the world around them that people were reminded of Jesus whenever they saw them. That is why they began to call the believers "Christians" at Antioch (see Acts 11:26).

If we become churches that are patterned after the New Testament Church, we will be filled with the power of the New Testament Church. Let us build according to the pattern.

Paul shows us part of that pattern in his letter to the church at Ephesus:

And He gave some as apostles, and some as prophets, and some as evangelists, and some as pastors and teachers, for the equipping of the saints for the work of service, to the building up of the body of Christ; until we all attain to the unity of the faith, and of the knowledge of the Son of God, to a mature man, to the measure of the stature which belongs to the fullness of Christ. Ephesians 4:11-13

It is quite clear that the church at Antioch was walking in the five-fold ministry. The ministry gifts — apostles, prophets, evangelists, pastors, and teachers — were functioning within this body of believers, equipping them to carry out the work of the service to the Lord. The fruit of this can be seen in the tremendous growth of the church, both numerically and spiritually. As the members of the body were equipped to carry out their ministries, this church was effective in reaching the world for Christ!

This is why we can view the church at Antioch as an apostolic church. This type of church may be defined as one that is functioning according to God's pattern and walking in His power. The only way we can have churches that function according to the pattern laid out in the New Testament is if we restore the five-fold ministry gifts and allow and encourage their operation.

The church at Antioch was led by the Holy Spirit and was releasing the miraculous into their community and beyond. They were showing forth the life of Jesus as disciples united by His grace. Although they were diverse in such areas as race, social position, background, education, and all the other things man sees, there was a unity in the Spirit that was clearly manifested.

How the Church in this day needs that kind of unity! What a lack this is in many of our churches — the very places where all should clearly see the reality of coming together in love for one another. Reach out to those the Lord brings to your church who seem to be different from those who already worship together. The unity that the Spirit of the Lord brings is shown forth as we are able to walk together and minister side by side even with those who are different from us.

If we are to be effective leaders walking in a second Acts experience, we must understand the pattern laid out for us. As we move ahead to see the leadership model the Lord has set into place, I will be using the term "apostolic church" in the context of the local body. What do I mean by this?

An apostolic church is a biblically-based fellowship that follows the pattern of the New Testament in living out the Great Commandment of loving the Lord, loving one's neighbors, and loving one's self. After all, the very essence of the New Testament Church is apostolic. Jesus was the foremost Apostle, and it is His DNA that is implanted in the Church. An apostolic church fulfills the Great Commission by evangelizing and discipling all nations of the earth, from the local (Jerusalem) and regional area (Judea and Samaria) to the ends of the earth (see Acts 1:8).

As a leader in the local church, you have the potential to lead the fellowship of which you are a part into the second Acts experience. Let's look at the pattern for leadership of the New Testament local church.

The Pastoral and Leadership Team

Much has been written and taught concerning the biblical foundation, basis, and structure of the five-fold ministry leadership gifts. We will simply review these areas here.

The first gift mentioned in Ephesians 4:11 is that of the *apostle*. This word is translated variously as "apostle," "messenger," or "one who is sent." It means a delegate, a messenger, or one who is sent forth with orders. The outworking of this gift is threefold: The apostle pastors cities and regions (rather than a single local church); he prepares people for the ministry; and he plants churches. God is moving today to restore apostolic leadership to His Church! This is the New Testament pattern.

The second gift is that of the *prophet*. In Greek writings, this is someone who is an interpreter of oracles or other hidden things. A prophet is one who, moved by the Spirit of God, becomes His voice to His people. He solemnly declares what he has received by inspiration, especially concerning future events. In particular, his messages will relate to the cause, to the Kingdom of God, and to the salvation of souls. The prophet seeks God's purposes, sees God's plan, and speaks it forth in faith.

The leadership ministry of apostles and prophets will set the House of God in order so that the Church can again function in the pattern, purpose, and power of the New Testament.

The third ministry gift, or office, is that of the *evangelist*. This term means "a bringer of good tidings." The evangelist proclaims the Good News, preaches the Gospel everywhere, and prepares converts to be discipled. The true biblical office of evangelist is not concerned with simply conducting meetings in churches for the stimulus of the saints. Rather, this leadership gift is telling "everyone, everywhere" about Jesus (see Mark 16:15, NLT).

The gifting of the *pastor* is the fourth mentioned. This word is translated as "pastor" or "shepherd." The word *pastor* carries the connotation of a herdsman, especially a shepherd. The tasks of the modern pastor parallel those of the shepherd of the biblical era. He was to watch for enemies; protect the sheep from attack; heal the wounded and sick animals; find and save the lost or trapped sheep; and to care for them, sharing their lives and so earning their trust. The pastor is to bring care, counsel, and comfort to those entrusted to him by the Great Shepherd.

"Pastor" is the most widely used title among the Church as a term of respect and identification of the leader. But it also creates confusion in that not all leaders are called to be pastors. Herein lies much of the problem with many in the ministry as they struggle with being a "pastor" when they are really called to be an apostle, or prophet, or evangelist, or teacher. It is not the title that I am concerned with, but the function. As long as we can edify people in our churches as to the biblical role of each of the five leadership offices, and those so called can walk in confidence and humility in their particular calling, then referring to the leader or leaders of a church as "pastor" is certainly appropriate and respectful.

The final ministry gift mentioned is that of the *teacher*. This word is variously translated as "Master" (of Jesus), "teacher," and "doctor." This is one who teaches concerning the things of God and the duties of man. A true teacher respects the Word of God, reveals the implications and tenets of the Word, and relates the Word to the people in practical terms.

Interestingly, the Bible refers to Jesus as filling each one of these offices in His ministry. He is the foremost Apostle, expanding the Kingdom of God; the Prophet of prophets, speaking the Word of God; the Evangelist, preaching the Good News to the poor; the Great Shepherd, pastoring the flock; and the Master Teacher, relating the truth in practical terms. Jesus Christ alone fills all these roles as only He alone can. Therefore, He alone has given "some" to be apostles, "some" prophets, "some" evangelists, "some" pastors, and "some" teachers.

Ministry Partnerships

Although there are five specific ministry gifts mentioned in this passage, it is imperative that one gift is not necessarily elevated above another. We must understand that God's plan is that those who do the work of the ministry do so in the context of partnership, not of competition.

Throughout the book of Acts and in the letters of Paul, we see no example of a local church body under the leadership of one person. Not a single one! No, the paradigm of the Word is that of leadership teams. Leaders are to come alongside one another, to join in partnership for the growth of the Kingdom of God. As leaders work together, they are able to grow in their ministry and in supporting one another in the furtherance of the cause of Christ.

Of course, this is often easier said than done. There are many reasons why ministers may not promote ministry partnerships. It is easier to do things alone; it may be quicker, at least in the short term; and there is no yielding of control.

A minister may be concerned that partnering in ministry will reduce his value in the eyes of the congregation. Functioning within a team structure may be a new way of doing things; there may have been no training, and expectations may be poorly understood. Too often there are no clear role models of this type of ministry functioning effectively.

In addition, ministry partnerships require a clear vision that can be articulated between the members of the team. As leaders make the transition into team ministry, their roles are redefined. None of these things is easy; most require death to the flesh. However, this type of change is necessary if we desire to enter into what God is doing and walk in the second Acts experience.

Why is this new way of doing things so essential? First, it is the biblical paradigm. No one person is to carry the load of ministering to a given church body alone; it is too much to ask. Leadership teams share the burden of ministry, reducing the stress placed upon each leader and enhancing the joy of serving. As they come together to discuss the vision of their particular fellowship, creativity is unleashed and innovation multiplied. Community is modeled for the people, and no one leader is seen as the "superhero." Finally, the giftings of the individual leaders are developed, since no one person has to lay aside his particular gift in order to attempt to fulfill all of the needs.

Forming Partnerships

So how can a local church leader implement partnering relationships with other leaders in the church body? One step is to begin with who you are. What are your giftings? What is your primary ministry gift? Are there other gifts that you have to offer as well? It may be helpful to take one of the gift assessment profiles that are available through various ministries. These will help you to pinpoint your strengths in ministry. Some will already be obvious to you; but there may be others of which you are not as aware.

Another step is to focus on developing relationships. Be aware that everything in true ministry hinges on relationship, both with God through Jesus Christ and with others in the Christian community. You must prioritize relationship as the basis for being a minister of the Lord and doing the work of the ministry. Relationship brings oneness, as Jesus stated and exemplified:

> *The glory which You have given Me I have given to them, that they may be one, just as We are one; I in them and You in Me, that they may be perfected in unity, so that the world may know that You sent Me, and loved them, even as You have loved Me.*   John 17:22-23

Relationship does several other things as well. First, your relationship with God through Christ and your relationship with others in Christian community shows who you are in the church.

Second, relationship determines our role and involvement in the local church. With whom do people relate? Do some people seem to gravitate toward certain ministries or people? Can you see the relationships among people, and how that determines their areas of involvement in the church?

Third, your role determines your responsibilities and your investment in the church; it defines what you are responsible for and to whom you are responsible. Finally, faithfulness in fulfilling your responsibilities determines your reward.

The next step you need to take is developing your ministry team. This requires much prayer as you seek out those who function in the other five-fold ministry gifts. These may be people in your church, or they may be others who are willing to support you and your church's ministry by filling up that which is lacking in the body. It could be helpful to you to ask the church to take a ministry gift assessment so that you can uncover the various gifts within the body.

Along with the five-fold ministry gifts, there are other qualities to consider as you seek to build a working ministry team. In particular, a team would do well to have directing, strategic, team-building, and operational leaders. Let's look at what these leaders have to offer.

A directing leader is the person with the vision. He sees the big picture of what God desires to accomplish through the body in a particular geographical region. He is the risk-taker who makes the difficult decisions. He is willing to do so because he is not looking at the risks involved, but rather has his eyes on what God is doing.

The strategic leader is the necessary accompaniment to the directing leader. He is the one who looks at the details, who analyzes plans and decisions. He is often a perfectionist; in general, he is more cautious and rarely takes risks. While he is also attuned to what God is doing and to fulfilling the vision God has for that people and place, he also has an eye to the details of facts and figures. He keeps the team's feet on the ground.

The team-building leader is a motivator. He is usually not very detail-oriented — he may not even have a specific plan for the things he does. His strength is his interest in people. He is the motivator who helps keep everyone working in the same direction. A people person, he networks among the believers, helping each to find his place in the plan of God. He is also a peacemaker who is attuned to the relationships within the body and strives to see the church walking with one another in love.

The operational leader is a process person. He is the planner, the one who thinks through how to implement the vision. He thinks systematically and plans accordingly. He has some of the leanings of both the strategic and the directing leaders. However, he must be careful not to lose sight of the big picture as he looks at how to implement the various facets of the plan.[2]

The Preparation of the Church by the Leadership

We need to look at the ministry gifts and relationships of those on the leadership team. Then we need to look at what, specifically, they are to do.

When we lived in Virginia, I had a vanity license plate that read "SPINPL8." People would ask me what it meant. Most of them thought it implied that I was a disc jockey or something of the sort. Never did anyone connect it with my pastoring a church.

What's the connection? Well, picture a circus, with everyone gathered under the big top. The show is about to begin in the center ring. As the spotlight comes on, a man is standing behind a table. Eight or ten rods protrude upward from the top of the table, evenly spaced. Beside him is a stack of plates. Suddenly he grabs a plate, positions it atop one of the poles, and begins to spin it as fast as he can. Then he grabs another plate and does the same thing atop the next pole. Then another, and another, until it is obvious he is endeavoring to put a plate on every pole and keep them all spinning.

The whole thing appears to be set up to keep him busy spinning plates. There are enough poles and plates that just as he has got them all spinning, the first one he placed is now starting to wobble. So he races to that end of the table to give it another spin. Now the next one needs another spin, and on and on it goes. Occasionally he's not able to keep up the pace and one of the plates falls and crashes on the ground. But without any hesitation, another plate is placed and spun.

The crowd is both amused and amazed. People start to wonder just how long he can keep going at that pace. But somehow he does, because he has practiced well this art of plate spinning.

"SPINPL8" seemed to define my ministry for me. As far as I was aware, my purpose as a pastor was to get all the people into some place of ministry and to keep them motivated. Without fail, about the time I thought I had everything going, a few here and there would start to wobble and would need another spin.

Worse yet were the times when I just couldn't get there quickly enough — I was busy spinning other plates — and one would fall and crash! But I would quickly grab another person, throw him or her atop the program, and give that person a spin.

Platespinning might have a place in the circus, but it can never be performed in the church! Leaders aren't called to just throw people into a ministry and give them a shove. Paul tells us what our purpose is in Ephesians:

> *For the equipping of the saints for the work of service, to the building up of the body of Christ; until we all attain to the unity of the faith, and of the knowledge of the Son of God, to a mature man, to the measure of the stature which belongs to the fullness of Christ.*
>
> Ephesians 4:12-13

This word *"equipping"* may also be translated as *"preparing."* But its meaning goes deeper than either of these words. It means "to mend in a medical capacity something that has been broken, such as a bone, or dislocated, such as a joint, so it can function as it was intended."

In other words, ministry leaders are to provide an environment where people can be made whole. They are to help people to find their life purpose, and help them to mature in Christ. It's a great responsibility, one not to be entered into lightly. But the Lord who gives the vision is the One who enables us to carry out the things He has given us to do.

As leaders, we must never become so caught up in "our" programs or "our" ministries that we fail to see the greater purpose to which we have been called. We are in the people-building business, not the program-building business. Our job is that of Christ-bearers. We are to bear

the life of Christ within us, pouring it forth to touch and to build into the lives of those who have been entrusted to our care in the Lord.
It may be time for a leader-shift!

1. From a teaching delivered by Stuart Ross of Bethel Temple, Hampton, VA.
2. Adapted from *Building Effective Lay Leadership Teams* workbook by George Barna, (Ventura, CA: 2000).

[Chapter Four]
The Potential for Leading and Changing

The angel answered and said to her, "The Holy Spirit will come upon you, and the power of the Most High will overshadow you; and for that reason the holy Child shall be called the Son of God."   Luke 1:35

When my wife was pregnant with our first child, it became obvious that changes were taking place in her body. The nine-month period of our son's growth and development inside her womb meant she had to change her wardrobe and what she ate, as well as the way she walked.

Clothes she easily fit into were fine until she was a couple of months into the pregnancy, when she started to "show." Now she needed new clothes to accommodate her changing form. She just couldn't fit into her pre-pregnancy wardrobe any more!

Not only that, but what she wore when she was three months into her pregnancy couldn't be worn at seven months. Over the course of those nine months, she had to continue to find clothes that were appropriate for the stage of development she was in.

Another interesting aspect of her pregnancy was her unusual cravings, as well as her need to eat a healthier diet. It seemed she couldn't get enough ice cream to satisfy her craving!

Women who are nearing the end of their pregnancy don't walk. They sort of waddle along. I know I'm treading on thin ice here, but it's true. It was especially noticeable when Jo Ann was pregnant with our second son, Corey. Carrying Corey at two weeks overdue was quite a chore for my wife. Our son was above average in size, and Jo Ann, toward the end, kind of walked a little hunched over with one hand on her protruding stomach and the other on her painful back! Eventually, our healthy eleven-pound, thirteen-ounce boy was born.

Leaders and churches that become pregnant with God's purpose soon begin to experience the changes that result. It isn't long until we discover that a new vision requires a new wardrobe of ministries because what we've been wearing just doesn't fit any more.

We also begin to have spiritual cravings that we have never experienced before. We soon realize we've got to be more careful about what we're feeding the church. Even the way we carry ourselves is much different from the way we used to walk in ministry.

These things have become very pronounced in the church of which I am now a part. The leadership here has been implementing a strategy to found, form, and facilitate the church to be a second Acts church. We have become pregnant with God's purpose, and we have had to change to accommodate this pregnancy.

Every church leader and every church has the potential to become pregnant with God's purpose, but it means we are going to have to be responsible and be ready to make some changes!

Failing to Adjust to Change

The world is caught up in change. It has always been this way; but in recent times the pace has accelerated. Unfortunately, humans are not usually comfortable with change. There is often some pain in the process of having to shift one's thinking or one's position. Someone has observed: "I don't mind change. I just don't want to be there when it happens!" Deep down, quite a few people would agree.

Leaders and churches that become pregnant with God's purpose soon discover that this can be one of the most frustrating times of ministry. Their frustrations are the result of the ever-expanding purpose of God that is rising up within the Church.

One of those errors is trying to fit this expanding vision into the structures of the church that always seemed to work before. Well, just as bringing an infant home requires some changes in the house, so it is in the church.

> *"Enlarge the place of your tent;*
> *Stretch out the curtains of your dwellings, spare not;*
> *Lengthen your cords*
> *And strengthen your pegs.*
> *For you will spread abroad to the right and to the left.*
> *And your descendants will possess nations*
> *And will resettle the desolate cities."*   Isaiah 54:2-3

The first part of this verse could be paraphrased, *"Enlarge your house, build an addition, spread out your home! For you will soon be bursting at the seams."* Sadly, we often don't facilitate the changes about which we preach. People begin to experience a new move of God in their lives and express their desire to step out into ministry in a new way, and we as leaders try to fit them into the old style of "the way we do things around here." New wine requires new wineskins! Don't make the mistake of trying to put the new thing that God is doing in the old containers!

On the other hand, we can tailor the purpose to accommodate people rather than tailoring people to fit the purpose. I have made this mistake in leadership by placing someone in a position of leadership for which he really was not qualified. What often happens in such cases is that the standard of leadership continually erodes as we try to plug holes. Every time this happens, we are altering the standard or purpose of leadership to fit the person, rather than realizing that one size does not fit all. In this case, the standard or purpose cannot change. Instead, leadership must develop to meet the mark!

Another error we can make is not "feeding" this new thing God is doing so that it can be nurtured and developed to maturity. Too many leaders and churches make the mistake of thinking that discipleship and developing proper spiritual habits happen by osmosis. If one of the responsibilities of church leadership is to *"feed the sheep,"* then what we feed them is critically important to their proper spiritual development and maturity.

We need to teach the biblical foundation and practical applications of this new thing that God is bringing upon us. Without that knowledge, people will perish! We cannot afford to have malnourished visions and churches.

There is also the error of not regularly and consistently monitoring and examining the health and status of what is being carried. Just as a pregnant woman requires regular checkups, so the leadership must constantly check on the status of the development of the vision and purpose of the church in every area of ministry. We cannot assume that everyone knows what is going on in the ministry of the church.

One of the mistakes I made in our church was expounding the new vision to the congregation through a series of messages without checking with the leadership to see how they were doing with all the changes. I made the assumption that because the leaders had initially been enthusiastic about my vision for the body and the potential changes it would bring, they would support everything that followed.

Instead, while I was preaching the changes and making them, they were dealing with the impact for the very first time, right along with everyone else. I should have been more careful in "checking up" on the leadership so they'd be prepared for all the possible reactions that come when change really changes things!

Leaders and churches need to prepare for the arrival of God's purpose. How will we facilitate what God has brought forth? Another significant mistake is not preparing people for what is currently happening and what is coming. Along with regularly checking up on people, especially the leadership, regarding all the changes that the new vision requires, it is important to further prepare the church from an administrative and organizational perspective.

I have found that typically many leaders do not communicate change very well, nor do we tend to set ourselves up structurally to accommodate it. A baby in the house requires major attention and adjustment. From decorating the nursery to making room in the refrigerator for all the infant food and formula, the baby's needs must be facilitated.

Sadly, many churches are not facilitating God's vision and purpose for the church, and the "baby" may be suffering considerably because both the leaders and the people are ill-prepared. We have had to make some major administrative, staff, and facilities adjustments in order to accommodate not only what God is doing right now, but also what we expect Him to do in the future. As a matter of fact, our church is currently somewhat overstaffed in some key areas because we believe we need to be prepared for what is coming as the result of becoming a second Acts church.

This also speaks to the error of not being able to "walk" appropriately so that we can accommodate the responsibility we're carrying as a second Acts church. By this I mean that it isn't enough to talk about the vision and communicate it well, but we must intentionally walk in it. Talk has to do with where you're thinking about going and what you're thinking about doing when you get there. Walk has to do with where you're actually going and what you're actually doing! You can "talk the talk," but "walking the walk" is where the real proof of any purpose is evidenced.

Many leaders and churches can talk it up, put it on paper, and plaster it on front of the pulpit; but carrying out what God has given you to do is an entirely different thing. This is the point at which many leaders stop. This is the place that requires a huge step of faith. You can sit and talk about getting out of the boat and walking on water ... or you can really get out there on the waves and walk with Jesus. This is a bigger problem than we care to admit — talking but not walking in what God has called us to do!

Another error we can make is not recognizing the onset of labor, when contractions begin to take place and the water breaks! I believe God does give us signs that this new thing He has been forming in us is well on the way. For a pregnant woman, her "water," the protective sac of fluids around the baby, breaks and signals that it is time for the birth. Her contractions grow more intense and are more frequent. For a leader or church that has been carrying God's purpose around for quite a while, sudden breakthroughs start to occur and the sense that something is perhaps about to happen gets very intense.

Our church has recently come through a time of finding new insight into how God is forming us as a New Testament church. With those things has come a greater intensity of being "squeezed," as an indicator that something new is birthing. We must be careful not to overlook it or to try to offer every possible excuse for what is happening.

This brings me to a final error we make. When God begins squeezing us, we need to get into the delivery room right away! The delivery room is that place of pushing, pain, and finally, posterity! The delivery room is the place of travail! A major mistake we cannot afford to make is not partnering in God's purpose with prayer. As a matter of fact, as we begin to see God's purpose come forth, we need to pray even more. The devil couldn't keep Jesus from being born, but that didn't stop him from trying to kill the Christ Child after His birth (see Matthew 2:13-18).

We often don't realize just how powerful the protections of fasting and intercessory prayer are to the work of the Kingdom. We fail to prioritize prayer in our own lives as leaders. We fail to organize our churches for prayer. We fail to preach and teach on the importance and various aspects of prayer. We simply fail to pray, and that's a major mistake.

Preventing Potential Pitfalls[1]

One of the major pitfalls made by leaders espousing a new vision for the body lies in the area of allowing too much complacency. While we do want people to be comfortable in our churches — able to reach out to others, able to share and to use their gifts — we must guard against becoming comfortable to the point of complacency.

Leaders, too, cannot afford to be complacent. There really is no time to sit back and put our feet up, content in the knowledge that everything is going well with our flocks. Yes, there is a place of rest; but it should be a place of watchful rest, lest the enemy come in to cause trouble. God is getting ready to move, to do a new thing. Surely the enemy will not simply sit back and enjoy the show.

Another common pitfall is failing to empower lay leadership. Too often people are hindered in moving forward in what God is asking them to do because the church leadership cannot fully let go and empower them to minister.

Leaders are to equip and to resource, but they are not to do all of the work of the ministry. They simply cannot! God is doing too much! Is God raising up people to minister in your local church body? Watch those people. See where you can help to train them, to equip them, to give them the resources they need. And once they are prepared, release them into what God has for them. Then stand and watch what God will do.

Another potential pitfall lies in underestimating the power of vision. Vision empowers people to go forth. It gives them something to aim for. Set the vision before the people. Remind them of it. Teach the vision, pray the vision, speak the vision. Every person in every local church should know why he is there and where the church is going. Jesus Himself planted the vision: to make disciples of all nations — locally, regionally, and globally.

Once the vision has been communicated effectively, do not lose focus. Don't allow obstacles to block the vision and purpose God has given you. Is there a city ordinance against concerts in the park? Is there a lack of funds for the projects that will enhance your purpose? Is there a dissenting faction that doesn't want to change to flow with the vision? Do not focus on these things. Yes, there will be opposition any time a local church becomes serious about accomplishing God's purpose on the earth. But that doesn't change His purpose, nor should it change our determination. Meet the challenges and move on.

As we move forward, it is helpful to create short-term wins. This helps to keep everyone focused on the vision. Perhaps the whole city can't be won to Christ during the first month's effort; but maybe some can be reached through a mom's day out service, or through a children's fair, or through a youth concert, or through a family movie night. While the long-term goal is wonderful, there must be some short-term goals along the way. Otherwise, people will give up before things even get started.

However, while establishing short-term goals, we must also guard against declaring victory too soon. This also will discourage people, as they look around and see that the "victory" is not as lasting as they had thought. Why not? Because when victory is declared too soon, it is not a true victory. The fight is not over, and the enemy will redouble his efforts when our guard is let down.

Finally, we must not neglect to anchor changes firmly in the culture of the church. The new things that God is bringing to pass must become a part of church life. They must be seen as integral to the life of the church, not as temporary measures that will soon pass away.

Effecting Change in the Church

It really doesn't matter where we are as churches; we can count on the fact that change will be necessary as we seek to become those bodies of believers who experience a second Acts. There will be transitions along the way. In the natural, "transition" is when the baby has crowned. It's the time when the mother most wants to give up because it's the most painful part of the delivery process. If we truly seek to follow the Lord, then we must understand that transitions may not always be easy.

The beginning of change is to recognize the gap between present reality and the vision of where God wants to take us. What has He shown you that He wants, for you or for the congregation of which you are a part? What things will have to change to get to that place? This is your starting point; it will be different for each person, every situation.

Leaders will face personal challenges. It simply won't work to ask others to change while we ourselves remain entrenched where we have always been. Leaders must first deal with their own personal issues before they can with integrity ask others to change. Supportive relationships — among leadership teams or accountability relationships — will help with this process. Leaders who are changing personally can in turn lead others to change. Personal change will always precede corporate change.

In a corporate setting, leaders must evaluate the present situation before moving on. Why do people support or oppose potential change? What issues are being dealt with? What about the societal culture surrounding the church? Factors such as the political situation, social issues, economic factors, significant trends, and external challenges all play a part. Finally, look at the strengths and weaknesses, opportunities and hindrances that face a local church.

After you have evaluated the church's current situation, it is time to look to the future. Biblical mandate should be the foundation of any future vision for a local church. In other words, we can only look at what we want the church to be in light of the Word. Any other standard fails. In conjunction with the leadership team members, ask the Lord to give you a clear, focused vision that is desirable, flexible, concise, challenging, and inspiring.

Now the vision is to be presented before the people consistently and clearly. Everyone needs to know and understand the direction of the church. This also creates a longing for the vision, or the preferred future, of a twenty-first century New Testament church. Change rarely happens when everyone is comfortable and complacent, but it will always precede progress. If all are satisfied with how things are now, why should they want to make the effort to change?

In addition to considering the vision and the church's present status, we must also consider the people involved. Who will embrace the change? Who will resist it? How can the process be made more positive?

Keep in mind that you should never try to institute change alone. This process is best accomplished when brought forth within the context of the partnering together of a leadership team. Each member of the team should be in agreement with and support the vision.

Trust should be developed within the team as common goals are set and all work together to achieve these goals. The team members should be people of integrity who have credibility with the congregation. As a supplement to the leadership team, other people can be great resources of help.

Once you have set a clear vision, have evaluated the church's current position, and have recruited people to help facilitate change, it is time to look at several possible scenarios for implementing change. Prayerfully, with the team, determine the best course of action. Understanding the areas in which God is moving throughout the Body regionally or nationally will enable you to flow with what He is already doing. This will make transitions somewhat easier, as you can better focus your energy on just a few things.

Leaders will face several challenges during the implementation phase. Time and resources will need to be freed. Relationships must be strengthened, or they may fall apart under the stress of change. There will probably be a diversity of visions which must be unified and refocused. A specific plan, complete with a timeline, will help people to get started.

Finally, once everything is in place and the congregation and leaders are moving in the right direction, be sure to fan the fire. Remind the people of how the change has helped to fulfill the vision and mission of the church. Provide opportunities for everyone to take part in the new thing God is doing. Craft a church structure that will hold and support the change, if necessary.

Change can be difficult in the life of any congregation. But it can be tremendously rewarding, as well. If the change is bringing the body more fully into the purposes of God, then it will be well worth the cost.

So, open your heart to the Seed of the Spirit so you can become pregnant with God's purposes for your life as a leader. As your mind, soul, and spirit are developed through the nutrition of God's Word, you will emerge as God's leader to lead His church in becoming a twenty-first century New Testament church. Your potential and your church's potential to penetrate the community and change the culture will become a powerful reality.

1. Adapted from John Kotter, *Leading Change*, (Boston, MA: Harvard Business School Press, 1996).

Part Two

The Ministry Foundation of the Second Acts Church

[Chapter Five]
The Scriptural Pattern for the Church

So then you are no longer strangers and aliens, but you are fellow citizens with the saints, and are of God's household, having been built on the foundation of the apostles and prophets, Christ Jesus Himself being the corner stone, in whom the whole building, being fitted together, is growing into a holy temple in the Lord, in whom you also are being built together into a dwelling of God in the Spirit.

Ephesians 2:19-22

God is doing a new thing! A second Reformation is taking place in the Church that Jesus Christ is building! I believe we are about to see a dramatic recovery of New Testament spiritual life and purpose in the lives of local churches. In some places, this is already happening, with the fruits evident. After all, it is the local church that will change the world, as we shall see.

Yet it cannot be denied that within the life of the local church, everything rises and falls on the leadership. The church cannot fulfill its intended purpose unless God's anointed and appointed leaders are in place. As we have seen, this may involve change on the part of individuals, or it may involve repositioning of individuals within the body. Either way, God is working to position His leaders so that His people can enter into the second Acts experience and become a twenty-first century New Testament Church.

In the first section of this book, we reviewed some of the basic elements of the leadership of the New Testament Church. Certainly having God's leaders in place is a crucial part of the foundational structure of the Church God is raising up in this day. Now let us turn our attention to some of the other significant elements that make up the ministry foundation of the Church of the new Reformation.

The Biblical Mandate

Do you recall the two lab mice, Pinky and the Brain? Pinky continually asks, "What are we going to do today, Brain?" Even so, church leaders must ask and answer that question often. What is the church going to do today? The same thing we do every day: Make disciples! It all becomes very simple when we realize the Church has a single ultimate purpose.

I am always amazed when I speak with pastors and they cannot truly identify or articulate the business of the Church. Some believe our business is to conduct meetings on Sunday mornings. Others suggest that we are here to meet people's needs. Perhaps our ultimate purpose is worship, or inner healing, or any of a myriad of other things. However important these and many other things may be to the life of the Church, it is made very clear in the Scriptures that the Church is in the business of making disciples.

The biblical mandate for the Church has not changed since Jesus Himself delivered it to the believers just prior to His ascension into Heaven. We find this mandate in the gospels:

And Jesus came up and spoke to them, saying, "All authority has been given to Me in heaven and on earth. Go therefore and make disciples of all the nations, baptizing them in the name of the Father and the Son and the Holy Spirit, teaching them to observe all that I commanded you; and lo, I am with you always, even to the end of the age."
                                                                Matthew 28:18-20

Our mandate is the Great Commission. We are called by the Lord to *"make disciples of all nations."* Let's take a closer look at this divine directive. What exactly is it that He wants us to do? What is the business of the Church?

First, we are to be walking in God's purpose for us. The scriptural mandate is clear: *"Go and make disciples."* This is not optional; it is a command. It requires a commitment of obedience on our part. It also requires a commitment of time and energy as we come into an intentional disciple-making process. This goes much farther than simply giving an altar call. Discipleship is the on-purpose process of re-creating people to possess the mind of Christ. It is developing the influence of Christ in people's lives so they in turn can influence others with the life of Christ. We are asked to sow into people's lives; we are to create, not converts, but disciples. This takes time and a commitment to intentionally work with new believers to bring them into the place God has for them in the Body.

God's purpose for the Church is also far-reaching: We are to make disciples *"of all the nations."* This encompasses the local, regional, and global levels. Our church bodies, no matter how small or obscure they may seem to us in the natural, are to have local, regional and global impact. We may not be able to see how to accomplish this, but God will surely bring it to pass as we believe His Word and walk in obedience to what He has already given us to do. Certainly through partnerships with other leaders and networks with other churches His purpose can be accomplished.

The Great Commission does not only reveal God's purpose for us, His people; it also shows us God's process for accomplishing this purpose. We are to *"baptize them."* As they are joined with a local church, new believers will be helped to grow in relationship both with Christ and with the people who make up His visible Body on the earth. As new believers are immersed in the waters of baptism, so they are to be immersed into the life of the local church. This means bringing people into fellowship.

In addition, we are to *"teach them to observe all that I commanded you."* As leaders, it is our responsibility to make certain that those under our care are receiving sound, biblically based teaching. This is crucial! The priests of our society cry out on the streets, through television, movies, magazines, the Internet, secular pop psychology, the self-esteem movement, humanism, paganism — the list goes on and on. These things indoctrinate people with worldly thoughts. So many are asserting with such certainty that which is not truth! No wonder believers are sometimes confused by what they hear. They need a place where they can receive, respect, and relate the truth of the Word — a place where the priority is to teach people to think like Jesus thinks. Our part is to ensure that they are given God's principles by which to live, His purpose that gives our lives meaning, and His plan to live lives that reflect and represent Christ.

Finally, our mandate gives us God's pledge: *"I am with you always, even to the end of the age."* God's promise is contingent on our partnering with Him to perform His purposes. And His promise brings with it His peace. When we truly believe and know that He is with us, we no longer need feel pressured or overwhelmed by the many tasks that go along with our ministry. We know that what we do will be fruitful. How can it not, if we are walking in obedience to the One whom we serve and who is with us to guide us? We must partner with Him if we are going to perform His purpose!

Just before Barnabas went to Antioch to help with the ministry there, the Word states that the hand of the Lord was upon the believers there (see Acts 11:21). What enabled the Christians in Antioch to impact their culture and see converts come to Christ? It was because Christ was with them, just as He had promised He would be. You see, to have the hand of the Lord on your life is to have His embrace, His favor, and His involvement in what you are doing. Jesus is near to those who are near to Him (see James 4:7-8). His hand is on those who are submitting to His Lordship and serving His purpose. After all, the Church is simply the multiplication of His ministry in the world (see John 14:12-14). We cannot fulfill His ministry without Him. Neither will He fulfill our ministry if it is not all about Him!

How's Business?

Now we know what our business is. Next we must look at how that work will be accomplished. How we conduct our business of making disciples is as critical as what we actually do. The work of the ministry is done primarily through the power and passion of the Holy Spirit.

> *"But you will receive power when the Holy Spirit has come upon you; and you shall be My witnesses both in Jerusalem, and in all Judea and Samaria, and even to the remotest part of the earth."*   Acts 1:8

"You will receive power." What is this power for? Is it to be used to gain our own way, or to coerce God through our prayers? No! God has given us the power to be His witnesses. We are empowered to be true representatives of Christ, showing forth His life to those around us. We are empowered to run with the revelation given to us by Christ. We are empowered to live righteously in Christ. And we are empowered to risk our lives for Christ, who said:

> *Truly, truly, I say to you, he who believes in Me, the works that I do, he will do also; and greater works than these he will do; because I go to the Father. Whatever you ask in My name, that will I do, so that the Father may be glorified in the Son. If you ask Me anything in My name, I will do it.*   John 14:12-14

The power that the Holy Spirit brings is the power to do the work of Christ. The ministry of Jesus is manifested through us. We are ambassadors of Christ, bringing a little bit of Heaven to Earth. This is not simply a nice thought; it is actual reality! We are God-bearers, carrying the presence and the Spirit of God within us everywhere we go! This is how the ministry of Christ is multiplied through the Church.

When Jesus came to earth, He lived as one Man. When He gave up His life, the seed of that life fell to the ground, and He completed the process by which the abundant life could come forth. His seed has been multiplied over and over again — we can see this seed in every Christian throughout the world. Christ is now dwelling within every believer, and His work is being multiplied throughout the earth!

And He said to him, " 'You shall love the Lord your God with all your heart, and with all your soul, and with all your mind.' This is the great and foremost commandment. The second is like it, "'You shall love your neighbor as yourself.'" Matthew 22:37-39

The Spirit imparts the power to show His way! God's love is the motivation for all true ministry. *Agape* love is the way of the Lord. And it is shown in us and through us by His power — not by our own capacity for love and caring. We must rely on the power of His love, for that is what moves people toward Christ. This spiritual act of worship requires the Spirit of God. This is how we do business in the church!

The scriptural pattern for ministry obviously includes some other things as well. For instance, we know that the New Testament believers walked in the power of the Holy Spirit. One way we will recognize the second Acts experience is by the manifestation of that power again today. Jesus told them:

"But you will receive power when the Holy Spirit has come upon you; and you shall be My witnesses both in Jerusalem, and in all Judea and Samaria, and even to the remotest part of the earth." Acts 1:8

This is a place where many have stumbled. The manifestation of the power of the Lord is not given to exalt one person or one ministry; it is not given because we are more "spiritual" than the church down the block, or because we have fasted and prayed enough to earn it. It is a gift; we are to receive it. If we are to display the glory of the Lord, if we are to truly be His witnesses on the Earth and cause His will to be done here as it is in Heaven, then we must walk carefully. We must walk in humility, not allowing pride to enter in, and we must walk in the Spirit.

If the power of the Holy Spirit is not given to exalt our ministry, or to show who is "right," then why is it given? Quite simply, if we are to accomplish all that God has for us, we cannot do it without His power! We need His power if we are to do His work. If we are to minister and bear fruit, if we are to make disciples who are growing in a vital relationship with God, if we are to bring healing and life to those around us and to the world, then we must have His power. If we are to rightly love the Lord and man, then we must have His power.

Trying to accomplish His work by our own strength and ability would be like trying to use a broom to stop the tide from coming in. The ministry of Jesus is to be manifested through us. Which of us can do this on his own?

Modern Models of Ministry

The church I pastor has had a great history of strong leadership and missions support. However, over time as many churches do, it became institutionalized and program-driven. This often happens as churches develop a maintenance mentality, rather than a ministry mobilization mindset to take possession of their communities in Jesus' name. These kinds of churches may seem to have good programs; but for the most part they're really only inwardly focused.

Without any clear purpose or biblical mandate, churches can settle into a place of convenient, comfortable Christianity. Looking around the church, I noticed some striking features. We were exclusively white, mostly upper middle class, and very religious about our routine.

It also struck me that we were spiritually immature in many ways. This was noticeable in one instance when we had four different groups meeting in one of our larger rooms, and each of these groups had equipped themselves with their own coffee makers, coffee, and other such supplies. I actually ended up with appointments wherein leaders came to inform me that someone had used their coffee and they had a suspicion as to who it was! From the staff to those in the sanctuary, we were dealing with a model of ministry that was causing the church to look more like a gated community with exclusive membership than a community center where everyone was welcome. Change was definitely needed to faithfully fulfill the biblical mandate given by Jesus for the Church. By God's grace, over the past five years we have seen our church move closer and closer to the New Testament model.

Churches really operate under two modern models of ministry. The first is the "mall" model of ministry which can be described as many separate ministries sharing the same roof, but not sharing the same purpose, philosophy, or profits of ministry.

In the mall model, people have many doors by which they may wander in and out of a ministry without ever having to enter or encounter the other ministries or other people. They may be aware of them without really being concerned about them. That's just not where they "shop."

In the mall model, every ministry is looking out for its own interest, setting its own agenda, and making itself accountable only to itself. People can come and go in these ministries because there are so many separate entrances and exits. The mall lets me shop at the Foot Locker without ever having to go through The Bon Ton. Men like the mall! But the mall is a poor way to do ministry in the church. It is one of the main reasons why there are so many problems in our churches. That was Bethel's primary problem too, but we set out to change it by implementing a better model.

That other, far more effective modern model of ministry is the Wal-Mart model. Have you ever noticed that there is only one main entrance to go into and out of a Wal-Mart? And in the Super Wal-Marts — the stores that carry groceries — the food, the bread and milk and all of those things, are lurking all the way in the back corner of the store. Why is that? Well, the store managers want you to have to walk through all those other departments to get to what you need. Otherwise, you might not walk through the clothes department, the shoes section, or the sporting goods aisles. In your quest to get to the milk, you just might happen to see and purchase that outfit, those shoes, and while you're at it, some tennis balls! The Wal-Mart model of ministry involves many ministries under one roof, or umbrella of oversight and authority, all sharing the same purpose, philosophy, and profits of ministry.

Interestingly, in the mall some stores will always do better than others, no matter what. And some stores will do better at particular times of the year due to their seasonal merchandise. In each case, the individual companies reap most of the benefits. In the mall model, everything is focused on "my ministry."

In the Wal-Mart model, some departments may consistently do better than others throughout the year, while others may do better on a seasonal basis; but every department is combining to support the overall purpose, philosophy, and profit margin of the store.

Is your church more like the mall model of ministry or the Wal-Mart model? As helpful as these models are, there is another model that puts it all into perspective: the biblical model.

The Biblical Model for Ministry

Our biblical model for the New Testament church is the church at Antioch. I believe we can see in their example at least seven distinctive characteristics for our churches today to embrace and exhibit if we desire to be twenty-first century New Testament churches in a second Acts experience.

A Growing Church

First, the church at Antioch was a growing church. This was a church that was growing both in numbers and in Christ-likeness. They ministered outward, sending gifts to those in need (see Acts 11:21, 26, 27-30). Their fruit, watered by the Word, multiplied and was a blessing both to them and to others. As Isaiah prophesied:

"For as the rain and the snow come down from heaven,
And do not return there without watering the earth
And making it bear and sprout,
And furnishing seed to the sower and bread to the eater;
So will My word be which goes forth from My mouth;
It will not return to Me empty,
Without accomplishing what I desire,
And without succeeding in the matter for which I sent it."

Isaiah 55:10-11

The church at Antioch lived this reality, and they were fruitful because of it. The time for feeding without doing the work of the ministry — especially in carrying out the Great Commission — is over! We must seek God's Presence and with God's power go forth to produce fruit ... lest we be cut off from the vine (see John 15).

This church was a healthy, growing church. This fellowship of believers had a distinctive apostolic message and mission. They understood that theirs was a message the world needed to hear. It is quite evident from the accounts in the book of Acts that there is a direct correlation between the message being proclaimed and the growth of the local church.

Now when they heard this, they were pierced to the heart, and said ...,
"Brethren, what shall we do?" Peter said to them, "Repent, and each of

you be baptized in the name of Jesus Christ for the forgiveness of your sins; and you will receive the gift of the Holy Spirit. For the promise is for you and your children and for all who are far off, as many as the Lord our God will call to Himself." And with many other words he solemnly testified and kept on exhorting them, saying, "Be saved from this perverse generation!" So then, those who had received his word were baptized; and that day there were added about three thousand souls. They were continually devoting themselves to the apostles' teaching and to fellowship, to the breaking of bread and to prayer. ... And the Lord was adding to their number day by day those who were being saved. Acts 2:37- 42, 47

At Pentecost some 3,000 received the Word (Acts 2:41). Acts 4:4 reveals that the church grew to 5,000 believers. The sixth chapter of Acts again illustrates the link between the Word going forth and the Lord being received:

The word of God kept on spreading; and the number of the disciples continued to increase greatly in Jerusalem, and a great many of the priests were becoming obedient to the faith. Acts 6:7

If our churches are stagnant, if they are not growing, we need to examine the message being given. If it is the apostolic message bearing the truth of the Gospel, then it will draw the hearts of those around to hear. If we are handing out life, many will come to lay hold of it.

A Grassroots Church

So then those who were scattered because of the persecution that occurred in connection with Stephen made their way to Phoenicia and Cyprus and Antioch, speaking the word to no one except to Jews alone. But there were some of them, men of Cyprus and Cyrene, who came to Antioch and began speaking to the Greeks also, preaching the Lord Jesus. And the hand of the Lord was with them, and a large number who believed turned to the Lord. Acts 11:19-21

The church at Antioch was a grassroots church. How was it begun? It was started by "some believers" who had been scattered by persecution, who went there from Cyprus and Cyrene and began to preach to the Gentiles. It wasn't started by the apostles, or by any of the people whose names are so familiar to us in the book of Acts. It was founded upon the teaching of the Word by believers who knew and loved Christ and who were sharing it with everyone everywhere.

This church was one which could adapt to changing circumstances. The body changed and grew as the Lord directed. As we have seen, the founding of this church marked the first time the Gospel had been preached to Jews and Gentiles together. This was a very dramatic adaptation for these new believers. Prior to this, the Jews would not even sit to eat a meal with the Gentiles; now they were partaking of the same spiritual food, loving one another as they did so. What a witness for those around them! This had never before been seen — Jew and Gentile worshiping together, seeking after one God. No wonder the church was increasing in numbers; this was something so startlingly new that it was obvious to everyone who saw it that God was doing a work in the hearts of these people.

Rather than being entrapped in the ruts of tradition and convention, we need to be able to respond to what God is doing and saying. We must be able to develop and adapt to changing cultures and circumstances while maintaining our essential nature and mission. We must also be wary of falling into the trap of continually changing merely for the sake of change. Change in and of itself is not the goal; hearing from God and responding to Him is what we are to seek.

What was obvious to all observers is that the church at Antioch expressed a deep commitment to Christ. Because of the very real relationship these believers had with their Lord, they were able to lay hold of the character of Christ. Everywhere they went, they reminded others of Christ — by their words, their character, their very lives. This was so evident that the believers first became known as Christians — little Christs — in Antioch (Acts 11:26).

The influence of Christ on these people could also be seen in the diversity of the fellowship of believers. Just look at their leadership team: Barnabas, a Jew and a Levite; Simeon, a black man; Lucius, a Gentile from Cyrene; Manaen, who was from the highest level of society, having been educated with Herod the Tetrarch; and Paul, the Jewish Pharisee, highly educated and brought up in the Gentile city of Tarsus. The commitment of this church to Christ had captured the souls of those of various races and social classes. Yet they walked in a unity that is not often seen today. This local church was remarkably representative of its community coming together to be a community of devoted followers of Christ.

A Grounded Church

The church at Antioch was grounded, built on a stable and sure foundation. These believers were devoted to the teaching of the apostles, hungry for the teaching of the Scriptures. They were seeing and hearing the Word anew. Jewish believers were learning to see Jesus in the Scriptures they had already heard. Gentiles were hearing, many doubtless for the first time, what the Scriptures teach.

They were continually devoting themselves to the apostles' teaching and to fellowship, to the breaking of bread and to prayer.   Acts 2:42

As the believers devoted themselves to the teaching of the apostles, they were being grounded in the true foundation, the cornerstone of which is Christ Himself:

Both of them stayed there with the church for a full year, teaching great numbers of people. 'It was there at Antioch that the believers were first called Christians.'   Acts 11:26, NLT

So then you are no longer strangers and aliens, but you are fellow citizens with the saints, and are of God's household, having been built on the foundation of the apostles and prophets, Christ Jesus Himself being the corner stone, in whom the whole building, being fitted together, is growing into a holy temple in the Lord, in whom you also are being built together into a dwelling of God in the Spirit.
                                                    Ephesians 2:19-22

The leaders of each local body must examine themselves and their churches. Is Christ the Cornerstone? Are the teachings that are going forth helping believers to be grounded in the sure truth of the Scriptures, or do they lead to conjecture and to being hearers rather than doers? What is going forth? If we are to experience what God has for us in this day, we must be those who honor the Lord and the Word in our meetings, bringing forth words that bear fruit for the Kingdom. Now is not the time to tickle itching ears, but rather to feed and to prepare the people to reach out and to serve others. Only so can we truly make disciples of all nations.

These believers were willing to step out in faith to do the work of evangelizing and discipling. Not only were they committed to the Lord, they were also committed to helping others to become fully devoted followers of Jesus Christ. These early believers understood that the primary task of the Church is to reach all people with the Gospel; our priority is to be that of making disciples, not merely winning converts. This one simple fact can revolutionize the missions models of most churches! We are not simply to see people come to Christ; we are to walk with them and help them to discover His saving, healing, and delivering power as He transforms their lives and relationships.

This is tied closely with the identity of a local church with the five-fold ministry. The apostolic church encourages the flow of the five-fold equipping ministers in the life of the church, both for the maturation of the believers and for equipping them for the ministry to which God has called them. As those within the church are equipped to walk out their giftings, so may they help in encouraging and equipping others.

A Giving Church

The church at Antioch was, fourthly, a giving church. These were a generous people, obedient in the bringing forth of their tithes and offerings. They were willing to give of their own supply to invest in the building of the Kingdom of God in this world. Nowhere do we see even a hint of compulsion or of coercion by man. These people were so enthralled with the Lord and with what they saw Him doing that they freely gave with a joyous and thankful spirit.

> *And in the proportion that any of the disciples* [or, believers] *had means, each of them determined to send a contribution for the relief of the brethren living in Judea. And this they did, sending it in charge of Barnabas and Saul to the elders.* Acts 11:29-30

Each of the believers determined to give. This was not a directive, and there is no sign of a bake sale or car wash; no one pledged a certain amount in order to receive a blessing. These people were in love with their Lord and wanted to bless Him ... and so they did.

A Gifted Church

The church at Antioch was a gifted church; that is, it was fully functioning in the ministry and giftings of the Holy Spirit. There is no sense at all that ministry was something to be "done" by the leaders. It was a shared activity, with the gifts and callings of all encouraged. If we are to experience a second Acts, we must do away with the artificial distinctions between clergy and laity — between the leaders and the people —

that would seek to shut people out from ministering. Each member is to operate and to grow in his or her spiritual gifts.

The leaders' place is not to hinder such ministry, nor is it to take over all places of ministry; apostolic leaders are to equip the body to do the work of the ministry. And as the members are equipped, they are to be released to minister. This was the result of the working of the Holy Spirit among them — Jesus' gift to the Church.

A primary hallmark of the early Church is that is was a Spirit-filled Church. This was a body birthed with the baptism of the Holy Spirit (see Acts 2), a family of believers who understood that there was no possible way for them to accomplish what God had set before them to do unless they went forward in the power of the Spirit of God.

We sometimes lose some of the meaning of the Scriptures if we simply take them at their word in the English translations. For instance, Paul wrote to the Ephesians:

> *And do not get drunk with wine, for that is dissipation, but be filled with the Spirit....*   Ephesians 5:18

Is that all? We are simply to be filled with the Spirit one time and then move forward? Not at all! For the Word here says, if we look to what Paul was really writing, *"Be continually filled with the Spirit,"* or *"Be being filled with the Spirit."* This is not a one-time affair; it is an experience to be walked out continually, day by day. We cannot rely on our gifts, our talents, or our abilities; we cannot lean upon our technology or our programs or our buildings. We must rely only upon the Lord, inviting Him to fill us continually and to give us the grace to obey His call upon our lives.

The Antioch church was a people of spiritual sensitivity, maturity, and giftedness, a body that allowed the Holy Spirit to lead and direct. Endowed with the power and the Presence of the Lord, these people walked softly before God in obedience to His guiding.

> *Now there were at Antioch, in the church that was there, prophets and teachers: Barnabas, and Simeon who was called Niger, and Lucius of Cyrene, and Manaen who had been brought up with Herod the tetrarch, and Saul. While they were ministering to the Lord and fasting, the Holy Spirit said, "Set apart for Me Barnabas and Saul for the work to which I have called them." Then, when they had fasted and prayed and laid their hands on them, they sent them away.*   Acts 13:1-3

As the believers sought the Lord's direction, the Holy Spirit spoke to them, most likely through prophecy or through tongues given with interpretation, telling them to set apart Barnabas and Saul. They did this, it seems, almost immediately. When the Spirit spoke, the people obeyed. No wonder they witnessed God doing such great works! They were growing under the apostles' teaching, they were moving in their gifts, and they were going forth in obedience. What might we see in our day if we followed that pattern? We cannot afford to leave this great gift of the Spirit unopened.

The Church that will see the coming of the Lord will manifest a greater glory as we live and operate in the presence and power of the Holy Spirit. The Church will be a people who hunger for the Word of the Lord as the Scriptures are clearly taught; it will be a people who evangelize and serve others; a people of ministry going forth. It will be a people filled with the Holy Spirit, God's gift, who in turn gifts the Church for ministry.

A Going-Out Church

Finally, the church at Antioch was one that understood the importance of fulfilling the Great Commission. They had a missionary mindset. Theirs was a church that had been founded and planted by those who had been sent forth because of the persecution in Jerusalem.

> *So then those who were scattered because of the persecution that occurred in connection with Stephen made their way to Phoenicia and Cyprus and Antioch, speaking the word to no one except to Jews alone. But there were some of them, men of Cyprus and Cyrene, who came to Antioch and began speaking to the Greeks also, preaching the Lord Jesus.*
>
> Acts 11:19-20

As they were planted, so they grew, sending missionaries to preach the Word. In fact, this became the home church for Paul and Barnabas as they went out to plant new works for the Gospel.

Too often the church is content to sit within its own walls, crafting programs and "outreaches" geared toward bringing people into the church. Yet our call is not to sit safely within our comfort zones; it is to go forth! We are to be going out to where the people are, not simply expecting them to come to us. The Church is to be sent; our nature and identity are only to be found in being sent to do the work and will of the One who calls out and sends us forth. Our goal is to plant that which will reproduce itself, and to equip the ministries to be used in this task.

Our church addresses this need with ministries such as Real Life Cleaners, Real Life Movers, and Real Life Meals. These ministries, and many more like them, have been created to serve people in the community. The people involved in these ministries simply go wherever the needs are — they take meals to the elderly, clean homes for the sick, help people to move. They clean yards, fix porches, and serve a variety of other practical needs. Most of those who are served do not attend our church … yet! But perhaps, as we share and express the love of God, they will encounter Christ and become a part of His Church!

One couple comes to mind as I write. The husband has battled sickness; his wife is confined to a wheelchair. Yet they were so hungry for love and fellowship! After they had experienced this type of love in service through the ministry of the church, they began coming to the meetings. He was pushing her in her wheelchair a couple of miles to get to church! Those are people who hunger for God and for His people!

Once we found out about the lack of transportation, we started to pick them up before services. Now this lovely, precious couple is part of the choir, singing praises to the Lord God. They help with grounds maintenance: He trims the bushes, and she bags. Everyone is significant in the Body of Christ. But if the church does not reach out, we will not be able to touch those who perhaps need us the most.

The church at Antioch gladly sent out workers into the harvest. Those they sent were equipped to do the work of the ministry. How was this possible in the days before Christian seminaries, before evangelism conferences, before equipping seminars? They were able to do this because there was a balance of ministries found within the leadership team of the local church. As the leaders responded to the call of God on their lives, the church was graced to respond to the call of God corporately.

A Grateful Church

Finally, we know that Antioch was a church that worshiped God! Worship was alive. Hearts were filled with thanksgiving and praise. As important as love is to the motivation to ministry, an attitude of gratitude is just as critical as the mindset for ministry. This church was filled with people of grateful hearts who realized what Christ meant to them.

We need an infusion of gratefulness in the Church today. Americans especially seem to have lost perspective on how good God has been to us and how grateful we should be. Grateful churches will be churches full of life, soaring high above the morass of mumbling and grumbling that seems to so easily prevail. There is an attitude of gratitude that enables altitude. We are like an airplane that cannot fly unless the nose of the plane is up. We will have no altitude in God without the right attitude.

The church at Antioch is the New Testament model of the local church's role and responsibility in fulfilling the Great Commission and expanding the Kingdom of God. There are still so many who have not heard the Gospel; isn't it time that we take the scriptural example to heart and allow the Lord to birth new Antiochs? If we do, we will rediscover our purpose, renew our passion, and revitalize our people to change the world!

[Chapter Six]
The Strategic Commitments of the Church

You may have heard the phrase "Beauty is in the eye of the beholder." It's a fairly common phrase in America. What this basically states is that there is no objective standard for beauty — beauty depends on the observer. What one may see as beautiful, another may see as hideous. The trouble with this phrase is that the world today has transferred the basic philosophy behind it to the way we think about nearly everything — including truth.

When we paraphrase the familiar saying on beauty to reflect the modern view of truth, we get "Truth is in the mind of the individual." This is the postmodern view of truth. This mindset concerning truth has become more and more the accepted view of many in the world today.

David F. Wells writes in his book *God in the Wasteland: The Reality of Truth in a World of Fading Dreams* that boundaries and distinctions fall rapidly within the postmodern way of thinking. Wells states that while some of the losses of these boundaries and distinctions have not amounted to anything serious, other losses have been earthshaking."[1] People can no longer tell where truth exists and where it doesn't.

On a trip to India to conduct a leadership conference and crusade, I encountered a vivid picture of the challenge facing a New Testament church in this postmodern twenty-first century. As we traveled to our hotel in Tenali, it became clear to me that there was no distinction between the right side of the road, the left side of the road, and the shoulder of the road. Neither did it matter if you were a water buffalo, a pedestrian, a bicyclist, or a motorcyclist, or a driver in a car, van, truck, or bus or even on a tractor! Everyone had the right of way as far as they were concerned. It was absolute chaos.

What made it even more incredible was seeing an Indian police officer standing in an intersection blowing a whistle and pointing a stick in the midst of this mayhem, and no one paying the slightest bit of attention to him. Seemingly, the only salvation was that every vehicle, from bike to bus, was equipped with a horn that sounded to warn others, "I'm coming through!" No lines, no boundaries, no rules.

This is fairly representative of the world we find ourselves endeavoring to reach. A new mindset has consumed the masses, and it calls into question all notions of truth, structure, authority, and reality. It makes everything absolutely subjective and states there are no absolutes. But how can they be absolutely sure? To assert there are no absolutes *is* an absolute in itself. Oh, how the god of this age has blinded people's minds so that they cannot see the Way (see Second Corinthians 4:4).

What are we to do? We can either stand in the intersection (like the Indian policeman) waving our Bible while influencing no one, or we can begin to turn the tide of the postmodern mindset by invading the thoughts, minds, and lives of people with the message and mind of Christ. As we influence individuals, we influence families, communities, and ultimately, entire cultures.

This can only be accomplished if we return to the sure foundation of the Scriptures as our rule for life. There needs to develop in our lives as leaders a love for the law of God. Only then, with a renewed passion for God's Word, can we keep ourselves and others from stumbling down life's streets without direction.

Passion for God and His Word

One of the outstanding attributes of the early Church was the passion of the people for the Word of the Lord — the Scriptures. As many people came to Christ, there was a great hunger for the Scriptures, as people wanted to know more about their Lord. But this was no mere search for intellectual stimulation; they wanted to know Christ more fully!

This was a time of great consistency in the preaching of the Word of God. Consider the account of Paul at Ephesus:

> *And he* [Paul] *entered the synagogue and continued speaking out boldly for three months, reasoning and persuading them about the kingdom of God. But when some were becoming hardened and disobedient, speaking evil of the Way before the people, he withdrew from them and took away the disciples, reasoning daily in the school of Tyrannus. This took place*

for two years, so that all who lived in Asia heard the word of the Lord,
both Jews and Greeks.   Acts 19:8-10

Paul consistently taught these people the Word for over two years. Notice how often he spoke to them: *"reasoning daily...."* This was not Sunday-morning Christianity! These people carried a great hunger and thirst for the Scriptures, and the leaders of the church were instrumental in ministering to this need. Paul wrote to the Colossians:

Therefore as you have received Christ Jesus the Lord, so walk in Him, having been firmly rooted and now being built up in Him and established in your faith, just as you were instructed, and overflowing with gratitude.   Colossians 2:6-7

How were the Colossian believers to be built up and established in the faith? *"Just as you were instructed,"* Paul said. In other words, they would grow through the teaching and expounding of the Scriptures. This intensive teaching and preaching of the Word of God was to be found throughout the early Church. We read of this in many places where the apostles had gone. What was the result of all this teaching? Let's look back to our passage in Acts.

This took place for two years, so that all who lived in Asia heard the word of the Lord, both Jews and Greeks.   Acts 19:10

As the Scriptures were taught, the Word became a living part of each believer. The Word was once again made flesh! Soon the entire geographic region — "all who lived in Asia" — was impacted by the Gospel of the Lord Jesus Christ.

This is our starting place as well. No congregation, no member of the body, will move into true Spirit-enabled functionality apart from a strong foundation and grounding in the Word of God. We need to stir up within ourselves and within those whom we serve a new hunger and thirst for the Bible. Too often reading the Scriptures, if it is done at all, is done under a sense of duty. How different this is from the recognition that the Scriptures are a life-giving source to be cultivated and partaken of daily! We need to recognize that, no matter how wonderful our meetings may seem to be, without the Word it is all pointless and visionless.

What was the fruit of all of this focus on the teaching of the Word in the early Church? What can we expect to see in our own local churches when we emphasize the teaching of the Word, allowing time for teaching and preaching, and encouraging the study of the Scriptures? First, as we have seen, the people were filled with the Scriptures and the apostles' teaching and were showing forth the Word of truth wherever they went. Secondly, or perhaps as a specific facet of this, there was a confirmation of the Word through miracles.

> *God was performing extraordinary miracles by the hands of Paul, so that handkerchiefs or aprons were even carried from his body to the sick, and the diseases left them and the evil spirits went out.*
>
> Acts 19:11-12

These believers were being schooled in a setting in which sound biblical teaching was joined with powerful encounters with the Holy Spirit. The sick were being healed; demons were being cast out; lives were being freed from the power of darkness. Miracles were taking place! This was a church of supernatural power, rooted in the supernatural reality of God's Word being birthed to life both in and through people.

A further outgrowth of the passion of the people for God and His Word is the confession by believers of sin in their lives. We see this happening after the questionable "ministry" of Sceva's sons.

> *But also some of the Jewish exorcists, who went from place to place, attempted to name over those who had the evil spirits the name of the Lord Jesus, saying, "I adjure you by Jesus whom Paul preaches." Seven sons of one Sceva, a Jewish chief priest, were doing this. And the evil spirit answered and said to them, "I recognize Jesus, and I know about Paul, but who are you?" And the man, in whom was the evil spirit, leaped on them and subdued all of them and overpowered them, so that they fled out of that house naked and wounded.* Acts 19:13-16

These men were trying to show the power, yet they didn't have the passion. They were trying to make use of the name of Jesus without actually taking on the name by walking in relationship with Him. They thought that they could have the power of Paul by using the name of Paul. Why should they go to the effort of walking in Jesus for themselves? They thought they had figured out a shortcut to accessing the power of God.

These few verses contain a strong warning to all who seek to display works of power apart from the deep, abiding life of Christ within. It is the Word within that causes the wonders without. Let's see what happened next.

> *This became known to all, both Jews and Greeks, who lived in Ephesus;*
> *and fear fell upon them all and the name of the Lord Jesus was being*
> *magnified. Many also of those who had believed kept coming, confessing*
> *and disclosing their practices. And many of those who practiced magic*
> *brought their books together and began burning them in the sight of*
> *everyone; and they counted up the price of them and found it fifty*
> *thousand pieces of silver. So the word of the Lord was growing mightily*
> *and prevailing.* Acts 19:17-20

A quick reading of this passage may cause us to overlook some key wording. We may tend to think that this great bonfire of occult and demonic literature, was built as people were coming to Christ. However, that is not what is said. In fact, it was *"many … of those who had believed"* who were bringing forth these occult books.

The failure of the sons of Sceva to cast out demons unmasked the emptiness of religious tradition. Those who had already received Christ saw that there was more to their walk with Him than simply confessing Him as Savior. They realized that they could not just get by on the strength of their leaders' spirituality. This confrontation with compromise and spiritual blindness in the church resulted in the bonfire.

A supernatural purification was taking place, breaking the powers of darkness that had been allowed to remain in the lives of the believers. The end result was that the Word of the Lord was growing in strength and was prevailing over the spiritual darkness. The Kingdom of God was being manifested in that place as a direct result of the repentance and purification of the Christians there.

We live in a time when the occult may be seen all around us. We seem to be surrounded by reminders of it. Our society, as postmodern as it is, has never been more spiritual. Everyone everywhere is searching for spiritual truth; unfortunately, as people determine that the Church or Jesus is not what they want, they are looking in all sorts of other places. Occult fare is featured in books, plays, and movies; on television; and in ads, toys, paintings, and sculptures.

With such influences surrounding us as we live in a fallen culture, we need to ask ourselves to what degree the supernatural life of our churches is being eroded because of the corrupt or occult influences that infest our lives. Perhaps it is time for us to ask the Lord what we are to burn and purge from our lives and from the life of the Church so the Word of God can burn in our hearts.

The final result of the supernatural passions of God's people for Him is that Christian development takes place. The church in Ephesus is one example. As the Ephesian church began to live out the principles of the Word — Kingdom love, grace, and power — great changes occurred in their city.

Strategic Fundamental Commitments

Having a passion for God and His Word is not enough. Many wrongs, even evils, have been done in the name of a passion for God or God's law. Along with that passion must come a spiritual sensitivity and submission to the Lord to live out His Word in a Christ-like, contemporary capacity without compromising truth. There are certain strategic fundamentals to which the Church must commit if the relationship we profess and the results we expect are to match the biblical pattern and example.

First, we must be committed to communicating Scripture.

And he entered the synagogue and continued speaking out boldly for three months, reasoning and persuading them about the kingdom of God. But when some were becoming hardened and disobedient, speaking evil of the Way before the people, he withdrew from them and took away the disciples, reasoning daily in the school of Tyrannus. This took place for two years, so that all who lived in Asia heard the word of the Lord, both Jews and Greeks. Acts 19:8-10

The church leaders were teaching and preaching the Word of God in every church over a two-year period. According to this passage, all who lived in Asia heard the Word — every person! These believers were being grounded in the Word of God. Their lives in God were rooted in the Scriptures in a way that most of the Church today does not even comprehend. These believers were hungry and thirsty for the Word of God. As a result of their desire for that Word, they were being transformed. Jesus was being made flesh in these people, and the entire geographic region was impacted by the Gospel.

The place of beginning is the same for all of us. No congregation, no believer, will move into true, Spirit-enabled functionality apart from grounding in the Scriptures (see Second Timothy 3:14-17).

A second fundamental commitment is to confront sin. We can see this in the account of the sons of Sceva. Recall that the occult books were not brought to be burned as people were coming to Christ; no, these things were brought forth by those who *"had believed."* In other words, as the itinerant Jewish exorcists had failed to cast out the demons, the emptiness of mere religion was revealed. These believers realized that there is more to walking with Christ than confessing Him as Savior; one must also confess Him as Lord, repenting of sin and allowing Him to forgive and to cleanse.

This event seemed to provoke many believers to become serious about their lives in God. This confrontation with compromise and spiritual blindness in the church occasioned the bonfire. A supernatural purification was taking place, one that broke the dark powers which, tolerated by believers, obstructed the flow and the power of the life of Christ Jesus through His body.

It is no different today. We need to take a clear, hard look at our churches. To what degree is the spiritual life of local church bodies being hindered and eroded because of corrupt or occult influences that infest our lives?

Thirdly, we must be committed to calling people to salvation.

Many also of those who had believed kept coming, confessing and disclosing their practices. And many of those who practiced magic brought their books together and began burning them in the sight of everyone; and they counted up the price of them and found it fifty thousand pieces of silver. So the word of the Lord was growing mightily and prevailing. Acts 19:18-20

As sin was dealt with in the church and appropriate steps were taken, there was a profound effect on the surrounding community. Many were coming to the Lord as *"the word of the Lord was growing mightily and prevailing."*

A fourth commitment that is required of the Church is that of being conditioned to sanctification. As these believers were physically burning their books, they were also burning and purging the sin from their lives. They were renouncing the sin and getting rid of its evidence; no longer would their homes be given over to such things ... and no more would their hearts be, either. These believers were being sanctified, or made pure and cleansed from their sin. They were becoming more holy, which is to say, more like Jesus. This is an immediate and an ongoing process in the life of the believer. Like these Christians, we must simply do away with our sinful behavior and practices.

Fifth, we can see in this passage that the people were committed to being characterized by God's sovereignty.

God was performing extraordinary miracles by the hands of Paul, so that handkerchiefs or aprons were even carried from his body to the sick, and the diseases left them and the evil spirits went out.

Acts 19:11-12

God had given Paul the ability to perform unusual miracles. Was this so that the apostle could become better known? Was it to increase offerings? Maybe then Paul could buy one of those faster new chariots. No! God gave Paul this ministry in order that many people would see and come to believe in the Lord Jesus. The miracles were there to lead and attract people to Christ.

No matter what it is that God gives us to do, we must do it under His authority and sovereignty, for the furthering of His Kingdom — not ours.

Sixth, we are to be committed to cultivating spirituality. It is not enough to be good people doing good works; we must be those who are filled with the Spirit of God Himself. Only as such will the things that we do be filled with the breath and the love of God to minister to the spirits and souls of others.

It happened that while Apollos was at Corinth, Paul passed through the upper country and came to Ephesus, and found some disciples. He said to them, "Did you receive the Holy Spirit when you believed?" And they said to him, "No, we have not even heard whether there is a Holy Spirit."

Acts 19:1-2

Paul asked the crucial question: "Did you receive the Holy Spirit when you believed?" Mental assent is not enough; we must receive of the Spirit of God. These hungry people were willing to come into the baptism of Jesus as soon as they had heard the truth.

And he said, "Into what then were you baptized?" And they said, "Into John's baptism." Paul said, "John baptized with the baptism of repentance, telling the people to believe in Him who was coming after him, that is, in Jesus." When they heard this, they were baptized in the name of the Lord Jesus. And when Paul had laid his hands upon them, the Holy Spirit came on them, and they began speaking with tongues and prophesying.

Acts 19:3-6

And the Holy Spirit came upon them. We need the Holy Spirit! The lack of power and of love in the Church is due to the lack of the Spirit of God in our lives and in our churches. We must have His Person if we are to receive of His power to carry forth His purposes.

May we be among those who hunger after God … and are filled.

Finally, a twenty-first century New Testament church is committed to commissioning people for service (see Acts 19:21-41). The culture of the Ephesians was very similar to American culture today. Commerce and trade were very important to them, as Ephesus was the commercial center of Asia Minor. The people of that city were very religious, full of zeal in their worship of Diana, or Artemis. The magnificent temple to Artemis is known as one of the seven wonders of the ancient world. The practice of magic as well as the local economy was related to this temple. So a form of religion mixed with magic and money held sway there as the people bowed down to what they themselves had created. Sound familiar?

Yet God chose to touch that culture, and in doing so He has shown us how to reach ours as well. How? He used a congregation that was led by an apostle and teacher, Paul, who was nurturing and cultivating their ministries as well as exercising his own. These people had been saved; they knew the Gospel of salvation and had seen its power. Their lives had been transformed as they were taught to live Christ in their homes and in the marketplace and as they were equipped to minister Christ in their personal contacts with those around them.

The accounts in Acts show a group of mature believers who could reach people not only with the Gospel of salvation, but also with the Gospel of healing, deliverance, and works of power. Was all of Asia reached by Paul alone? No, for he was teaching daily at the school of Tyrannus. It was as he taught and the others received and went forth that the Gospel was furthered.

These strategic fundamental commitments, absolutely adhered to by the New Testament Church, changed the culture and robbed the world of its gods. It *can* happen again.

By the way, through the conference and the crusade in India, several thousand people made decisions to follow Christ, the vast majority of whom had never heard the Gospel of Jesus Christ before, and thirty-two churches were planted in that previously unreached region.

If we will love God's Word and passionately share it with the world without reservation as the absolutely only means of salvation, we *will* experience New Testament results!

---

1 David Wells, *God in the Wasteland: The Reality of Truth in a World of Fading Dreams*, Wm. B. Eerdsman Publishing Co. (Grand Rapids, MI: Wm. B. Eerdmans, 1994), p. 48.

[Chapter Seven]

The Supernatural Potential
of the Church

Upon this rock I will build My church.   Matthew 16:18

God has something for you.

It may be a new sphere of ministry. It may be a new way of ministering. It may be a new type of ministry. He may have a whole new outlook ready for you, or a revelation that will propel you forward to reach lives for Him.

God is ready to release a second Acts experience. All of Heaven is poised, ready to help His people as they walk into this new thing He is about to do. And make no mistake; what He desires is to reach every person with the Gospel, His message of life and of truth.

There's just one little thing we should keep in mind: We cannot do what God is asking us to do.

Not on our own, that is.

You see, the Church is the most unique, unusual, and yet so dynamically universal agency in the world. Nothing else like it exists; nothing else even comes close! That's because the Church exists in the world yet also out of the world. Although it consists of that which seems natural, it is profoundly supernatural. Nothing else on this Earth has the same level of purpose, power, and potential to change the world. There's truly nothing like a local church when it is functioning in the pattern, purpose, and power of the New Testament!

Nothing man can create or imagine — no government, no philosophy, no corporation, no technology — can do what only the Church can do: impart real life — abundant, amazing, eternal life!

Why is the Church so purposeful and powerful, with such supernatural potential? Because only the Triune God can cause the Church to be what it is! Let's look at the Church, this supernatural "building" originated by the Lord God. How is it being built? Who is putting it together?

God the Father: The Architect

"For God so loved the world, that He gave His only begotten Son, that whoever believes in Him shall not perish, but have eternal life."

John 3:16

This is the blueprint! God the Father is the One who initiated the plan of redemption. He predetermined the role and responsibility of the Church that would be born out of relationship with Him through Jesus Christ. It is His blueprint that we see throughout the pages of the Old and New Testaments. By His sovereign design, the Church discovers her destiny as the instrument of God's invasion into darkness, penetrating the world and producing people of supernatural promise!

As the Architect, God has already planned how the Church is to be founded, formed, and facilitated. He has determined every integral part of the Church, and knows where each part will be placed. Just as God has designed the human body, He has designed the Body of Christ to be fully functioning, mature, and ministering.

Just as there cannot be a building unless there is first a blueprint, so it is with the Church. God has given us in His blueprint, the Bible, the plan for the Church!

God the Son: The Builder

You see, God has a supernatural plan for His people. His plan is as it has always been … the building of His Kingdom, person by person, soul by soul. This purpose can only be fully accomplished through a people of supernatural power. Jesus' Presence is to be made known throughout the earth through the supernaturally empowered body we call the Church.

And God the Son is the Builder, building the New Testament Church.

As the Builder, Jesus has determined the trueness of the building, or its soundness. He is the Cornerstone of the Church. What's a cornerstone? It is the critical part of a building made of stone. The cornerstone was the first block laid after the footer had been formed, and the builders were very careful about how they set it into place. All other blocks were fitted based on the positioning of that one stone. The cornerstone had to be perfectly true, level, and straight, since the framework and the entire structure would be built according to how the cornerstone had been set.

God has set our Cornerstone — Jesus Christ. We all align to Him; He doesn't align Himself to us. Only by aligning ourselves with Him and with His will for us can we build the Church. We find our trueness in His truth. We have strength because He is strong. We have become living stones (see First Peter 2:5), purchased and placed by Jesus, connected to Him and to other living stones according to God's blueprint. Every believer is joined to Christ. But we are also strategically joined together with other believers in local churches, missions efforts, and apostolic networks, just to name some of the possibilities!

Also, as the Builder, it is Jesus Himself who determines the territory of the Church. He has all authority! There is no rule, no realm of power, no government greater than His (see Ephesians 1:15-23). According to Paul, we are seated in the heavenly places in Christ — that is, we are seated with Jesus in His authority (see Ephesians 2:6). God's mystery revealed is that the Church, a supernatural people by virtue of God's plan, Jesus' power, and the presence of the Holy Spirit, can overcome all darkness with the light of the Gospel!

When Jesus determines to build His Church, there is no city code, no zoning law, no right of way regulation that can halt her. The Church will take the territory that she has a right of "the Way" to take possession of! She will move forward based on God's code, God's law, and God's righteousness.

The Church is constantly taking back lost territory — lost souls, lost communities, lost nations — and expanding into all those places. Hell cannot erect any barrier or gate that is able to stand against the Church! Just as God promised Joshua that Israel would be given every place on which their feet stepped in the Promised Land, so it is for the Church today (see Joshua 1:1-3).

We have the authority, signed with the blood of Jesus, to take territory in families, cities, and nations to expand the Kingdom through the building of the Church!

Upon this rock I will build My church.　　　　　　　Matthew 16:18

This familiar Scripture is taken from a discussion Jesus had with His disciples. We can read this account in Matthew's gospel. Jesus is questioning His disciples, asking them who others say that He is. He then presses in deeper, asking who they themselves believe Him to be.

*Simon Peter answered, "You are the Christ, the Son of the living God."
And Jesus said to him, "Blessed are you, Simon Barjona, because flesh
and blood did not reveal this to you, but My Father who is in heaven. I
also say to you that you are Peter, and upon this rock I will build My
church; and the gates of Hades will not overpower it. I will give you the
keys of the kingdom of heaven; and whatever you bind on earth shall
have been bound in heaven, and whatever you loose on earth shall have
been loosed in heaven."* Matthew 16:16-19

The word Jesus used here in referring to the church is *ekklesia*. This
Greek word has its roots in the term for the original citizens of the first
city-state in ancient Greece. What is the significance of this? This citi-
zenry together determined the issues and policies of public life. It was
up to each individual to help chart the direction of that culture. Jesus
was saying here that His intent is to make every member of the body
significant. Each has a place, each has a role, each has a purpose. None
is left out.

As God calls each to His purpose, we would do well to keep in
mind Paul's words:

I can do all things through Him who strengthens me.
Philippians 4:13

Does this mean we are capable of anything if we are really spiritual? Of course not! A more literal translation is this:

I can do all things God asks [or, requires] *of me through the power of
Christ who is resident within me.* [Author's paraphrase]

This is the source of that supernatural power of which we must lay
hold. The power to do what God asks is found in the resident, indwell-
ing Spirit of Christ.

Along with the power we need, Jesus also gives us the authority we
need to carry out His building project on the earth. The keys to the Kingdom to which Jesus referred in His conversation with the disciples are
more than just symbols. This was no mere figure of speech! Jesus was
not one to say what He did not mean. These keys are the powerful principles of the Word. What keys did Christ use when He was tempted in
the wilderness? *"It is written!"* (See Matthew 4:1-11.)

These are the same keys that have been given to us — not mere written words on a page, but true, God-breathed words that spring to life in

the power of the Spirit. These are the Words that bring the authority to unlock what the enemy has locked away, be it a life, a home, a city, or a nation. Christ-empowered prayer, preaching, prophesying, and praise — Christ-empowered lives — belong to those armed with the keys of the Kingdom.

When we are able to go forth in God's plan with God's power, then we shall be people of God's victory. Jesus, as He was speaking with His disciples, revealed His intent: *"Upon this rock I will build My church; and the gates of Hades will not overpower it."* Jesus has promised supernatural victory wherever His people take a stand against the dark powers of hell. The only effective way we can take a stand against Hell's dominions is through the power of prayer.

Just what are these "gates of Hades"? In the world of the ancients, the gates of a city were quite important. There the elders of the city sat to discuss legal matters and to make decisions regarding the city and its people. The government, the courts, the economic center, and the councils of war were all centered at the gates of the city. I believe Jesus envisioned a community of believers whose spiritual acts of binding and loosing would be a force capable of successfully resisting the powers of Hell's rule over human lives and circumstances. How is this binding and loosing achieved? Again, it is through the power of prayer.

If we are to see God bringing forth a revival that will shake the world, a new Reformation, a second Acts experience, then we must become a people of prayer. Prayer is the pillar upon which everything else in the Christian experience rests. Powerful prayer that makes use of the keys that Jesus Himself has given us is necessary for us if we are to be victorious when the enemy comes against us. Looking into the heavenlies, we need to become those who are able to pray with the words of Isaiah:

"The Spirit of the Lord is upon Me,
Because He anointed Me to preach the gospel to the poor.
He has sent Me to proclaim release to the captives,
And recovery of sight to the blind,
To set free those who are oppressed,
To proclaim the favorable year of the Lord."   Luke 4:18-19

Isaiah prophesied these words by the Holy Spirit; Jesus read them in the Temple. He was sent to be the fulfillment of this scripture. He came to preach, to proclaim release, to speak forth recovery of sight and freedom and the favorable year of the Lord. As we read the Scriptures, we can see Him doing all of these things as He went about ministering, doing the will of His Father.

Do you want to know something incredible? We are sent for these things, too! We are to preach, to proclaim, to see that things of this world conform to the will of the Father in Heaven. I believe there is more for us than a nice, comfortable state of unity with one another in the Church. God desires that we reach out to others and that we go forth in faith, bringing release and freedom and vision as we come to them. We are to proclaim today the favorable year of the Lord!

We are joined with Jesus, as co-workers, building His Church — the mobilized, multiplied, manifested ministry of Jesus in the world!

God the Spirit: The Construction Foreman

Finally, God the Spirit is the Construction Foreman of the Church. He is the Overseer, the One who makes sure that each worker is doing his job. He also makes certain that each worker is equipped to carry out his part of the project. What construction foreman would expect a new building to be created without the use of excavators and dump trucks? From the electrical wiring through the laying of tile and the painting of the rooms, the construction foreman has to keep the project moving through its various stages. This is what the Holy Spirit does.

As the construction foreman makes certain that every facet of construction is going according to schedule, so the Holy Spirit moves according to God's time. And just as it is the job of the construction foreman to handle any problems that may arise, so the Holy Spirit works according to His own plan to overcome what we see as insurmountable obstacles.

We cannot be a true New Testament Church by recognizing God the Father's role and God the Son's role while exempting the work of God the Spirit. It was not the Father's intent that the Church should rise up and replace the Spirit by walking in its own strength. It is in this Church Age, the time between Pentecost and the Rapture, that the Holy Spirit's function is so critical. As we have been looking to the biblical model of a supernatural Church, there is one central concept, one crucial experience, that we really need to grasp if we want to be a New Testament Church in this twenty-first century. We must have supernatural power! We can see this revealed in the account of the church at Ephesus.

The book of Acts in chapters 18 and 19 explains that Paul did not come to Ephesus to begin a new work; he came to what was already a believing flock. These Christians had a level of biblical faith, but Paul recognized that it was not enough. After seeing what was going on in and around the church there, he asked a crucial question.

It happened that while Apollos was at Corinth, Paul passed through the upper country and came to Ephesus, and found some disciples. He said to them, "Did you receive the Holy Spirit when you believed?" And they said to him, "No, we have not even heard whether there is a Holy Spirit."   Acts 19:1-2

In other words, God's plan was in place; Jesus was building up the church; but where was the Spirit bringing facilitation? Paul's response to this was immediate:

And he said, "Into what then were you baptized?" And they said, "Into John's baptism." Paul said, "John baptized with the baptism of repentance, telling the people to believe in Him who was coming after him, that is, in Jesus." When they heard this, they were baptized in the name of the Lord Jesus. And when Paul had laid his hands upon them, the Holy Spirit came on them, and they began speaking with tongues and prophesying.   Acts 19:3-6

"Did you receive the Holy Spirit when you believed?" The answer of these believers, who did know salvation, and Paul's response to them teaches us two absolutes that are needed if we are to understand the pattern for a supernatural church.

First, people need more than religious ideas about the Lord; they need more than a secondhand knowledge. They need to know Him intimately! God desires that every believer have a unique and personal relationship with Him.

Secondly, newborn believers not only need to hear about the Holy Spirit, but they also need an experiential encounter with His power. For it is this imparting of power that propels people to boldly proclaim the Good News to the ends of the earth (see Acts 1:8; 4:29-31).

Central to this teaching, crucial to the idea of the second Acts experience, is the reality that a supernatural church depends upon more than teaching and grounding people in God's Word. It also depends on every individual having an encounter and ongoing experience with the Holy Spirit. The ministry of the Spirit rests upon each believer having an encounter with the Lord Jesus Christ. Yet how many of our programs and meetings do not lead people to encounter God in the fullness of His Spirit?

Being filled with the Holy Spirit is not an option, but a necessity if Jesus is to build us together into a *"dwelling of God in the Spirit"* (Ephesians 2:21-22) and if His Church is to be *"strengthened with power through His Spirit in the inner man"* and *"filled up to all the fullness of God"* (Ephesians 3:16, 19). We cannot expect to walk in a supernatural plan with supernatural power if we are not living supernatural lives. And that is possible only when we are supernaturally filled with the Holy Spirit Himself.

As leaders we are charged with more than simply educating God's people; we are appointed to lead in an incarnating. What do I mean by that? I mean simply that we are, in reality, the Body of Christ. As we walk in obedience and death to self, His life may flow through us, so that He lives His life in us and through us to reach those around us. We have heard many times that we are Christ's hands and feet to minister to others; yet without the Spirit, the Body is dead (see James 2:26). The building has no function or facilitation.

As the Church is led into a supernatural empowering for ministry by the Holy Spirit, it will result in a biblical Church with supernatural vitality, as Christ-replicating ministry is realized and released. This is how we become a Spirit-formed Church — a second Acts Church.

We are to be a people formed of the Holy Spirit:

He saved us, not on the basis of deeds which we have done in righteousness, but according to His mercy, by the washing of regeneration and renewing by the Holy Spirit, whom He poured out upon us richly through Jesus Christ our Savior. Titus 3:5-6

We are to be a people filled with the Holy Spirit:

And do not get drunk with wine, for that is dissipation, but be filled with the Spirit, speaking to one another in psalms and hymns and spiritual songs, singing and making melody with your heart to the Lord; always giving thanks for all things in the name of our Lord Jesus Christ to God, even the Father. Ephesians 5:18-20

And we are to be a people facilitated by the Holy Spirit:
Now the Lord is the Spirit, and where the Spirit of the Lord is, there is liberty. But we all, with unveiled face, beholding as in a mirror the glory of the Lord, are being transformed into the same image from glory to glory, just as from the Lord, the Spirit. Therefore, since we have this ministry, as we received mercy, we do not lose heart. Second Corinthians 3:17-4:1

Let us encourage and embrace all that God has for His Church! As we move forward in the things He has for us, we will become the second Acts Church, experiencing life in Christ in much the same way our brothers and sisters in the early Church did.

Let us continue to walk with our Lord, growing in our passion for Him, for His people, and for the expansion of His Kingdom. May we be, as the New Testament Church was, firmly rooted in the Lord.

Therefore as you have received Christ Jesus the Lord, so walk in Him, having been firmly rooted and now being built up in Him and established in your faith, just as you were instructed, and overflowing with gratitude.   Colossians 2:6-7

May we lay hold of what He has for us, and may His Kingdom come and expand into all the earth!

[Chapter Eight]
The Seven Pillars of Ministry Foundation

Wisdom has built her house,
She has hewn out her seven pillars .   Proverbs 9:1

When my wife and I were first married, we lived in a 12' x 70' trailer on an acre of land that my father-in-law had given to us. We lived in that trailer for three years, and I have to confess that I didn't exactly enjoy the experience. First of all, every time there were high winds the trailer would rock back and forth until I almost felt seasick! And pieces of the skirting — the aluminum attached around the base of the trailer to hide the area underneath and give the impression of a foundation — would invariably blow off and end up scattered wherever the wind would blow them!

Secondly, every time it rained, the metal roof would leak like a sieve. No matter how many times I tarred that roof, it still leaked. Finally we had to completely cover it over with a new shingled wooden roof that the trailer really wasn't structurally capable of handling. Imagine lying in bed and asking yourself whether the roof is going to hold up, or if it will come crashing down on you at any moment!

And since we lived in an area where we experienced some rather cold temperatures in the winter, the water pipes under the trailer sometimes froze and burst. Mice were frequent visitors, since trailers without foundations are easy to get into! We couldn't get that trailer to be warm enough in the winter or cool enough in the summer!

Now, I was grateful to have a roof over my head, as long as it stayed up there. And I was thankful for a floor under my feet, as long as it didn't shake too badly when the wind blew. But what I was really looking forward to was living in a house — a nice, solid house.

That trailer was certainly more than a place to stay; even with all of its problems, it was our home. Still, there was a considerable difference between that trailer and a house.

We saved up until we were finally able to build a house on the same lot, behind the trailer. I was rejoicing the day we moved in. Imagine! We were moving into a house — a house with a foundation, with a basement, with hallways where we could actually turn to the right or to the left, a house with two stories, firmly set on a solid foundation!

The first night in our new home there were no thoughts of the roof falling in on us, or of the walls and floor shaking from the wind, or of water leaking, or of it being too cold or too hot. Instead, there was a profound sense of security and peace, for we were living in a house that had been built according to a blueprint and the right specifications. Everything, from the footer to the framing to the floors to the flashing on the roof was built according to the plan. It took some time to build. We just didn't pull it up onto the lot and park it! No, it was built from the ground up and it was built to accommodate our growing family. What a blessing!

Both Wisdom and Folly have houses to which mankind is invited. We each choose to which house we will go. Wisdom has "built" her house; she has worked at it, followed a plan, established it. Her house is spacious, for it has been built on seven pillars. These foundational pillars are just as vital to the Church today as they were to the early Church, or to the Jews for whom this description was first written. I believe these pillars exist to support all the ministries we see in the accounts of the early Church ... and beyond, even to today.

Jesus said: *"I will build My church"* (Matthew 16:18). I believe He began the building of His Church at Pentecost (see Acts 2) by building it on seven specific pillars. These pillars make up the ministry foundation of the second Acts Church.

The book of Acts contains a beautiful picture of the early believers as they came together to form the Body of Christ. If we examine a few verses of chapter two, we can find the seven foundational pillars upon which those early believers based their experience of life in Christ — pillars that have supported the expanding ministry of the New Testament Church to this day. Here we can see the foundational support for what God is doing in the Church today.

They were continually devoting themselves to the apostles' teaching and to fellowship, to the breaking of bread and to prayer.
Everyone kept feeling a sense of awe; and many wonders and signs

were taking place through the apostles. And all those who had believed were together and had all things in common; and they began selling their property and possessions and were sharing them with all, as anyone might have need. Day by day continuing with one mind in the temple, and breaking bread from house to house, they were taking their meals together with gladness and sincerity of heart, praising God and having favor with all the people. And the Lord was adding to their number day by day those who were being saved. Acts 2:42-47

This passage refers to the church at Jerusalem. We know that God had given them the pattern for the Church He was — and is — building. They were faithful to the pattern, building the Church in the world. What was the result? God was moving greatly in that church. Many were being saved, the church was being added to daily, and they were meeting together in their homes and at the Temple. This was a church of ingathering. They were gathering people in as many more believed the Word of truth. This was a vibrant body, growing in numbers and in maturity, knowledge, and influence.

But then something happened: The believers began to be persecuted. Suddenly the believers were scattered about, going to Judea and Samaria, and to the outer reaches of their world. But they had gone through the time of gathering in; they had grown and learned. So they were not defeated — not at all. Many churches were planted and the Word of God was spread.

Again, this is where we see the paradigm shift in the book of Acts. No longer is the focus primarily upon Peter and his work at the church in Jerusalem; now we see more and more of Paul and his work among the Gentiles. We read more of the church at Antioch. And instead of a gathering-in church, Antioch became a going-out church. This is our pattern for ministry. If we want to see what the church at Antioch saw, if we want to experience the book of Acts in our own churches and in our own lives, then we must be faithful to build according to the pattern that God has set before us.

As we examine the seven pillars of ministry foundation, we have three areas of concern with each pillar: foundation, formation, and facilitation.

Foundation, Formation, and Facilitation

First, we must understand that the foundation is the one God Himself has laid. We cannot build our own foundation, nor can we add to the foundation that has been established for us; if we are to be co-workers with Christ, building God's Church, it must be on God's foundation. Each of the pillars must be built on the true foundation. We must be sure that our foundation is built on the truth of the Word, with Christ Jesus Himself as the Cornerstone.

> *So then you are no longer strangers and aliens, but you are fellow citizens with the saints, and are of God's household, having been built on the foundation of the apostles and prophets, Christ Jesus Himself being the corner stone, in whom the whole building, being fitted together, is growing into a holy temple in the Lord, in whom you also are being built together into a dwelling of God in the Spirit.*
>
> Ephesians 2:19-22

Once the foundation is in place, we may begin to build. It is at this point that we must be careful about formation. What is the plan? No one would build a home without first having some idea of what it is to look like when it is finished. While the building is going up, it won't look like it will at the end. While the plumbing and electrical lines are being put into place, while the scaffolding is still up, while the carpenters and painters are doing their jobs, the house certainly doesn't look finished. But each worker is concerned with doing his part so that the whole will be according to the plan. So it is with us. In everything we do, we must keep the plan in place. God has already given us a blueprint. Our task is to follow it.

This brings us to the facilitation of the plan. Just how are we to build? What can we do to facilitate that building? We know that building the Church is beyond our ability; we need the power of the Holy Ghost. The transformation of lives is a spiritual matter, not a physical one. That is why is it so crucial to build on the pattern given to us by our supernatural God.

That pattern begins with seven pillars, which speak of foundation and structure — the kind of structure and strength that are needed to support the work of God. The Church is wonderfully large, and God is continually adding to it. Therefore the House that God is building is huge, founded upon seven pillars. These pillars must be the foundation on which all of the ministries of the Church rest. No matter what name you give them or how they are organized, a New Testament Church capable of changing its world will be built on these seven foundational pillars of ministry.

We will look at each of the seven pillars briefly in this chapter; later we will examine them more carefully, one by one.

The Pillar of Passion for God

The Church in Acts was a passionate church. The early believers were passionate about their relationship with God and their relationships with one another. The Church was devoted to coming together to worship their God. Believers met together at the Temple on a regular basis; they met together in one another's homes. They came together to fellowship, to worship, to learn. They met together to share their passion for God.

Look at what the Bible says about this group of believers:

> *They joined with the other believers and devoted themselves...*
> *A deep sense of awe came over them all...*
> *All the believers were meeting together constantly...*
> *They worshiped together at the Temple...*
> *...all the while praising God...*
> *...the believers met regularly at the Temple...*
> *...these men were worshiping the Lord...*
> Acts 2:42,43,44,46,47; 5:12; 13:2, NLT

These believers were passionate about God. Our churches need to be built on worship gatherings, on times of coming together with one another and expressing our passion for God.

The Pillar of Partnering With Other Believers

The New Testament Church was a body of believers who were devoted to one another. They came together frequently in small groups to fellowship with one another, support one another, and grow in their relationship with Jesus Christ. How do we grow? We grow in the context of fellowship.

If we want to grow as Christians, we need to have fellowship with Jesus Christ. If we want to become more like Jesus, we need to be with Him; we need to see Him so that we can grow to be more like Him (see First John 3:2). How is Jesus on display in the world today? Although He is not literally walking among us in physical form, He is walking among us by His Spirit in every believer's life and heart. Therefore we need to fellowship on a regular basis with other believers so that we can more clearly see Jesus.

We should be providing opportunities for believers to meet together regularly in small groups. This provides the opportunity for sharing, for being open with one another, for speaking into one another's lives that a larger weekly gathering cannot provide.

In the local church I serve, we have LIFE groups that meet regularly. These small groups support the concept of *Living In Focus Everyday*, as members help to keep one another focused on the Lord Jesus and on His plan and purpose in the earth. As leaders, we are committed to encouraging and supporting these groups, as we believe they are an excellent vehicle for personal growth, for training in ministry, for mentoring, for counseling, and for fellowship.

The Pillar of Power Through Prayer

The New Testament Church was a community of believers who declared a bold faith through the power of prayer. They were committed to strategically praying for the power to boldly advance the Kingdom of God.

There is a direct relationship between our prayer life and our strength, both individually and corporately. If we have spent little time in the Presence of God, we will have little strength; but thank God that the opposite is true! When we are spending time before the Lord, praying to Him, listening to His voice, surrounded by His presence, then we will grow in spiritual strength.

Why is there a lack of power in some churches today? I believe it is because of the lack of time spent in prayer and fasting (Matthew 17:14-21).

We must also have a proper approach, a right mindset, when we come before the Lord. When the Christians we read of in the New Testament came up against opposition, they brought it to the Lord in prayer. But did they pray as many today do? "Oh, Lord, please make the devil go away!" No! They understood that while they were on the earth they would have the enemy and his schemes to deal with, especially if they were very supernaturally and strategically penetrating the enemy's lines with the power of God!

Instead, they implored God, "Please, O Lord, make us stronger. Give us Your power to resist the works of the enemy, and help us to stand firm in You!" This is proclaiming a strong faith through the power of prayer.

That's why we call our prayer ministry in our church SWAT Operations. We identify the very purpose for our praying with this acrostic. It stands for *Spiritual Warfare Attack Teams* and also for *Spiritual Warfare Action Times*. In this way, we are mobilized in prayer teams of intercessors, and also corporately for strategic times of prayer.

What was and is God's response to this type of prayer?

And when they had prayed, the place where they had gathered together was shaken, and they were all filled with the Holy Spirit and began to speak the word of God with boldness. Acts 4:31

Let's be careful not to be so concerned with looking for the shaking that we neglect to see the boldness the Lord would release to us as we come to Him.

The Church in Acts was a praying people. They were following the pattern modeled by Christ Jesus Himself when He walked the earth. There was a relationship between the time that Jesus spent in fasting and prayer and the things He was able to accomplish for the glory of the Father.

The second Acts experience will never be ours if we neglect to spend time on our knees before the Lord. We need to be on our faces before God for everything else springs from our relationship with Him.

How vital are the prayer meetings in our churches? Do we encourage the prayer warriors? Are we involved with prayer teams, with intercessory prayer, with deliverance prayer, with community-wide prayer gatherings? Are we helping the churches we serve to be praying churches?

The Pillar of Principles by Which to Live

The New Testament Church was a community of believers walking together and developing a strong character as the people of God. The apostles, as we have seen, were devoting themselves to the teaching of the Word, and so were the people. They were listening to the teaching and prophecy going forth, and these were becoming the principles by which they lived their lives.

Is it natural human nature to sell all of our possessions and share the money with those who have need? Is it human nature to invite all kinds of people from various races and societal classes to come into our homes, regularly sharing our hospitality and our time? Is it a normally accepted thing for us to drop what we are doing to go help others, or to pray with others, or to hear the Word of the Lord? Oh, that it were! But these things are only "natural" by the Spirit of God.

As these believers were devoting themselves to the hearing of the Word, it was entering into their minds and spirits and becoming the principles by which they lived. This was a community of believers that was developing a strong character of righteousness.

Even more so today, we need to be careful of the principles by which we live our lives. It is easy in our culture to slip into materialism or commercialism, easy to believe the lie that it is what we see that is reality. Yet God has more for us.

Our purpose is to make disciples, and it must be an on-purpose purpose. Discipleship does not happen by osmosis. We don't naturally gravitate upward! We need to be devoting ourselves to the discipline of making disciples.

In addition to our LIFE groups (what we call our cell groups), our local church is developing a process of discipleship called the LIFE Institute, which includes three levels: Foundations of LIFE, Formation for LIFE, and Facilitation in LIFE. We also have an Advanced Ministry Level for interns and others desiring to enter into full-time ministry. These classes can help believers to grow in their relationship with the Lord and in the use of their ministry gifts. As we train believers to be disciples, the fruit in their lives is evident. Only true disciples can make disciples.

The Pillar of Providing for the Needs of Others

The New Testament believers cared for others both inside and outside the church. They did not allow themselves to be limited by what they could do; they looked to what God could do through them.

Examples of such ministry are evident throughout the book of Acts, as well as through the rest of the New Testament:

> *And all those who had believed were together and had all things in common; and they began selling their property and possessions and were sharing them with all, as anyone might have need.* Acts 2:44-45
> *And the congregation of those who believed were of one heart and soul; and not one of them claimed that anything belonging to him was his own, but all things were common property to them. ... For there was not a needy person among them, for all who were owners of land or houses would sell them and bring the proceeds of the sales and lay them at the apostles' feet, and they would be distributed to each as any had need.* Acts 4:32, 34-35

So the twelve summoned the congregation of the disciples and said, "It is not desirable for us to neglect the word of God in order to serve tables. Therefore, brethren, select from among you seven men of good reputation, full of the Spirit and of wisdom, whom we may put in charge of this task. But we will devote ourselves to prayer and to the ministry of the word."

Acts 6:2-4

And in the proportion that any of the disciples had means, each of them determined to send a contribution for the relief of the brethren living in Judea.   Acts 11:29

God was moving among this body, raising up those who would engage in care ministry, visiting the sick, counseling, and giving. These are the ones the Lord uses to love people into the Kingdom. Care ministry is to bless believer and nonbeliever alike:

So then, while we have opportunity, let us do good to all people, and especially to those who are of the household of the faith.

Galatians 6:10

This pillar is one that is sometimes overlooked in the busyness of our lives. Yet it is an important part of God's plan for His people, a foundational pillar in the Church. We need those who will take the time to care for others, thus expressing God's love in a tangible way. As leaders we need to reach out to strengthen, encourage, and support those God is raising up in the Body of Christ who will have that kind of compassion, heart, and desire to minister to others.

The Pillar of Planting Churches

This foundational pillar involves reproduction through Kingdom expansion efforts. The early Church was consistently reproducing itself as many people came to the Lord. And God desires no less for us today.

God is still using the apostolic ministry in the Church, because the very essence of the New Testament Church is apostolic. The first-century Christians were committed to expanding the Kingdom by sending out people to plant churches. God was giving this parent Church favor around its world. As people were being saved, new offspring churches were planted, leaders were trained, and those offspring churches began planting churches as well. This was the apostolic gift in action, and this is what God wants us to do today.

We can see the first part of this cycle in the book of Acts. First, we find the disciples walking in love with the Lord and with one another, fellowshipping together and going daily to the Temple for prayer and worship.

Day by day continuing with one mind in the temple, and breaking bread from house to house, they were taking their meals together with gladness and sincerity of heart, praising God and having favor with all the people. And the Lord was adding to their number day by day those who were being saved.   Acts 2:46-47

The response is clear: People were being added to the Kingdom and the Church was walking in favor with the people. The next step of the cycle is seen in Acts 13:

While they were ministering to the Lord and fasting, the Holy Spirit said, "Set apart for Me Barnabas and Saul for the work to which I have called them." Then, when they had fasted and prayed and laid their hands on them, they sent them away.   Acts 13:2-3

Finally, Acts 13 to 28 is a record of city after city in which churches were planted through apostolic ministry.

If we desire to see our churches walking in a second Acts experience, we must commit to making disciples locally, regionally, and globally through our Kingdom expansion efforts. Within our churches, we are called to impart the vision for Kingdom expansion, sharing what God is calling us to do. We must intercede, that God would show us His path. Where are we to go? Where does God want us to begin a new work? Or maybe a replant is necessary (revitalizing an existing, yet struggling church, and turning it around by installing Spirit-anointed and appointed people, programs, and purpose that will effect health, growth and fruit). Next, we must investigate the strategic place the Lord shows us, looking for any special directives the Lord may have for us there.

Our next task is to identify the key people who will go, as well as the people God is raising up there among the new believers. Finally, we can implement the church planting process — making disciples, not just converts — and involve others in ministry partnerships as they are trained, in turn, to go forth.

The Pillar of Promoting Jesus in a REAL Way

We are to reach the lost. This is closely related to Kingdom expansion, but does not necessarily require the establishment of a new local church. Rather, our churches should be places where new believers are coming in to grow in God. People should be being saved; our churches should be growing. Why? Is it so we can have large churches? No; this is simply the normal, healthy life of the Church. We are to evangelize the world in the most effective way possible.

How can we promote Jesus in a "real" way? By providing evangelism efforts that are REAL; that is to say, *R*elevant, *E*ffective, *A*ccountable, and *L*oving.

Our efforts should be relevant to our culture, connecting with people where they are. We must be effective in our commission, keeping our purpose and focus clear. We should at all times be accountable to our Christianity, keeping our words and conduct above reproach. Finally, we should be loving in our conduct toward all, that we may win some.

We cannot simply reuse the same old programs we have always used if they are no longer relevant, effective, accountable, or loving to those we are trying to reach. How absurd it is to keep doing the same things over and over, yet expect the results to suddenly be different than they have always been!

I've seen churches try just about everything they can think of to grow — the latest this, the greatest that. I've been there myself, and there's nothing more frustrating when the results keep turning out the same. Some just keep doing it the same old way with the same old results, while others try all the ways that seemed to work for this or that church with little or no success. What is the key? It is Jesus' formula: *"Ask, seek, knock!"* Jesus said,

> *"Ask and it will be given to you; seek and you will find; knock and the door will be opened to you. For everyone who asks receives; he who seeks finds; and to him who knocks, the door will be opened."*
> Matthew 7:7-8, NIV

Ask yourself, "What is our purpose as a church in this local community, and are we functioning in a New Testament pattern and power in a REAL way?"

Seek methods of fulfilling the Great Commission that are REAL: *R*elevant to the culture your church is in; *E*ffective in the commission to make disciples by being contemporary to your culture; *A*ccountable to Christ by never compromising truth; *L*oving in your conduct towards those you are endeavoring to reach.

Knock on doors. I have a friend who delivers packages for Fed Ex.

He doesn't just leave important packages at people's doors. He is required to knock or ring doorbells to ensure that packages are delivered personally to whomever they are addressed. We have a greater responsibility to deliver God's gift of salvation to every person, every family in our community. We just don't leave this Gift lying at the door! We knock on the door of people's hearts and enter into their lives through REAL ministries and personally deliver Jesus Christ!

This final pillar is the one that brings all seven together under one purpose: to go and make disciples, locally, regionally, and globally. This is the purpose Christ Himself gave the Church; this is our reason for being.

By founding the ministries of our churches on these seven pillars — worship gatherings, LIFE groups, prayer priorities, discipleship processes, care providers, Kingdom expansion, and evangelism efforts — we will always be right on target with God's blueprint. Then our churches can be communities of believers devoted to God and to one another. We can be those who are declaring a bold faith, developing a strong character, delivering a servant's heart, and demonstrating a global mission in relating the reality of Jesus in a REAL way.

Chapter Nine

The Strategic Plan for the Church

Remember our lab mice? In the *Pinky and the Brain* cartoon it is obvious what the partners intend to do, even if Pinky has to ask his question every episode. The problem isn't with their purpose, but with their plan! The purpose is to "take over the world"; but the plan just never seems to work! Inevitably, both Pinky and Brain end up the victims of their own poor planning.

The Church is called to "take over the world" in Jesus' name. We know Jesus commanded us to *"make disciples of all nations."* Although much of the Church seems to have lost that sense of purpose, there are also those who know the purpose but don't seem to have a very good strategy for implementing it. Perhaps Pinky should have told Brain, "Listen, I've finally figured out that every day we're going to try to take over the world. But do you think we could find a better plan than the ones we've been using? It's just not working! And I'm tired of getting blown up, or run over, or flattened every week!"

Now, we live in real life, and the Sunday service isn't just another episode of some stumbling people who may feel like mice as they bumble around trying this and that to win against the world. We are the Body of Christ! Not only do we have a strategic purpose, but God has also given us a strategic plan that will work and won't leave us crushed every week!

Perhaps we may need to ask ourselves every week just what it is we are trying to accomplish. Beyond that, how are we going to accomplish it? I believe the reason so many churches seem to be joyless, defeated places is that the plan isn't working. Are we willing to change the plan? Are we ready for a strategic plan?

Now there were at Antioch, in the church that was there, prophets and teachers: Barnabas, and Simeon who was called Niger, and Lucius of

Cyrene, and Manaen who had been brought up with Herod the tetrarch, and Saul. While they were ministering to the Lord and fasting, the Holy Spirit said, "Set apart for Me Barnabas and Saul for the work to which I have called them." Then, when they had fasted and prayed and laid their hands on them, they sent them away.   Acts 13:1-3

Have you sensed the intensity of these times? This is such a strategic time on God's timetable. We may look to the first century Church as having lived in an exciting time; but we live in what may be an even more exciting era in terms of the expansion of the Kingdom of God. There are more people today who need Jesus than at any other time in history. Aren't you glad God has a plan?

Just as Jesus stood and looked out over the city of Jerusalem, weeping because of its spiritual blindness, so He stands to look out over the Church today. What are His emotions? We too are experiencing a *kairos* time, a time of visitation where we are being examined and our path is being determined. *Kairos* times are God-appointed times when a situation can go one way or the other. May God find us faithful, obedient, diligently seeking after Him with all that is within us so an explosion of His power and an expansion of His purpose can be realized like never before — even in the first century Church!

The Church has literally come full circle in history. The New Testament Church originated in the midst of a pre-Christian culture. People of the time had no idea of who Jesus was or of what Christianity was about.

Is it much different in America today, or in other places throughout the world? Yes, we have a lot of church buildings, and here in the United States our currency claims that we place our trust in God; yet for every new church that opens, several close their doors. As we've already discussed in chapter five, society in general no longer sees the Church as relevant. Our culture is no longer the premodern culture of our founding fathers, when anything that had any meaning was possessed by authority (an example would be the Church of England) and the individual was dominated by tradition. Nor is our culture living any longer under a modern philosophy of enlightenment — humanist rejection of tradition and authority in favor of reason and natural science. In the modern mindset, God was the sole source of meaning and truth; the value of progress and novelty was enhanced within a linear conception of history — a history of a "real" world that was becoming increasingly real or objectified.

Now, in a postmodern society, especially in America, people reject

God as the Sovereign of the universe and emphasize anarchic, collective, anonymous experience. In other words, there's no rhyme or reason to anything! Collage, diversity, the mystical, "do what you think is right," is the focus of attention. It is an age of the dissolution of distinctions and the rejection of all attempts to define or denote the human subject. We are more hopelessly lost than we have ever been.

And to this culture we are sent out as "sheep among wolves" — but not without an ultimate plan, purpose, passion, and power! By returning to the New Testament model and renewing it in this twenty-first century, we can and should expect the same, if not greater, results than we read about in the book of Acts. Our results will be that we won't be able to contain all the people who will come into our churches.

Today, too often in our churches, we see tired, dry, barren, joyless people who confess God, but are not consumed with God. Yet Jesus told us He came to give us abundant life. In the midst of barrenness and brokenness we are to have wells of living water flowing out from us that will overwhelm everyone around us. This may not be happening in very many places right now, but God wants to make us alive again. How is that possible?

We need to return to our foundation. We need to go back to the pattern and the power that God has given us. As we become the kind of Church that God has called us to be, a New Testament Church, we will experience His power ... and His life.

> *"But you will receive power when the Holy Spirit has come upon you; and you shall be My witnesses both in Jerusalem, and in all Judea and Samaria, and even to the remotest part of the earth."*   Acts 1:8

What is this power for? Is it to show how spiritual we are, how in tune with God? Is it to be used to impress or frighten others, or to expand our own kingdoms? No; it is given that we might expand His Kingdom, both in ourselves through growing in holiness and through witnessing to others.

As we begin to witness to our own Jerusalems and Judeas and Samarias — our own cities and regions — something exciting happens. The Spirit of God begins to well up from within.

What does the Lord God want to do through your local church? As the body walks according to the pattern the Lord has given, the power of God will so come upon you that you won't be able to contain it. It will overwhelm your city and your region. It will begin to build so greatly upon you that it will flow forth to the ends of the earth.

If we will fall on our faces before the Lord to pray, believing that He is the God who wants to pour out His Spirit in a greater capacity than ever before, He will respond to His people. His heart is toward His people, and He desires that none should be lost. He will pour out His Spirit in places like your church and mine. No matter how small or large the congregation, no matter how prominent or obscure the place, God desires to move among and through His people. Let us become desperate for God. Now is His strategic time.

Strategic times require strategic people. We need to understand and impart to the congregations we serve the truth that we are, each one of us, divinely anointed and appointed for such a time and place as this. This is exciting! So many people are living purposeless lives, moving from one round of activity to the next without understanding that there is a purpose behind their being. Yet there is a divine intent, and we are part of it!

God is a strategic God. He has placed each member of the Body where He wills and given each one the gifts He desires. He has assigned us the days and times of our lives. Let's look at how He was working strategically in the church at Antioch.

Then, when they had fasted and prayed and laid their hands on them, they sent them away.   Acts 13:3

Paul and Barnabas were chosen by God to do a certain work. The believers, with fasting and prayer, laid their hands on these two men and sent them out to accomplish what God had assigned them. And the Lord used them to establish new works for the expansion of the Kingdom.

We must continually remember that we have a business in this world, if we are to partner with God in the fulfilling of His purposes. Our business, our goal, is to reach the world with the message of Jesus Christ. We are called to be a supernatural Church, filled with supernatural people who carry within themselves the supernatural power of God. We are also to be a balanced Church, a people who values relationship above cold religion and God's presence above programs. That is God's balance.

God has a strategy for our world. He knows exactly what needs to be done; He knows the essentials necessary for His plan to be most effective. Our church activities are to support this plan and purpose of making disciples. As leaders in the local church, it is up to us to lay the foundation for the New Testament mission and ministries of the church through a strategic plan. This will incorporate preaching, prayer, purpose and people.

Strategic Preaching

"Now there were at Antioch, in the church that was there, prophets and teachers..." The New Testament Church was marked by a hunger and thirst for the Word of truth. And so God raised up teachers to do the work of ministry. These new believers needed those who were able to teach and who knew the truth.

Although Christians have abundant teaching resources available today, strategic preaching is still essential to the effectiveness of the local church. Strategic preaching sets a vision before the church so that all may know the priorities, programs, and purposes of the church.

Preaching strategically involves several factors. First and foremost is prayer. We must pray for God's direction and favor in sharing the vision. If there is no clarity of vision, people have nothing to which they can respond.

When it is time to share the vision, begin with the leaders. Ideally, all can come to a prayerful consensus. Then, when the vision for the church is presented to the people, it will have the authority of the full team, and all will be working in the same direction. Input from all of the leaders can also help to shape and mold the outworking of the vision. And if it a shared vision, all of the leaders can help to preach and teach various aspects of the message.

As the leadership team meets, it is important to evaluate the history and current status of the church. This will be your starting point. It is useless trying to build a full program to support the vision overnight if there is nothing there to begin to facilitate it now.

Share the vision with the congregation. If possible, present it as a shared vision among the leadership team. Be clear and positive, and communicate it often. The goal is that it will become a shared vision among all in the church.

It helps to have a preaching plan to communicate the message as often and in as many ways as possible. Invite people to participate in the new direction each time you preach, and ask others to preach the vision for you when there is the opportunity.

Unfortunately, you may need to accept the fact that not everyone will lay hold of the vision at first ... or at all. Some will withhold judgment for a while, to see how everything works out. Some may simply not want to move in the same direction and so will refuse to be a part of what the church is doing. Whatever the case, do not focus your preaching on the few who are negative toward the vision. Allow them to come to leadership meetings or to meet with one of the leaders to voice their concerns, and try to address each difficulty presented honestly. Do not tune these people out, for they may have valid points that should be considered. But do not allow any negativity to creep into the preaching or into the corporate meetings.

I consider myself a visionary leader. My tendency is to cast the vision before the people and then become totally carried away in pursuing it. The problem is that I sometimes do not consider the pace of the congregation when I do this.

I understood this more clearly once when I was bicycling with my wife, JoAnn. I ride more frequently than she does, and I'm somewhat stronger physically. But I also have a desire to do everything with great intensity — so I must always pedal when riding a bike, even when going downhill.

One day while we were riding I kept outpacing JoAnn. I was so focused on pedaling and on getting the most out of the ride that I would get way ahead of her. This happened several times. I would pedal back to her, only to find myself getting ahead of her again. After I had returned to her for the third time, she said something that has changed my life: "Terry, if you hadn't come back to ride with me, I was ready to turn around to go back home. I'm not going to ride alone. That wasn't our purpose when we started out!"

Then she added, "That's how you head the church at times, too." She wasn't criticizing me. Rather, she was speaking from her giftedness of discernment, and as a result, I learned a leadership lesson that day that I will never forget.

As leaders who carry God's vision, we can so intensely run with the revelation that we can run away with it. If we do this too often, people will have enough — even other leaders. We run off with the revelation, leaving the church to return to its place of comfort. Then we become frustrated with the problem we ourselves have caused.

That day of riding taught me that I need to set a pace that is intense, but is able to involve everyone, even if I have to pedal around and pick up the stragglers. After my wife's words, I set a pace with which we could both be satisfied. I slowed down a bit for her, and she sped up a bit for me. There are times when we each ride by ourselves, and then we each set our own pace. But when we ride together, we are together.

The Church needs visionary leadership that can pace the vision so everyone crosses the line a winner. God will help you cast that vision and carry it out with God-speed — the pace He sets for His Church.

Prior to speaking forth the vision to the congregation, while the people are processing what you have shared, and while you cope with dissenters or answer the questions of the enthused, there is one practice you should continually make use of, and that is prayer.

Strategic Prayer

God is causing a tide of prayer to well up in His Church. You see, prayer is essential to the strategy of God, and it will cause you to be effective in the purpose of God. He is bringing us more and more to a place of prayer that presses in to God, prayer that partners with God's will.

It is apparent from the accounts of the church at Antioch that the believers there spent much time in prayer, coming together for that purpose. Jesus Himself, quoting the prophet Isaiah, declared that His Father's House should be a House of prayer for all the nations (see Mark 11:17).

Prayer is one of the great privileges of the Church. It is our priority; it is our source of power. A praying person is one who is powerful in the Spirit. It is as we speak with the Lord that we reach out to Heaven for divine resource. Prayer is essential and effective when it becomes the priority of the Church because it releases the power we need to be the Church.

We know that prayer is one of the foundational pillars upon which the Church is built. We are to be engaged in strategic prayer — prayer that gets to the point. Jesus had told the disciples to go to the Upper Room to wait for the Spirit. So they went, they waited, and they prayed, as the Lord had told them to do. When Peter was sent to prison for preaching the Word, the believers again prayed ... and they continued day and night until they had received what they asked. We need to have a point to our prayer!

James discusses this very thing. In James chapter four, we are told that if we pray and do not receive, it is because we have been praying amiss; our prayers were pointless, being aimed not at God but at our own desires (see James 4:3). Our prayers — our very lives — should be partnering with God's purposes. Yet so often we try to get God to partner with our desires.

We went through a time in our local church life when we weren't sure of our direction, or of the means to get there. This was reflected in our leaders' meetings. We simply didn't know what to do! So we began to pride ourselves on being risk-takers. If we tried something and it didn't work, we'd say, "Well, at least we took a risk and tried something new." Although, we sometimes plowed into the wall at 90 m.p.h.! Finally the Lord said to us, "No. This is not what I want. Pray, and ask Me what I want you to do." Guess what? It worked. When we ask, He will answer. Strategic prayer allows us to get to the point; it also allows God to tell us what He wants us to do.

Prayer strategies are essential to effectiveness in prayer. In our churches we need to make prayer a priority, both during corporate prayer times and individually. There need to be strategic prayer times and strategic prayer teams for the purpose of enforcing Kingdom power and authority in spiritual warfare. We can teach on prayer, pray in small groups or in the corporate body, mentor or disciple new believers in prayer — whatever it takes to make prayer a priority in our lives.

As we pray, we should repent of both personal and corporate sin. Anything that might stand in the way of our relationship with God should be repented of and done away with. We are to be those who walk in holiness, "little Christs" who manifest Jesus' life. This cannot happen when we have unconfessed sin in our lives.

Prayer should include asking the Lord for corporate and personal revival and renewal. As we ask, expecting, we will see Him begin to move in this way. It may begin with the gentlest stirring of a hunger for Him, but as we continue in prayer and obedience, we will see God move.

And always, as we pray we should yield to the guidance of the Holy Spirit, who will teach us to pray as we should. My mother presented me with a Bible when I graduated from high school. On the inside cover she had written several things. One was this: "No prayer, no purpose, no power!" It's true!

Strategic Purpose

Strategic prayer gives birth to strategic purpose; it is as we come to the Lord asking His direction that He reveals it to us. We need a strategic purpose if we are to be effective. It isn't enough to look at one another and say, "Hey, I know! Let's be a second Acts church!" We need to look to the Word to find what that means, and we need to look to God to find out how to implement what He shows us by the Scriptures.

When we have a clearly articulated purpose, the people of God are released into freedom to minister, freedom to grow in what God has for them, freedom to help in expanding the Kingdom of God in the Earth.

There are strategies to purpose in the Church. We must pray for the revelation of God to the Church. If He will unveil the vision to the people, we won't need to persuade and cajole; the revelation of the Spirit will help the congregation to lay hold of it.

Strategic purpose involves understanding God's plan and how the local church is part of that plan. We cannot clearly communicate the plan if we ourselves do not fully understand it.

If we are to be the strategic people of God responding to the strategic plan of God, then we must respond to that plan with personal and corporate action. Let us step out in faith, participate in the ministry, and obey the purpose of God at His pace.

Strategic People

Strategic people are essential to the effectiveness of our churches in performing their ministries. Strategic people are those who are placed strategically for the carrying out of the purposes of God, and everyone in each body is essential.

God has a part for every person. Each one has a ministry, a gift. Leaders are to help each member of the body to discover that gift and to help in training people to use their gifts effectively. God has purpose for every life, and the purpose for every life fits within the framework of the purpose to which God has called His entire Church.

As every person does his or her part in the local church, the purpose of God is fulfilled and the Lord gets all the glory. That is what God is working right now. Although every person may be a strategic individual, the Lord is even now moving people into the right places, aligning His purposes with His Church. The Church in turn is aligning with His purpose. This will be a little uncomfortable at times, as people search for their positions in the local body as well as in the Body of Christ. But the result will be a people who are released to fulfill God's purposes for their lives.

As you work to develop strategic people and plans in the local church, keep in mind that programs don't develop people; people develop people. And God-empowered people develop God-empowered people! Mentoring, discipling, and ministry training all help to develop people of strategy in the local church.

Everyone has a ministry; everyone has a part to play as God is building His Church. As leaders, our goal is to help each person to find his or her place of ministry and effectiveness in the body. Only as people come into their strategic positions within the body can the purpose of the church be fulfilled. And only when a member is functioning effectively

in the way God created him or her to function can he or she be fulfilled.
   Strategic preaching, strategic prayer, strategic purpose, and strategic people are essential. Without God's strategy we will perish.

Where there is no vision, the people are unrestrained [perish],
But happy is he who keeps the law.   Proverbs 29:18

Part Three

The Ministry Formation of
the Second Acts Church

[Chapter Ten]
Formed Through Relationship

And He gave some as apostles, and some as prophets, and some as evangelists, and some as pastors and teachers, for the equipping of the saints for the work of service, to the building up of the body of Christ; until we all attain to the unity of the faith, and of the knowledge of the Son of God, to a mature man, to the measure of the stature which belongs to the fullness of Christ.   Ephesians 4:11-13

We have seen that God has a purpose for everything He does, an intent for every life.

He also has a purpose for His people. He has formed the Church specifically for His purpose, leaving out nothing that is needed. We read of the birth of the Church in Acts chapter two, at the coming of Pentecost. As Peter preached salvation, thousands were saved. A new thing was birthed, something the world had never seen before: the Church. This was a body of people called to come together to form one Body. These believers were joined together in unity and fellowship, regardless of race, regardless of status, regardless of language. God had put them together without consulting them; they became part of the one Body that God was creating.

For even as the body is one and yet has many members, and all the members of the body, though they are many, are one body, so also is Christ.   First Corinthians 12:12

As God looked upon His people, the Church, He chose the gifts He desired for each member of the body. Indeed, these were determined even before each person was born; yet God was stirring up these gifts, that they would be a blessing to the Church and to the world. He was bringing together diverse people of diverse giftings, that none should be lacking.

Now you are Christ's body, and individually members of it. And God has appointed in the church, first apostles, second prophets, third teachers, then miracles, then gifts of healings, helps, administrations, various kinds of tongues. All are not apostles, are they? All are not prophets, are they? All are not teachers, are they? All are not workers of miracles, are they? All do not have gifts of healings, do they? All do not speak with tongues, do they? All do not interpret, do they?
First Corinthians 12:27-30

This is not an exhaustive listing of the spiritual gifts available. Paul was giving us a sampler plate, showing us some of the gifts available to the Church. Have you ever gone to a restaurant and ordered a sampler? What do you get? You get a taste of several dishes — the best that eatery has to offer. The sampler gives us a taste of that restaurant, letting us know what the food is like there.

This is what Paul is doing. He is giving us a taste of some of the gifts God offers us. There are many diverse gifts. And we need to grow to maturity so that we can recognize and appreciate the significance of every part of the Body.

You see, in many cases we still need to grow up in Christ. He does not want His Body to remain in a childish state. When you were a child, you did not fully realize what all of your body parts were for. You thought your fingers were for sticking in your mouth … or your ears.

There are many churches that remain in this state. Even though we understand that God has put us together in local churches, we aren't really sure why some parts of the body are there. We devalue some people and use their gifts for the wrong purposes. Sometimes we even become harsh toward one another, not understanding why some people won't just stay put where they have been placed — whether they fit in those places or not. But God has not formed His Church to act in this way toward one another.

According to Paul, every part has significance; and God wants the Church to grow up to be like Jesus, fully mature (see Ephesians 4). When did Jesus come into the fullness of His ministry on the earth? It was when He reached maturity. This is what God desires for the Church — that we come into full maturity, that we may also come into a fullness of ministry. This includes growing together in the Lord.

When Paul wrote to the Ephesians concerning the Church coming into maturity, it was in a corporate sense: *"until we all attain to the unity of the faith ... we are to grow up ... the whole body, being fitted ... causes the growth of the body for the building up of itself in love"* (see Ephesians 4:13-17).

We are called to have a right relationship with Jesus Christ. We are also called to have a right relationship with those around us. Relationship is essential to the formation of the Church! Through right relationship we can relate to God and to one another in the Body of Christ as God intended.

Relationship determines our role; role determines our responsibility; and responsibility determines our reward, as we've already discussed. We were created, formed, and purposed for relationship. It is generally accepted that we were created for the purpose of fellowship with God; yet how can we become the Body or the Bride if we are not walking in right relationship with one another?

God Provides the Foundation

"I also say to you that you are Peter, and upon this rock I will build My church; and the gates of Hades will not overpower it."
Matthew 16:18

So then you are no longer strangers and aliens, but you are fellow citizens with the saints, and are of God's household, having been built on the foundation of the apostles and prophets, Christ Jesus Himself being the corner stone, in whom the whole building, being fitted together, is growing into a holy temple in the Lord, in whom you also are being built together into a dwelling of God in the Spirit.
Ephesians 2:19-22

God has provided a sure foundation for His Church. If there is any slipping, any crumbling out of place, we can know that it is due to our building, not to the foundation God has set in place.

Nevertheless, the firm foundation of God stands, having this seal, "The Lord knows those who are His," and, "Everyone who names the name of the Lord is to abstain from wickedness."   Second Timothy 2:19

When a building is being constructed, the foundation is the first part laid down. The foundation must be strong enough to hold the weight of the entire building. It must be straight and true, or the building will not be structurally sound; it will develop cracks and weaknesses, eventually resulting in ruin.

As I write, my family and I are living in what we are calling our transition home. We have recently sold our former house and property and are hoping to purchase some land and build a new house. That's how we came to be in our current house, one that was built before the Civil War on a large tract of land. It is essentially a farm house, and we love it.

My wife, especially, loves these old, historic buildings. It's one of those places that has character — at least, that's what people call it when a building is older. But if you were to come and examine the house, you would find that every wall is crooked, along with each window. Why? It's because the foundation is crooked. There is nothing "true" about the house. Still it stands, although in a state of crookedness that historians call character. Eventually, a thorough remodeling will need to take place if this house is to be occupied into the future.

You see, the Church doesn't derive her character from being old. It doesn't matter how historic a local church's building is or how long the people have been worshiping together — that isn't what's important. It isn't a number of years that matters. The Church doesn't derive her character from being historic, but from being Christ-like.

As we discussed in chapter six, the Church is described in Scriptures as a House that is being built by God. And He is not building His Church upon just anything. He has, rather, placed a solid and sure foundation, one that will never shift nor change; and the Cornerstone is Christ Jesus Himself (see Ephesians 2:20).

Scriptures tell us that a day is coming when everything that can be shaken will be shaken. Everything that is not built on the Word will collapse. But we are secure if we have been built up in Him. The Church is not set upon shifting sands, but has been founded upon the solid Rock of the Word of God.

Our foundation consists of the Word — both the written Word, the Bible, and the Living Word, Christ Jesus Himself. And in that written Word we read of the seven foundational pillars of the Church: passion for God, partnering with other believers, powerful prayer, principles by which to live, providing for the needs of others, planting churches, and promoting the reality of Jesus. These provide the foundation by which we are to live our daily lives in the Kingdom. These are our instructions, our directions for life.

Have you ever noticed that men sometimes have a difficult time following directions? For instance, a man purchases a new bike. When he gets it home, he takes all the pieces out of the box ... and he tosses the directions off into a corner. He puts the bike together, and he's proud of his work. Then his wife walks into the room and asks, "What are all those pieces for, honey?"

"Those? Oh, they're just the, uh, extra parts! The company sent them in case we needed spares."

God has given us His instructions. If only we would build by the Book, we would not have the problems that we often have! We must follow God's blueprint if we would begin to understand how He wants His Church to be built.

The Lord has provided all we need to build according to His plan. We have the instructions, the blueprint; we have the foundational pillars; we have the living stones. He has also given us the Cornerstone, Christ Jesus. And we have the Holy Spirit, who provides what we need to minister most effectively.

God Places People in Relationship

How has God brought us together within the Church? He has done it by bringing us out of the world. We are called in to come out ... to go back out and bring more in! He calls us out of darkness and into His light, bringing us together to become the people of God.

For those whom He foreknew, He also predestined to become conformed to the image of His Son, so that He would be the firstborn among many brethren; and these whom He predestined, He also called; and these whom He called, He also justified; and these whom He justified, He also glorified. Romans 8:29-30

We have been called out from many and various places; but God has brought us together to form one Body — for His glory! The reason He brings us together is so that He may be glorified, drawing more to Himself so that none should perish.

"Truly, truly, I say to you, he who believes in Me, the works that I do, he will do also; and greater works than these he will do; because I go to the Father. Whatever you ask in My name, that will I do, so that the Father may be glorified in the Son. If you ask Me anything in My name, I will do it." John 14:12-14

The commission of the Church is Kingdom expansion. The reason God has called us out and put us together is to expand His Kingdom.

The reason He has put us together with those in our local churches is the same: that we would go forth to make disciples. We may not always understand why we are placed into a specific body with the people who are there; but if God has indeed placed us there, then we can know that we are in the best place possible to use our gifts for His glory for this time. This is how we fit into the framework God has formed.

God Places People on Purpose

But now God has placed the members, each one of them, in the body, just as He desired. If they were all one member, where would the body be? But now there are many members, but one body.
First Corinthians 12:18-20

Now you are Christ's body, and individually members of it. And God has appointed in the church, first apostles, second prophets, third teachers, then miracles, then gifts of healings, helps, administrations, various kinds of tongues.
First Corinthians 12:27-28

God created the human body with wonderful complexity! From the eyelashes to the circulatory system, from the toes to the cerebral cortex, each part of the body is important. Now, I know what you're thinking: "What about the tonsils? How about the appendix? Surgeons remove those all the time." We once thought these body parts had no particular function, but guess what? Science recently has determined the purposes of those things too. God created them for a reason, yet for decades we believed they were unnecessary!

We have to be careful not to have this mindset in the Church. There are no unnecessary parts! There may be some parts that are not functioning properly yet; but that does not disqualify them from membership in the Body, nor does it mean they are needed less than others.

God wants us to work together. He wants us to understand that there are no spare parts in the Body of Christ. All are necessary; all have purpose; all have the potential to carry the glory of the Lord. You simply cannot have all the parts and not have a complete body; nor can you have a complete body without all the parts! Much of the Church today is operating and trying to function effectively with missing parts.

Much of the Church today is a handicapped Church. Handicapped originally meant, "cap in hand" — a person was not physically able to work, and so was asking for help. Rather than meeting the needs of those who are without, we ourselves are the ones who are lacking. The primary reason for this is that we have so many parts missing in the Church today that we have somehow decided we can do without them. And so we hobble along on one leg, or endeavor to reach out with one arm, or to see without eyes, or to run without feet. Certainly, we should be sensitive to those we meet who are physically or mentally handicapped. Usually one finds himself in such a state quite innocently.

But such is not the case with the Church. There can be no sympathy for us when we ourselves have cut off a hand, or plucked out an eye, or trampled a foot. If we believe that we do not need the apostles or the prophets today, we succumb to being a greatly dissected body. All the parts are necessary for His Body to function according to His purpose. That is why God has formed His Body, the Church, accordingly.

God has not formed the Church to lack that which is necessary. Even now He is strategically joining together various people and ministries to fill up the places that lack, that the Body may be whole.

But you are A CHOSEN RACE, A royal PRIESTHOOD, A HOLY NATION, A PEOPLE FOR God's OWN POSSESSION, so that you may proclaim the excellencies of Him who has called you out of darkness into His marvelous light; for you once were NOT A PEOPLE, but now you are THE PEOPLE OF GOD; you had NOT RECEIVED MERCY, but now you have RECEIVED MERCY.

First Peter 2:9-10

Why has God called us and put us together? According to Peter, God has done this so we can show others the goodness of God, who has called us out of darkness into His wonderful light.

The Greek word for the Church is *ekklesia,* which means "called-out ones." God is continually calling us out of one thing and into another; from darkness into light, from immaturity into maturity, from sin into holiness. He brings us out of the darkness of sin and bondage and darkness, and He brings us into His Kingdom.

When we are born again, He brings us into the Church, where we have a unique function and purpose. Then He calls the Church back out to go into the world and expand His Kingdom. We're called out, we're called in, and we're called back out. We are called out of the world, called in to be given purpose, then called back out to show the goodness of God in all the earth.

For those whom He foreknew, He also predestined to become conformed to the image of His Son, so that He would be the firstborn among many brethren; and these whom He predestined, He also called; and these

129

whom He called, He also justified; and these whom He justified, He also glorified. Romans 8:29-30

God did not send Jesus to the earth to be an entity unto Himself; He sent Him to bring many brothers and sisters into the Kingdom. This was not just for the Lord God; rather His heart was that a family should be born, a Church of brothers and sisters in Christ. And we share in the work of Christ as we go forth and bring more people into the family. Yes, the Church is the multiplied, mobilized, manifested ministry of Jesus in the world, but it is also the Family of families, working together to bring glory to the Father.

"Truly, truly, I say to you, he who believes in Me, the works that I do, he will do also; and greater works than these he will do; because I go to the Father. Whatever you ask in My name, that will I do, so that the Father may be glorified in the Son. If you ask Me anything in My name, I will do it." John 14:12-14

Jesus' words don't seem to make sense to the natural mind. How can we do greater works because He was going to the Father? Yet His implications are clear: When He went to His Father, His work was accomplished. He had overcome death, Hell, and the grave; all was finished, the victory won. Because of that victory, He was able to return to His Father; but He also was able to leave two things behind: the Church and the Comforter.

Jesus promised that He would not leave His disciples as orphans (see John 14:18). He has given us the spirit of adoption as sons (see Romans 8:15-23). His purpose was to create a family. He has given us His Spirit who lives within us and flows out of us; so now we can see this multiplication, mobilization, and manifestation of Christ's work on the earth. No longer is it restricted to one time and place, as when Christ walked the earth. Now His ministry, through the Church, covers the whole earth.

Do you want to see these "greater works" done on the earth today? Then start to do them! Every believer has the opportunity to see God working in and through his life as a vessel of God. When the life of Jesus is within you, the ministry of Jesus is free to flow from you. What is this ministry? Jesus Himself quoted from the prophet Isaiah:

"THE SPIRIT OF THE LORD IS UPON ME,
BECAUSE HE ANOINTED ME TO PREACH THE GOSPEL TO THE POOR.

HE HAS SENT ME TO PROCLAIM RELEASE TO THE CAPTIVES,
AND RECOVERY OF SIGHT TO THE BLIND,
TO SET FREE THOSE WHO ARE OPPRESSED,
TO PROCLAIM THE FAVORABLE YEAR OF THE LORD."   Luke 4:18-19

Every believer has the potential to have this kind of ministry flowing from his life! Each believer has significance. As leaders, we are to train and encourage, mentor and guide those under our care so that this can be the reality of their lives.

Do you recall the account of the poor widow in Elisha's time?

Now a certain woman of the wives of the sons of the prophets cried out to Elisha, "Your servant my husband is dead, and you know that your servant feared the LORD; and the creditor has come to take my two children to be his slaves." Elisha said to her, "What shall I do for you? Tell me, what do you have in the house?" And she said, "Your maidservant has nothing in the house except a jar of oil."

Second Kings 4:1-2

This poor woman was in need of funds. There were many ways in which she could have obtained what she needed in order to save her sons from slavery. But the prophet asked her what she had. Where was she starting from? What did she have in her possession that God could use to bless her and her sons?

This account contains a picture of the Church today. While people come knocking at our door to be provided for, we barely have enough for ourselves, or so we think. What is the key to overflowing resources? First, be willing to provide for the needs of those who come knocking at your church doors. Second, start pouring into the people you already have in your church. You won't get more vessels until you do! Third, after you have poured the oil of the Holy Spirit into the vessels in your house, go and take possession of the vessels outside your house and pour into their lives. Finally, never stop providing, pouring, and taking possession. If you do, the oil will cease.

"What do you have in the house?" God asks us that question, too. He has given us our purpose — to make disciples. Yet there are so many ways to go about that task! Like the widow, we are to redeem sons and daughters from slavery. But how we go about doing that depends on what and who God has put in the house. We have already been given the resources to complete our assignment. Leaders are to recognize the gifts God has placed in the house, provide the people with the resources

they need, and release them into ministry.

God Promotes the Health of the Body

We are to grow up in all aspects into Him who is the head, even Christ, from whom the whole body, being fitted and held together by what every joint supplies, according to the proper working of each individual part, causes the growth of the body for the building up of itself in love.
Ephesians 4:15-16

In the natural, physical human body, just what is a joint? It is a place where two parts of the body come together. Think about that. The Body of Christ is *"fitted and held together by what every joint supplies."* Every joint! There is no person, no relationship, that is not important within the Body of Christ. If we want our local churches to be healthy, then we need to look to the needs of individuals and also of relationships. We need to become the "joint" in the community where people connect, with God and with one another.

Do you remember *Cheers,* a sitcom popular several years ago? In this show, Cheers was the name of a small Boston pub. According to the show's theme song, it was the place where everyone knows your name. That idea profoundly captures the need and desire of every person on the planet. People are desperately searching for a place that is familiar, comforting, and welcoming.

Where I come from, places like Cheers are called "beer joints." These were the "joints" where many people went to connect in the community. In Cheers, every time one of the regular customers walked in, everyone would yell his name: "Norm!" There is something about being in a joint where everyone knows who you are. That's why people show up there. It's human nature; we want to be known! Sadly, the world offers too many joints for people to connect in that only bring destruction and a kind of fame that most people really don't want.

The Church is designed to be the joint where all of us can connect and truly be known for who God has created us to be. As the Body of Christ, every joint and every part is essential. What would happen if every time someone showed up at the church, we all yelled, "Norm!" or "Jim!" or "Sally!" After a time, people would begin to feel as though they belonged there, as though that church was the place they wanted to be, as though it was the one place where everyone knows their names!

How is that possible? It's simple, really. All it would take is every person reflecting Jesus in every area of the church, from greeters to pastors to teachers to nursery workers to every person in the pew. Your church can become the joint where everyone wants to connect — with God, who knows their name and everything else about them, and with others in Christ.

Establishing a local church is not enough. Converting people to Christ is not enough. Even gathering together the "right" mix of giftings is not enough. If we want to fulfill the will of the Lord, we must have churches — local expressions of the life of Christ — that are healthy. Christ's Body should be a healthy Body!

What comprises a healthy body? The absence of illness is a starting point, obviously. But how can we ensure that the local church body is well? The body God forms will be healthy as every person performs his part for God's glory. Each person must make a commitment to serve Jesus Christ, and to serve as Jesus Himself served.

A healthy body needs the proper food, and it needs to exercise. It also needs light and stimulation. In the same way, the Body of Christ needs these things. We need to feed on the Word and exercise our gifts. We must walk in the light and stimulate one another to love and good works.

God has created His Church to function beautifully, all parts working together. Every part is crucial. When each part is doing what God formed it to do, a healthy church is the result. And a healthy church will be a growing church. There are so many seminars about church growth. But do you know what? We don't need them. I'll let you in on a secret: God is not concerned about growth; He's concerned about health.

A healthy church is one that is living in the Word of God and doing His will. As a result, there will be inspiring worship, worship that rises beyond the level of singing another song, or even of catching a glimpse of God; it will draw us into closer relationship and communion with the Lord. Such a church will foster small groups and discipleship, prayer, relationships, understanding that the body needs *"that which every joint supplies."* Such a church will be reaching out to others, drawing them to Christ. And they will live in loving relationship with one another and expand the Kingdom.

A church is formed through relationships. Our relationship with God is important; our relationship with others in the body is also important. We cannot neglect — or allow those whom we serve to neglect — one for the other. Each person is crucially important to the Lord. Each one is also to be seen as crucially important to the church.

[Chapter Eleven]
Recognizing Each Person's Unique FORM

When I went into high school as a seventh grader, I didn't know quite what to expect. I remember having dreams, or rather nightmares, in which I couldn't get my locker open or I'd forgotten the combination to the lock, or I'd lost my books. It was a nerve-wracking experience the first couple of weeks at the new, bigger school. I was just a measly seventh grader, or so the seniors told me. I seemed to have no unique purpose except to be the subject of the upperclassmen's jokes.

But one day all of that changed! As I sat in one of my classes, the intercom buzzed with the secretary's words: "Terry Broadwater, please report to the office." What had I done? Why did they want me? Was I in trouble? Down the hallway I went to the office. I told the school secretary that I was reporting as requested. To my surprise, she didn't know why I was there. So I explained to her that someone had asked for me over the intercom: "Terry Broadwater, please report to the office." So to the office I had come.

That's when the secretary started to laugh. What she said would become the unique feature of my life at Valley High School for the next three years.

"Oh, you must be Terry Broadwater, the boy!" Uh, yes. "Well," she said, "we wanted Terri Broadwater, the girl. She's in the principal's office right now!"

I found out that day that there was another Terri Broadwater; only she was a she, and she was a tenth grader! From that day on until she graduated, every time they wanted her in the office there would be an announcement: "Terri Broadwater, the girl, please report to the office!" And every time it would happen, all of my friends would say, "Hey, dude, they want you again! Ha, ha, ha!"

Thankfully, when they really did want me, they would ask for "Terry

Broadwater, the boy!" That was what set me apart and made me unique from the other Terri Broadwater.

Well, every child of God is unique too. We may all have the same Jesus Christ in us and we may all be Christians, but we all have a very special and unique role to serve in His Body. Think of all the "Joe Smiths" in the world who are Christians. God knows the uniqueness of every one. God may call for "Joe Smith, the pastor," or "Joe Smith, the evangelist." He may call "Joe Smith, the administrator, please report to the office," or "Joe Smith, the teacher, please report to Christian Education," or "Joe Smith, the tenor, please report to the choir room."

Every person God has placed in the Church, His Body, is uniquely formed for service!

Living then, as every one of you does, in pure grace, it's important that you not misinterpret yourselves as people who are bringing this goodness to God. No, God brings it all to you. The only accurate way to understand ourselves is by what God is and by what he does for us, not by what we are and what we do for him.

In this way we are like the various parts of a human body. Each part gets its meaning from the body as a whole, not the other way around. The body we're talking about is Christ's body of chosen people. Each of us finds our meaning and function as a part of his body. But as a chopped-off finger or cut-off toe we wouldn't amount to much, would we? So since we find ourselves fashioned into all these excellently formed and marvelously functioning parts in Christ's body, let's just go ahead and be what we were made to be, without enviously or pridefully comparing ourselves with each other, or trying to be something we aren't.

Romans 12:3-6, MES

God is forming us to be a New Testament Church, a Body that will walk in the second Acts experience. If we will follow the New Testament pattern, we will receive the New Testament power. This is what God is doing. He is forming the Church with purpose; He is forming lives with purpose. He has brought us out of the world to make us part of His family. He has given us an identity as His children, and He has given us purpose. And He sends us out to fulfill that purpose: to make disciples — locally, regionally and globally.

God has placed you in a very strategic place in life. Your heart, mind, spiritual gifts, and ministry gifts are all to be used for the glory of God. Every believer has been called into the ministry. Everyone may not be called to full-time ministry, and everyone may not hold a five-fold ministry office. But all are called into ministry, and God has specially gifted each member to fulfill the purpose He has set for him from before the beginning of time.

God is releasing His people to be who He has fashioned them to be. We needn't be like anyone else. We don't have to sing or preach or talk or act like anyone else; God is releasing us from all of that! He has created each one of us for His own good pleasure. Do you consider yourself a little too short or too tall? Is your hair a continual source of irritation? Do you dislike your voice, or something about your looks? What about your spiritual gifts? Do you secretly envy someone else's gift? Well, I have news for you: God did not create you to please you; He created you to please Him. He has formed each of us uniquely and is releasing us to be who He has formed us to be for His own glory. When we discover this clue, we discover the confidence to fulfill His call on our lives.

We don't always understand the things we go through in this life. We often see ourselves as being very limited in what we can accomplish; but that is our perspective, not God's.

Beloved, now we are children of God, and it has not appeared as yet what we will be. We know that when He appears, we will be like Him, because we will see Him just as He is. And everyone who has this hope fixed on Him purifies himself, just as He is pure. First John 3:2-3

We may not always be content with who we are right now, but we know that when He appears, we'll be like Him. Even now we are being made more like Him as we grow in maturity and Christ-likeness. As we grow in Him, we fulfill the purpose and the function for which we were created. Maturity comes when we come to the understanding of who we are in Jesus Christ, and when we begin to walk in the purpose for which we were created.

We may not always see exactly who we are becoming or who God intended us to be; but we can release ourselves to God by faith and allow Him to work in our lives.

It has taken me forty years to realize what God has formed me to be. Now I understand that there is an apostolic call on my life, that I am to train and encourage leaders in the Body of Christ. This understanding has brought tremendous excitement to my wife and me. Now we know our purpose! We can walk in what God has called us to because now we are beginning to understand what that is.

I remember when I was taking art in high school. We were given some clay, and we were supposed to mold it into something. The teacher walked by and asked me what I was going to make. I said, "I'm going to make a dog. It's going to be the best-looking dog you've ever seen!" I started molding and shaping and working with that clay. But the longer I worked on it and the more effort I put into it, well ... it wasn't looking exactly as I had envisioned it. The teacher came by again. She said, "I thought you were going to make a dog."

"Well, obviously you were mistaken!" I replied. (It turned out to be a mouse with large ears.)

I still have that sculpture in my office. It serves as a reminder to me. Sometimes what we think God is doing in our lives isn't what He's really doing. He is molding us and shaping us ... and sometimes things don't turn out as we thought they would. Then we worry about that. Sometimes we even try to fight with God. Yet God has never lost.

Eventually we give in and say, "Lord, have Your will in me!" It's the "nevertheless" prayer that Jesus prayed, and it's the key to our realizing God's destiny for our lives.

As we learn to pray, "Nevertheless, Your will be done," God replies, "Are you sure that's what you want? It will be painful. It won't be what you think it should be."

But the only possible response is to ask Him to have His way in us — "nevertheless!"

This is what He is doing throughout the Body of Christ today. He is molding us and shaping us and releasing us into our destiny. This has always been His plan; this is what His House is about. These are strategic times; these are the times of the coming of the Lord.

God is calling us to our destiny. Each believer is a part of that. No one is insignificant, for all play important parts in God's plan. Otherwise, God would not have put you in His House at such a time.

A Unique FORM for Ministry

In our local church we have developed the REAL LIFE Commitments Process, or RLCP This is a tool to help people to fit into the place the Lord has for them. RLCP is a three-part foundational class that takes the believer through three aspects of ministry partnership.

The foundation level deals with those aspects of our Christian life that we need to implement in our lives personally and corporately as a church in order to grow spiritually and become fully devoted followers of Jesus Christ. The formation level helps us discover how God has uniquely formed us to fit into the Body of Christ, the Church. And the facilitation process then shows how the ministry is facilitated through our lives and in the church.

The class provides information about our local church, our vision, and our mission. It addresses what Bethel is about, how we are going to bring the vision to reality, and what the believer's individual role is in that.

Leaders must recognize that every person in the local church has been formed for ministry, created to play a unique part in God's purpose. What does that FORM entail? It involves *Focus, Opportunities, Resources,* and *Ministry* gifts.

Focus

We already know that God has created each person to be a person of purpose. But understanding that we have purpose and knowing what that purpose may be are two different things.

Sometimes the focus of one's life may be unclear. When this happens, we can pray for our spiritual eyes to be enlightened, that we may clearly see what it is that God has for us to do. As we evaluate our lives with the help of the Holy Spirit, we will discover our purpose. What is it that God wants to do in your life? What is His good and acceptable and perfect will for you? (See Romans 12:1-2.)

One of the first things to look at in discovering purpose is passion. What are you passionate about? What is it that consumes your life? Passion is an intense emotion. It compels us to action, and it brings with it a strong devotion. Passion is the energy of our souls. God created us to be passionate people — passionate about Him. The first place to focus our passion is in God. A passion for God will give you a purpose for life.

So begin by looking at what stirs your passion. What makes you want to get up every morning? What is the absolute best part of your day? Ask the Lord if this is a God-given passion. If it is, then give yourself to it. Focus on that area, and begin to release that passion as it is filtered through His Holy Spirit. As He works in you and through you, you will come to a place where that passion provides purpose for your life.

Your passion will rate your priorities. Joshua said it well: *"As for me and my house, we will serve the LORD"* (see Joshua 24:15). Joshua's passion was for God, and that became his priority.

Passion will also resolve your schedule. Take a look at how you spend your time. That's an indicator of your passion. We do what we're passionate about, what we deem important.

Your thought life is ruled by your passion. Paul's passion was for God. What did his mind dwell on?

> *Finally, brethren, whatever is true, whatever is honorable, whatever is right, whatever is pure, whatever is lovely, whatever is of good repute, if there is any excellence and if anything worthy of praise, dwell on these things.* Philippians 4:8

When you begin to think about something throughout the day, when you can't take your mind off of that certain thing, then you will have found your passion.

Passion will often lead us to do things that don't seem to be quite rational. It requires the unexpected. The book of Judges contains the account of a man whose passion for God led him to do the unexpected. Do you recall the account of Gideon? That young man was called to do battle on behalf of the Lord's people. He sent out messengers and raised a large army. He was set!

But his passion for God wouldn't leave it at that. When God spoke, Gideon obeyed. He sent home 22,000 men. Now that was unexpected! Then God spoke again, Gideon once more obeyed, and he was left with only 300 men — a mere handful compared to the number he had started with. But with 300 men and a passion to obey God, Gideon was victorious! (See Judges 7 for the full account.)

God still works like this today. God-given passion will still lead us to do things that are illogical or unconventional. But when we are passionate for God, we will step out in faith. Passion deepens our convictions, discloses our core values, and determines our lives' purposes:

> *But life is worth nothing unless I use it for doing the work assigned me by the Lord Jesus — the work of telling others the Good News about God's mighty kindness and love.* Acts 20:24, TLB

Focus also has to do with one's personality. The leaders with whom I serve are men of passionate, intense conviction. They love the Lord, and they love the people they serve. Sounds rather boringly similar, doesn't it? But it isn't. They each have very different personalities.

What was it the Lord said to His prophet Jeremiah? *"Before I formed you in the womb I knew you"* (see Jeremiah 1:5).

Psychologists speak in terms of four distinct personality types. Lions are the dominant type, very direct and decisive. These are usually strong leaders who know what to do. They organize and delegate. Lions are determined and driven to succeed.

The second personality type is the otter. Otters are the fun-loving people. They thrive on personal interaction. Very social, otters can be inspiring, influential, enthusiastic, talkative, expressive, creative and colorful. They're fun to be around! Otters need a lot of personal interaction.

A third type of personality is the golden retriever. People who have this type of personality are faithful, steady, submissive, stable, calm, and patient. These are the peacemakers and the good listeners.

The final type is the beaver. These people tend to be competent, compliant, cautious, very deep, thoughtful, very organized, very orderly and driven by rules. They may also be somewhat pessimistic.

God has created each of these personality types, and He has done so because all are necessary to the Kingdom. Most people will tend to be stronger in one type, but will possess the traits of several or even all of the four types. Determining one's personality type may be helpful in taking stock of strengths and weaknesses; however, we cannot place ourselves or others into nice, tight little boxes based on these types. God did not create us to be so limited!

God uses all of these personalities in His Kingdom. He partners your passion with your personality because He has formed you. Too often we think we should be like someone else or God can't use us. But God wants each one of us to be released to be who He has created us to be.

Living then, as every one of you does, in pure grace, it's important that you not misinterpret yourselves as people who are bringing this goodness to God. No, God brings it all to you. The only accurate way to understand ourselves is by what God is and by what he does for us, not by what we are and what we do for him.   Romans 12:3, MES

God has made each one of us who we are. And He continues to work in our lives:

For I am confident of this very thing, that He who began a good work in you will perfect it until the day of Christ Jesus.   Philippians 1:6

Opportunity

An opportunity may be defined as an advantageous combination of circumstances. People's lives are comprised of many different sets of circumstances. Some we did not choose: where to be born and to whom; what we would look like; our physical traits; how our minds function. However, most of a person's circumstances come about as a direct result of the choices he makes. What kinds of experiences shape our lives? We have all gone through difficult experiences. But these struggles in life can sometimes turn out to be wonderful opportunities for ministering to others who face similar experiences. Opportunities are God's way of proving us responsible. Ministry starts with opportunity, but it succeeds as responsibility. Opportunity gives us options, but responsibility is what is required of us — that's true ministry!

Blessed be the God and Father of our Lord Jesus Christ, the Father of mercies and God of all comfort, who comforts us in all our affliction so that we will be able to comfort those who are in any affliction with the comfort with which we ourselves are comforted by God.
Second Corinthians 1:3-4

Often God uses those who have already gone through a particular difficulty to help another who is facing the same thing. Many times, this is the only kind of ministry the person facing the problem can receive. The world understands this; that is why there are support groups for every conceivable illness, addiction, or situation. Now, there is nothing wrong with support groups, at least in theory. But wouldn't you rather be helped by a support group that includes a supernatural God who loves you enough to have sent His Son for you? That's why LIFE groups can be so effective. It is crucial that we allow the Lord to flow through us in ministry!

We also have experiences of achievement. These are the memorable, enjoyable highlights of life: scoring the winning point, getting that longed-for promotion, graduation. We overcame some obstacle to be victorious in life. These experiences can also be seen as opportunities to connect with others in similar circumstances and to share the faithfulness of the Lord.

Relationship experiences may be positive or negative, depending on the situation. These can also provide valuable opportunities to share and lead to the responsibility to minister. In fact, most ministry takes place in the context of relationship. In all of our relationships, we are to be God-bearers, those who carry the Lord within them and who respond out of a heart of love. There is no relationship that would not be the better for allowing the love and light of Christ to shine into it.

Like relationship experiences, ministry experiences may be positive or negative; and they always provide an opportunity to grow and the responsibility to do so. These experiences include the many situations people have encountered in ministry: the Sunday school class, the food bank outreach, the neighbor next door. Sometimes ministry can be difficult; many have simply given up and determined to no longer even try. But the Lord can take those negative experiences, if we will yield them to Him, and turn them around for our good so that we can be more gracious as we reach out to others who have gone through similar things. These experiences are opportunities to learn and grow in ministry, so we can become more responsible in better representing Jesus in all we say and do.

All of these types of experiences help to form people's lives and contribute to who they are and what they do. But having an experience is not enough; it must be paired with a proper attitude, lest the maturing and growing process be lost.

You see, the experiences we have will form our lives, for better or for worse. It all depends upon our outlook and our attitude. When things are going well, is it because of God's presence in our lives, or because of our own talents, charms, and abilities? When things aren't going so well, is it because God has something to teach us, or is it that everyone is against us and God no longer loves us?

There is one primary difference between those who see that everything is working out for their good and those who believe it's all for the worse. It all comes down to whether or not we have an expectation of God's love and faithfulness in our lives. As children of God, we can expect the extraordinary in every experience. God has plans — good plans — for us! As Christians, we're responsible for having a Christ-like attitude!

> *"'For I know the plans that I have for you,' declares the LORD, 'plans for welfare and not for calamity to give you a future and a hope.'"*
> Jeremiah 29:11

There are many things over which we have no control in this life. People will hurt us; we will hurt others. We all need God's grace and His mercy. But even though we cannot control all of our circumstances, we can and must be responsible for controlling our attitude.

The Lord takes all the experiences of our lives and uses them for opportunities to mold and shape us into responsible ministers of His grace for His glory. None of us have had precisely the same experiences or opportunities; no one has made the same choices in life as another has. But all of us are responsible! All of us have access to the One God who can take it all and use it for our good, and to bless those around us.

Resources

Our personal resources are those things we're naturally good at, our talents and abilities. This includes such things as mechanical ability, hospitality, organizing, leadership, singing, artistic ability ... the list is practically endless, as God has created us with so many diverse giftings. While these are not, strictly speaking, spiritual gifts, they may still be used in the ministry and in the service of the Lord. All of these contribute to our FORM in God.

We have some choices about our experiences and expectations, but God gave us our personality and abilities. We didn't get to choose the things in which we would do well; we can choose whether or not to develop these talents. But a violinist who decides to no longer play has no advantage over someone who cannot play well; we must use the gifts God gave us if we want our lives to be fulfilled lives. God did not simply put together a heavenly grab bag from which He pulls a package for each soul to unwrap; He designed every person with certain abilities because He had certain actions in mind.

God has given each of us the ability to do certain things well.
Romans 12:6, TLB

The things that you do well are another way of knowing how God wants to minister through you.

For we are His workmanship, created in Christ Jesus for good works, which God prepared beforehand so that we would walk in them.
Ephesians 2:10

Think about the abilities people have. God formed them that way because He wanted to use them that way. He puts people in His House for His purposes; and He equips us to fulfill those purposes. Our natural abilities often involve the things we most enjoy doing. God has created us in this way so that we can be glad and enjoy the things that He gives us to do. In this way, our natural abilities can be used for His glory.

Yet it is not enough simply to have an ability. Are we available to the Lord? Will we allow our gifts to be used for His glory? Some hide their abilities out of a fear of rejection or a misguided sense of modesty. Others use their abilities everywhere except in the House of the Lord. But ministry is what those in the House are meant for! Ministry is not to be given over to a few professionals. Ministry is the responsibility of every member of the Body of Christ.

God wants to use the leadership teams in His House to equip people for ministry so they can build up those in the church and reach out to those around them — by doing what they were formed to do. This is the intentional process of discipleship that I've noted earlier in this book. Leaders must encourage people to ...

... present your bodies a living and holy sacrifice, acceptable to God, which is your spiritual service of worship. And do not be conformed to this world, but be transformed by the renewing of your mind, so that you may prove what the will of God is, that which is good and acceptable and perfect. Romans 12:1-2

Ministry Gifts

Ministry gifts are the special abilities given by God to accomplish His purpose.

Now there are varieties of gifts, but the same Spirit. And there are varieties of ministries, and the same Lord. There are varieties of effects, but the same God who works all things in all persons. But to each one is given the manifestation of the Spirit for the common good. First Corinthians 12:4-7

Spiritual gifts are given to every believer for two primary purposes: to edify the body and to equip believers for ministry. As with our resource gifts, our ministry gifts are to be used and honed, and are to be available to the Lord for His use. Some teach, some lead, some administrate, but all are equipped to edify the Church (see Romans 12:6).

Spiritual gifts are gifts of grace that God has given to the Church for its edification and expansion. These gifts come by way of the Spirit to those who are born of and filled with the Spirit. We are encouraged to seek the *"greater gifts,"* (First Corinthians 12:31), which are those gifts that have been determined necessary by God for us to fulfill His purpose for our lives in the greatest way possible. Gifts are not given to us for our own honor or our own fame, but rather to honor God and to bring Him glory that He alone deserves.

The "best gifts" are those by which God is most exalted and the Church is most edified. These are the spiritual gifts we should seek for our lives. And it is our role and responsibility as leaders to encourage those in our churches to do the same.

Wherever you have been in life, no matter your situation, God's desire is to mold you into a world-changer. He has given you the FORM — the focus, opportunities, resources and ministry gifts — that you need to minister as He has planned. Believe me, there can be nothing more exciting for you than a life lived to God's purpose! As a leader, one of your greatest pleasures will be helping people discover their FORM for ministry!

[Chapter Twelve]
Releasing People Into Ministry

You also, as living stones, are being built up as a spiritual house for a holy priesthood, to offer up spiritual sacrifices acceptable to God through Jesus Christ.   First Peter 2:5

Years ago I was traveling with what was then described as a contemporary Christian rock band. Most of our "gigs" were at youth rallies and other such events. But once we were invited to play at a maximum security prison. I was fairly frightened as we went through security checks and huge steel doors that were then shut behind us. I thought to myself how blessed I was not to be in such a place. Then I realized that I was in there! At least I only had to visit, sing a few songs, lead a few prisoners to Christ, and then leave.

As we set up the stage and prepared for our performance, I couldn't help feeling closed in — which is exactly what we were. Suddenly, sirens started going off and guards started running toward us. Immediately I shouted, "I didn't mean to take that pencil in sixth grade! I'll pay, I'll pay!" Be sure your sin will find you out!

But that wasn't what was happening. As the prisoners were walking across the courtyard on their way to the auditorium for the concert, one man had attempted to escape. The guards weren't sure where he was at that point. So they hurried us to a room and locked us in, for our own safety. After an hour or so some officers returned and told us they had caught the escapee. The concert would go on as scheduled. So we changed our clothes and headed for the stage.

As we began our first song, I noticed that several of the prisoners on the front row were pointing at me and making faces that seemed to me to be somewhat threatening. Others were pointing at me and laughing. Later, after we had finished our songs and were tearing down, I told several of the band members what I had experienced. That's when we realized what had been going on. Looking at my tee shirt, everyone began to laugh hysterically. I was wearing a shirt that was advertising a new album. In big letters across the front were the words "Soon to be released!"

With everything that had been going on, I hadn't paid any attention to what was on my shirt. To some I'm sure it seemed offensive, while others just got a laugh out of it. The truth was that some in that room were "soon to be released," while many others never would be!

How many people are sitting in our churches feeling as though they will never be released from all sorts of bondages or wounds, let alone be able to minister to others? How many have been told that they will soon be able to minister, they'll soon experience a breakthrough in their lives … yet it never happens? What would happen if we really set out to see people released from their fears or doubts or bondages? What if we truly intended to help them to be released into ministry to do their part in fulfilling God's purpose for the Church?

It might change the world!

God desires to use the local church — His church in your town and in mine — to touch the city, the region, the nations. Our part is to continue to follow the pattern He has given us in the Word.

Look at those who attend the local church of which you are a part. What do you see? A miscellaneous group thrown together by geography and chance? Look closer. These people have been hand-picked by God Himself to be part of that body. People do not come together in the local church by coincidence; they are there by divine appointment. God assigns the times of our lives.

We are living in a *kairos* time — a place where time and destiny meet. Just as God assigned Esther a special time and place through which salvation was brought to her people, I believe God is now making assignments for His people today. We are living in a strategic time in God's plan. He is bringing people together, bringing ministries together, gathering His people so that He may send them out … to make disciples of all the nations. To take possession is His purpose, with His plan, by His power.

Are we ready for what God is doing? Are we poised to take off into His purposes? Are we in proper formation?

Placing People Into Formation

We have seen that we are, truly, the Body of Christ. Each member has a function; all members fit together and work together. Significance is not gained by having a part, but by doing what that part requires.

One of the tasks of leadership within the local church is to release the people into ministry. This way, all are free to be who God has created them to be. As every person functions properly, other people are enabled to take the parts God intended for them. As we each do our part together with one another, a wondrous thing happens: Together we form the House of God under His direction and for His purpose.

God puts His people into formation as He desires. He assigns each one to a special place. But that place is according to His plan ... not yours. Sometimes as leaders we tend to jump ahead, trying to fit people into the programs we have developed. But the Lord already has a plan, He has a program in place, and He knows where everyone fits. He is building His House, using His living stones. Jesus is still the Cornerstone of the Church. And we still have to align ourselves with Him.

One of our tasks as leaders is to help the church get into formation to achieve God's purposes. What does that mean? It means we must determine people's gifts and equip them to serve. It means an intentional process of discipleship. It means people within the church are ready to edify, to serve, to go forth with the good news about Jesus Christ.

There may be some repositioning necessary. Just as leaders may be encountering changes as they move from a Moses to a Joshua state, so the congregation may also encounter some shifting as God positions each member of the body as He wills. Some people may need to come out of the positions they were placed into by man in order to come into the place God has for them. God's House must be set in order, from leadership to laity. This will require bold faith and obedience. And this is what God is doing today through apostolic leadership — setting His House in order.

God is moving. The second Acts Church is appearing. And as we've seen historically, moves of God can be messy. Sometimes it takes a while for us to find our places. Sometimes we are so caught up in what God is doing that we don't even really think about these things. But God is working and moving, placing people where He wills. And when people are in the right positions, it's obvious! Suddenly they are excited. Suddenly they are ministering. Suddenly they can't stop talking about what God is doing in their lives! This is the fruit of formation.

Have you ever seen an air show? Usually it includes several planes or jets flying in patterns at the same time. How do they begin? They are in formation. As each plane flies in its own pattern, it is working together with the others. Each pilot knows where he is to go at every moment. If one pilot gets out of formation, the results could be disastrous. All have to work together if there is to be success. Each pilot has been trained in what he is to do, equipped to do it, and resourced with the things necessary to his task. So it is with the church.

Many Parts, One Purpose

It often seems as though there are so many ministries. There are the five-fold ministry leadership offices, of course. And there are so many others: ministries for the poor, the orphaned, the divorced, the abused, the abuser, the prisoner; worship ministries, drama teams, interpreters for the deaf, administration, ministries of hospitality, and so on.

Yet in reality, there is only one ministry from which all others should, ideally, flow: We are to make disciples of all the nations, beginning where our church has been planted. That's all there really is. Everything should flow from this one purpose, and everything should have this as its point of reference: Does this ministry help to make disciples? Is it drawing people to Christ, or to a deeper walk with Him? There is one ministry, but many parts to that ministry. All of these parts are integral to the performance of the singular mission of the New Testament Church.

No matter where we are placed within the body, there are several things we need to understand. First, God has already determined what part we will have. We don't get to choose from a smorgasbord of giftings or ministries. The Lord already knows why we were created. Our fulfillment comes as we flow in our purpose.

> *For by grace you have been saved through faith; and that not of yourselves, it is the gift of God; not as a result of works, so that no one may boast. For we are His workmanship, created in Christ Jesus for good works, which God prepared beforehand so that we would walk in them.*   Ephesians 2:8-10

I don't know about you, but I find this passage comforting. God has already prepared our assignments. I don't have to worry about what I should do next, for God already has it planned for me. All I have to do is to walk in humility and obedience.

Secondly, we need to understand that we were created for a purpose, and that everyone else was also created for a purpose … and that one purpose is not more crucial than another. We need to walk in purpose for ourselves, of course. But just imagine what a difference it would make in the life of most churches if everyone treated all the other members as people of great purpose in the Kingdom of God — as ministry partners.

It is one thing for me to see that I have been created for a reason; but can I see the same about you? And can I truly value you and your part, whether I think it to be of greater or lesser importance than my own? We cannot be in formation for God's work if we have to step around from behind our own egos to see Him.

Finally, we must learn — with more than our heads — that we truly are dependent upon God and upon one another. Most believers would give a mental assent to that; and then they would go back to their isolated lives, struggling through difficulties on their own. But God has formed us to be people of community, a Family of families.

What happens when a car's engine is knocking? The car is taken to a mechanic. The engine has many parts all working together. Yet when one part is not functioning properly, it is noticeable. We try to get that part repaired.

In the same way, we all need one another, and we all need God. What a difference it would make if the Church would grasp this! A local church walking in this truth would attract people from miles around. Why? Because this truth would be presented: God has a place for us in His House, and it is a place of importance and fulfillment, a place where everyone knows our name, our passion, and our purpose!

We must help the congregations we serve to see the importance of every part to every other part. This is especially important in the leadership/congregational relationship. The church in which I serve as pastor is not "my" church; the ministry is not "my" ministry, and the people are not "my" people, either. Rather, it is Christ's church; it is His ministry through me, and it is His people to whom I'm ministering. The moment we seek to control these things, we lose the point. The Lord is not concerned with my taking ownership of my ministry; He is concerned with His taking ownership of me!

Whenever we try to build our own little kingdoms, they will fall into ruin every time.

The fear of the LORD *is the instruction for wisdom,*
And before honor comes humility.   Proverbs 15:33

Humble yourselves in the presence of the Lord, and He will exalt you.
                                                                        James 4:10

Humility precedes honor; we are to humble ourselves before God. Where, then, is room for pride of place or position? Remember, it is His Church that He is building.

We have changed the concept of membership in our local church. We no longer invite people to become members of our congregation. Instead, we invite them to become ministry partners. We are looking for those who want to partner with us in ministry, who want to support the ministry that is going forth. We want to help people to find what God has called them to do, through gift assessments and interviews. We want to equip people, give them the resources they need, and release them into ministry. In this way, we can truly be partners sharing in the one ministry: making disciples.

Believers in the American church often have a Lone Ranger mentality. "It's just me and the Lord. We'll do everything together. I don't need other people! God and I will do just fine." It's the curse of our culture. There is a spirit of independence in this country that is misplaced when it comes into the church. It doesn't belong there, for this is not God's heart for His people. He didn't create us to be Lone Rangers.

The Lord wants us to be more like the Three Musketeers: "All for one, and one for all!" There is to be a sense of community, of shared experience. We fight the battle together. We share our help, support and encouragement regardless of who needs it or when. The Christian life is not about toiling on alone, but about going forward in the company of many others, all heading straight for the purpose and vision God has given us.

I have a confession to make: I have sometimes been a "ball hog." Have you ever played basketball with a ball hog? Then you know what I mean. Actually, you also know that was a trick question. No one ever plays with a ball hog; he always plays by himself. The other people on his team are just there to make sure the ball gets to him. And no one wants to pass to him, because they know they won't ever get that ball back. Ball hogs are no fun. They want to do everything by themselves. But after a while, they'll have trouble finding people to play ball with them.

We can act like this in ministry, too, if we aren't careful. Sometimes we start to think that we're the only one playing on the field. All the people in the congregation are just there to make sure we get the ball. But that isn't Jesus' way. Christ lived to serve others. He was continually giving others opportunities to minister and to grow. I believe one of the greatest ministries is that of encouraging others in the use of their gifts and in their ministries.

As we support others in their ministries and help them to do what God has called them to, then we are truly ministering in a Christ-like way. There's a big difference between being a ball hog and being a team player. If we are to model Christ, then we must be team players — people on leadership teams, prayer teams, ministry teams — who understand our roles, who work for the victory of the team. That's how a second Acts church works.

Helping People to Find Their Part

Just as simply as the Church has the ultimate purpose — to make disciples of all the nations — so, too, leadership has a role of supreme significance: to disciple people to become disciple makers! How this simplifies the purpose of the Church!

Leaders are to help people to make the most of their part in the body. There must be room for each ministry and each gift to serve in some capacity. Every believer should have an outlet for ministry. This is true even for those who are very young in the Lord. If we follow Christ, we give, we serve; we don't simply take ministry into ourselves week after week, month after month.

The purpose of the leadership offices is ultimately to release the people into ministry. Like parents whose ultimate goal is to produce mature, responsible, godly adults, there is a process to go through before we can release people into ministry. A loving parent would not send a five-year-old child out to make his way in the world. He could be a wonderful child — smart, handsome, engaging, talented. But those things will not carry him through. He is too young, too immature. He has not been trained in how to care for himself or what his place is in the world. Even so, we must not send people out in ministry before they are ready (First Timothy 3:6). They must first be discipled.

What happens when mature, discipled, trained people are released into ministry?

First, they become more responsible. Only if everyone knows what their parts or roles are can they begin to fill them and be responsible for them. Once people's gifts are identified, they should be responsible to receive training in the use those gifts in order to minister.

Keep in mind that ministry is not opportunity; it is responsibility, and one's relationship with Christ has already determined one's role. If someone has signed up to work in the nursery, then he or she should do it for the glory of God, understanding that it is a wonderful opportunity to help make disciples of those little ones from an early age. If someone has volunteered to coordinate a young mothers' outreach, then that person should do that for God's glory as well, knowing that this role is important to the life of the church.

People who have been released into ministry become more reliable. As they see that their parts are important, they are more reliable to do their parts. As they see what God is doing in and through them, they are excited to show up to see what He will do next. They become responsible and reliable. Responsibility and reliability flow from a release into ministry that is born of relationship.

So those who are ministering are relational people. They recognize the importance of building relationships with those who are working in similar ministry, as well as with others throughout the Body of Christ. I may not be part of the youth ministry of our church; but I have a relationship with the youth pastor whereby we are ministering together. We are part of the same team, and we are in joint ministry, in relationship with Christ and with one another, serving responsibly.

Those who have been released are resourceful people. They use the gifts and abilities God has given them, and then they look around to see what God has given others that could also be used in ministry. They can be very creative with what they have, for it is God's creativity flowing in them to accomplish His purposes.

Finally, released people are respectful people. They respect the gifts of others. They respect others' ministries, because they have seen the cost of ministry in their own lives. And they respect other people simply out of love for the God who created them.

Maturing in Ministry

The work of the leaders in the church is not over after they have gotten people into the right formation, helped them to make the most of their parts, and released them into ministry. Leaders have yet another task: to help people mature in ministry and measure up to Jesus' pattern:

> ... *until we all attain to the unity of the faith, and of the knowledge of the Son of God, to a mature man, to the measure of the stature which belongs to the fullness of Christ.*   Ephesians 4:13

God has blessed us abundantly with His salvation in Jesus. He has given us His Word, the Bible. The Holy Spirit dwells within us. We have been graced with spiritual gifts and natural abilities. Yet even with all of these things, the Church still is not fulfilling the Great Commission that Jesus gave His disciples so long ago. Why does so much of the Church function at the level of least effectiveness?

We can summarize all the possible reasons in one word: immaturity.

Would you ask a ten-year-old child to shingle your roof? I hope not! You would find someone who has been proven in that type of work, someone with experience. Please do not misunderstand me. I am not implying that children cannot minister or that they have no part in the Body of Christ. They can and they do. But God wants adults to function as fully mature adults in ministry. He asks that we leave our childish ways and grow up into maturity like Christ. Only then will we be able to fully function with the utmost effectiveness to accomplish His purpose. Immaturity stunts more ministry than anything else that I know of.

Sometimes we look at things that we think indicate maturity ... but we are mistaken. Maturity is not the same as age, either natural, physical age or the length of time someone has been saved. Putting in years is not the same as maturing. Maturity cannot be seen by one's appearance. We all know people who look very mature — until they start to speak. Maturity doesn't even lie in achievement, or in academics. Granted, maturity often comes with these things, but it would still be a mistake to confuse them.

So, what is maturity? Maturity speaks of that which is fully developed, completed, or perfected. What did Paul pray for the church at Thessalonica?

Now may the God of peace Himself sanctify you entirely; and may your spirit and soul and body be preserved complete, without blame at the coming of our Lord Jesus Christ. Faithful is He who calls you, and He also will bring it to pass.   First Thessalonians 5:23-24

When Paul prayed for the Thessalonians, he was yielded to the will of God. He prayed that the church would come to that place of yieldedness and in that place find His perfect peace. Maturity in Christ comes when you have accepted what He wants you to do and you are acting upon it with a confident attitude that is combined with Christlike wisdom.

James speaks of maturity as being confident under pressure (see James 1:2-4), being considerate of others (2:8), being in control of one's mouth (3:8-10), being consecrated to God (4:7-10), and being committed

155

to patience and prayer in ministry (5:7-8, 16).

Leadership, to be effective, must be a mature leadership that incorporates the insights revealed in God's Word and by the Spirit as necessary to complete the call that God has commissioned. But leadership must all take on the role and responsibility of developing maturity in the church.

This can be accomplished as leadership helps people recognize their FORM and function in the ministry of the church, and by connecting people in the right relationships for the most effective spiritual development and growth. Leaders must intentionally teach on the roles and responsibilities of people in the church, so there is proper appreciation of authority and respect for all the diverse parts of the body of Christ. Finally, by releasing people into the ministry that God has formed them for, people can begin to realize the fulfillment that God has intended for every life.

When people are released into ministry, the church can begin to function fully as God intended. We must place people in formation to serve the purpose of God!

Our goal in maturity, as in every area, is to be like Christ. How did Jesus live His life? We can look to the Word to find the example He left for us. First, we know that He spent a lot of time in prayer. He prayed with others, and He spent much time by Himself with His Father. Jesus stayed with His purpose. He did not take the easier road, but set His face to go where His Father sent Him.

Jesus sacrificed His royal position to serve people's needs — and some of the lowliest of people, at that. His life was one of praise to His Father, not one of gathering praise to Himself. Because of His relationship with His Father, He spoke with power and authority. And He saw the potential the Father had planted deep within each person He encountered. Because of this, He was able to call forth wholeness and health, healing and restoration.

Let us ask the Lord to help us as we seek to walk in maturity …

… until we all attain to the unity of the faith, and of the knowledge of the Son of God, to a mature man, to the measure of the stature which belongs to the fullness of Christ.   Ephesians 4:13

There's a story about a baby eagle that grew up in a chicken coop. No one knows for sure how he ended up there, but he did. His days were filled with all the things that chickens do. You see, he didn't know he wasn't a chicken. Life in a chicken coop was all he'd ever known. He scratched the ground like a chicken. He roosted like a chicken. He even strutted like a chicken.

But all that changed one day when high over the chicken coop, a Mighty Eagle soared in the sky. As that Eagle flew majestically along, He let out a call like only eagles can make. Down in the chicken coop, the young eagle experienced something he'd never known before. As he heard the cry of the Eagle above, his heart began to beat faster, his wings began to stretch out to full length, and he began to run and not strut. As the cry of the Eagle overhead grew stronger, the young eagle began to run faster and his wings began to move in a motion he'd never realized he was capable of before.

Suddenly, he was off the ground. He climbed up into the sky, excited because he'd never known he held this potential inside of himself. He became more courageous and confident as he soared higher and higher. Then he encountered the One who had made the call from above, recognizing that he'd never really looked like a chicken at all, but closely resembled the Mighty Eagle instead. As he joined the Majestic Eagle in flight, he knew for the first time what he was and that this is what he was meant to be.

God is calling to us today. We're not meant for the pecking, roosting, and strutting of the "chicken yard." We are meant to soar on eagles' wings, to run and not be weary, to walk and not faint, to be released into a multiplied, mobilized, manifested ministry of Jesus in the world. And we're meant for a higher place. We're meant to soar alongside the Mighty One on eagles' wings.

Part Four

Ministry Facilitation in
the Second Acts Church

[Chapter Thirteen]
Becoming a REAL Church

I do all things for the sake of the gospel, so that I may become a fellow partaker of it. First Corinthians 9:23

Our family once toured the back lot at Disney's MGM Studios. It was interesting. As we walked down the street, it looked like any normal street, with houses and landscaping. Everything looked very real. In fact, if it hadn't been part of a tour, we wouldn't have realized there was anything different about this particular street. But then they took our group around to the back of the houses. What a difference! The buildings weren't as substantial as they had seemed; in fact, they were just facades. There was absolutely no depth to them. The entire scene from the street was faked.

As we were looking at that, I couldn't help thinking of the Church. How much of the Church is like that? How often do we present ourselves as being very substantial, very honest, when, in reality we are faking things? How much depth do we have? How real are we?

As we continued, I asked the tour guide why they didn't build entire buildings. His answer carries a message to the Church: The studios only build what they want the camera to see. So many people are living their lives that way! They are only interested in building into their lives what they want others to see. They aren't really all that interested in what is going on inside, behind the scenes.

But there's a problem with that. Much in our lives in Christ has to do with what is behind the scenes. For us, it isn't so crucial what others see; our concern is for what God sees.

According to the tour guide, there were other considerations as well. You see, building the real thing takes too much time. It costs too much — certainly more than the studios are willing to pay. And it simply isn't necessary.

Perhaps that guide was a bit prophetic without realizing it.
Parts of today's Church may have a lot in common with a studio
back lot. But the Church in Acts did not. The early Church believed that
building the real thing was necessary, that it was worth the time and
personal cost involved. They invested whatever was necessary to make
their ministry substantial and significant ... and real.

*Even though I am free of the demands and expectations of everyone, I
have voluntarily become a servant to any and all in order to reach a
wide range of people: religious, nonreligious, meticulous moralists, loose-
living immoralists, the defeated, the demoralized — whoever. I didn't
take on their way of life. I kept my bearings in Christ — but I entered
their world and tried to experience things from their point of view. I've
become just about every sort of servant there is in my attempts to lead
those I meet into a God-saved life. I did all this because of the Message.
I didn't just want to talk about it; I wanted to be in on it!*
First Corinthians 9:19-23, MES

Paul obviously believed that people have real problems, and they
need the message of God's love to give them real life!

Paul wanted to do the work of the ministry in an honest, open, real
way. Why? Because the message he shared was honest, open, and real.
Paul said that he had become all things to all people, that he might by
all means save some. Think about that. As the Church, God has called
us to make disciples. So we provide worship gatherings, prayer times,
ministries in which people can go out to care for others. But we also
need to keep in mind that how we build is just as important as what we
are building.

My wife and I have moved several times in the course of our mar-
riage and ministry. Once we lived close to where our new home was
being built. So I would walk over every day to see how things were
progressing. Now, the plan looked wonderful. The picture showed that
this was going to be a great place to live. But every day I would find
that the builders were trying to cut corners. They used inferior supplies; in some places the boards weren't nailed down; the trim did not
meet properly in the corners. Even though they had a good plan, they
were undermining the final product by their quality of work.

Too often the Church knows what it's called to do, but we're not
putting our best into the work. We're not always too concerned with
how it gets done. Putting quality workmanship into the work of the
Church is what I mean by being real. How, then, do we relate Jesus in a

real way to the world? We do it by presenting a message that is *Relevant*, *Effective*, *Accountable*, and *Loving*.

Relevant to Our Culture

If we want to be real, to present the message of salvation in a way that will connect with people, then we must begin by being relevant. Now, the truth is the truth; it does not change. But speaking of the need for redemption and salvation and sanctification and the redeeming blood, in those terms, to a modern secular teen will be about as effective as if we were presenting the entire message in a foreign language. In effect, that is exactly what we would be doing!

In his first letter to the Corinthians, Paul explained that he tried to see the world from others' perspectives so that he could relate Jesus to them from their viewpoint without compromising the truth of the Word of God. Paul understood that there is a pattern in which people need to relate, a social context into which most interactions of a particular group fall. Relevance is the patterned way in which people relate, and Paul tried to enter into that as much as he could without compromising his relationship with his Lord.

When we were visiting in Florida, I took my children to a skate park. They carried their skateboards into the park, and I sat down where I could watch them. As I looked around, I thought, "I'm visiting another planet!" I had entered a culture of skateboarders who were tattooed from head to toe and had piercings everywhere possible. They even spoke an entirely different language than I do. As I sat and watched, a boarder sat down beside me. He was a colorful person — literally. His arms and face were covered with tattoos. His piercings made me wince.

Then he began to talk with me. He was smiling, but he was using words and terms I didn't understand. I was lost! What was this boarder talking about? I had no idea.

Now, I know that God created that young man and loves him, and that God wants him to be part of His Kingdom. But how can we reach him for Christ? Can I take him and toss him into the traditional church structure and expect him to fit right in? Will a few hymns or praise choruses set him right? I don't think so.

You see, what it takes to relate to a skateboarder is going to be very different than what it might take to reach a senior citizen or someone from another country. When I travel to other countries, I have to be careful in what I say. Some things simply don't translate well. They make no sense within the culture. So we have to find the connections that make the message relevant within the context of that culture. As we adapt to others' cultures, we are becoming *"all things to all people, that we may by all means win some."*

We in America are living in a postmodern culture — a culture in which truths or concepts that contain narrow paths are authoritative only to the person seeking them. So we need to find out how to relate Jesus in a culture that refuses to acknowledge the validity of statements such as "We believe" or "This is an absolute" or "The Scriptures say…." Postmodernists really don't care all that much what anyone believes since, really, it's all the same thing to them. It all boils down to whatever makes one happy being one's truth.

The postmodernist's view of God is not the God of Abraham and Isaac and Jacob. He isn't the One who sent His only Son, either. Many have exchanged secularism for pluralism and paganism. How are we going to convey to such a culture the reality of Jesus Christ?

People need to *see* that Jesus is real. They need to see that He is real in us. They should see people of integrity, people of honesty, people of truth. If people see in us the living reality of the Lord Jesus Christ, then we are living relevant lives in our society.

Paul advocated preaching Jesus by whatever means possible without compromise in order to reach people for the Lord. This is cultural relevance.

Your church must identify its culture or cultures, the community or context into which God has placed you. There is a harvest field waiting for you, ripe and ready to be brought in. Perhaps you believe that the opportunities just aren't there. Maybe if you lived in Chicago or in the Silicon Valley, you could have raised up a megachurch for God. But perhaps the reason others have been so successful elsewhere is that they have discovered the keys to unlock their communities. They have made the connections without the compromise, and many are coming to Christ. Perhaps you are settling for the row of potatoes that was planted fifty years ago when God wants to give you the whole garden! Or maybe you're simply using the potato plow to harvest corn. Relevance means relating in the right way.

Oh, about that skateboarder I mentioned earlier … I know someone who is heavily tattooed. He has his nose and ears pierced. But this young man is on fire for God! And I'm sure you can guess what he does. That's right; he goes into skate parks to tell those teens about Jesus Christ. And they listen to him.

That's cultural relevance.

Effective in Our Commission

If we will be relevant to our culture, we'll be effective in our commission. Paul says:

I do all things for the sake of the gospel, so that I may become a fellow partaker of it. First Corinthians 9:23

Paul didn't want to just talk about spreading the Gospel; he wanted to be the one doing the sharing. He understood that he had been given a commission.

So have we.

And Jesus came up and spoke to them, saying, "All authority has been given to Me in heaven and on earth. Go therefore and make disciples of all the nations, baptizing them in the name of the Father and the Son and the Holy Spirit, teaching them to observe all that I commanded you; and lo, I am with you always, even to the end of the age."
Matthew 28:18-20

We have been called to make disciples, to reach the nations, to share the Good News, to spread the love of God. We have been called to this. In order to fulfill that call, we need to be relevant to our culture. But we cannot stop there. Our purpose is not just to become friends with people, to connect with them, to "speak their language." If we are to bless them, we must go farther.

We must be effective in our commission.

The Church has supernatural purpose. We are to reach everyone, everywhere. No one is to be excluded. Is there someone to whom you cannot genuinely relate? Then find someone who can. Are your methods not reaching the people you need to reach? Then change the methods. The question is not "How can we do the Great Commission?" but "How effective are we in carrying out our commission?"

The Church in Acts was marked by the fact that people were being added to the Kingdom every day. The New Testament Church was effective in carrying out the Great Commission. Paul didn't reach out to the Gentiles in the same manner he endeavored to get through to the Jews. Nor did he reason with those in Ephesus in the same way he articulated with the Greeks. Yes, multitudes were being saved! And the same thing is happening in some areas of the world today.

Jesus spoke of a great harvest. I believe that harvest is beginning even now. People have discovered the key to being effective in carrying the message of Jesus to others.

Too many churches in America are closing their doors. Too often churches are growing only by transfer of membership. What does this say about the church in America? We are not being effective in sharing the good news of Jesus Christ! Research has shown that new churches usually begin as outreach-oriented works, but that within about twelve years they become inwardly focused.

But the Church is not a gated community! We are not here to exclude, but to invite. The gate is wide open to whosoever may come. When we see visitors at our churches, we cannot look askance and keep our distance. Jesus said, "Let them come." In fact, He said, "Go and find them and bring them in."

After the Resurrection, Jesus was seen by the disciples over a period of forty days. During this time, He gave them some directions.

Gathering them together, He commanded them not to leave Jerusalem, but to wait for what the Father had promised, "Which," He said, "you heard of from Me; for John baptized with water, but you will be baptized with the Holy Spirit not many days from now" ...

"...but you will receive power when the Holy Spirit has come upon you; and you shall be My witnesses both in Jerusalem, and in all Judea and Samaria, and even to the remotest part of the earth."   Acts 1:4-5, 8

Jesus sent the disciples out; but before they all left, He said, "Now, wait! Before you attempt to go and make disciples, wait for the power that I'm going to give you from on high. What I have called you to do cannot be done by human strength alone. You can only succeed through My supernatural power."

The same is true for us. We need His power if we are to do His will. Let's not hinder the church with natural human laws when she was created to respond to the supernatural. For instance, the shelves of Christian bookstores are loaded down with books about church growth. I'll save you some reading. If everyone in your church is on fire for God and living a life that shows a surpassing love for God, then the church will be overflowing with the Presence of the Lord. And then, if each person, knowing what a wonderful place the church is, will invite one person to come as his guest — well, you've just doubled your attendance. Instead of trying to manipulate numbers through various programs, let's welcome the supernatural power of God to transform lives by His Presence.

Remember the Church is the multiplied, mobilized, manifested ministry of Jesus in the world!

When we are filled with the Holy Spirit, He floods our hearts with love for the Lord and our minds with the knowledge of God. He teaches us of Jesus and ever whispers into our spirits of the nearness and the love of Christ. He releases His supernatural authority and power into various situations through us, because on our own we cannot do the work we are given. We must partner with His Presence to effectively accomplish His purpose.

Who among us can convict another of sin? Who among us can draw another to seek after God? Who among us can persuade another soul to come to the Lord? We can be tools, yes; but only the Holy Spirit can do these things.

The Lord has used my wife, Jo Ann, to speak into people's lives, as she has a very discerning, prophetic spirit. In the beginning, especially, she was somewhat hesitant to do so, as she did not want to say the wrong thing. I encouraged her to step out in faith. One incident especially was a blessing from the Lord, and encouraged her to continue to speak forth what He gave her.

A young lady came to me after a meeting. She was about five or six months along in her pregnancy. Unfortunately, she had been told by the doctors that there were several things wrong with the baby, medical problems that would be difficult to face. I said to her, "I'm not supposed to pray for you; my wife will pray." And I asked Jo Ann to pray for this lady. She prayed and she spoke into the young lady's life, and the girl seemed to be encouraged.

The following week, the lady and her husband came into a Bible study at the church. They had wonderful news for Jo Ann: The young woman had gone back to the doctor. He had done more tests, and they had all come back negative. The baby was healthy! What's more, they now knew that it was a girl. The couple was ecstatic.

Jo Ann, as wonderful as she is, could not have done this in her own power. Only God could heal a little baby still in her mother's womb. But as Jo Ann stepped out in faith, she was being effective in her commission.

Making disciples of the nations requires people who have been influenced by Christ and who will go forth to influence the world. Such people will have put on the mind, and the heart, of Christ. What was it that made the disciples stand out? Was it their church programs? Their eloquence? The fact that they met together in people's homes? No. They had spent time with Jesus ... and it showed (see Acts 4:13).

Not only do we need the moving of the Holy Spirit if we are to be effective in our commission, but we need the right methods of ministry. Are there more effective ways of reaching people than some we may be utilizing right now? Again, this goes back to relevance; having the right methods also makes us more effective. We should not only be concerned with the commission to make disciples, but also with being as effective as possible in doing it.

My father-in-law has always been very effective in business. He had one man working for him who would not hesitate to spend money on equipment. His motto was, "You have to have the right tools for the job if you want it done right." Oh that the Church would develop that kind of mindset! We limit our effectiveness when we use outdated methods. We must wake up and adapt our methods to a changing world. Technological advances have impacted our youth, yet much of the church remains mired in the "new thing" of twenty or thirty years ago. What will make us most effective in our commission is the moving of the Spirit in methods that are making the most of ministry!

Just as an American embassy is a little bit of America a long way from home, so is the Church to be a little bit of Heaven a long way from home. We represent God in the world. We are not of this world; our home is somewhere else. But while we are in the world, we represent Christ, our King. Let's do so in an effective manner that brings many more people to our Lord and King.

Accountable to Our Christianity

For if I preach the gospel, I have nothing to boast of, for I am under compulsion; for woe is me if I do not preach the gospel. ...
Therefore I run in such a way, as not without aim; I box in such a way, as not beating the air; but I discipline my body and make it my slave, so that, after I have preached to others, I myself will not be disqualified.
First Corinthians 9:16, 26-27

If we want our ministry to others to be real, then we need to keep Jesus at the center. Church life is not about us; it is not about the Sunday services, or the spiritual warfare, or the stained glass, or the sermons. All of these things may be wonderful, but they aren't Jesus. We need to make certain that Jesus Himself is the center of all that we do, of who we are. He cannot be the passion of the church if He is not the passion of each individual member; for the church is not the organization — it is the people.

We must be accountable to our Christianity. If we are Christians, then we are Christians first, and our light shines undimmed. Our message also will be pure and unadulterated, not continually bending to the world's current tastes. Relevant, yes; compromised — never!

The New Testament Church was always unapologetically clear about Who they were preaching. Unfortunately, there has been a muddying of the waters in our day. Some have suggested that God seems to be back in style in America, especially since 9/11. That may be true to a degree. However, while "God" may be back in our culture, that doesn't necessarily mean Jesus is welcome.

We must be absolutely clear in presenting our message. Jesus is the Salvation-Bearer. There are not many ways up the mountain, only One. And that Way is Jesus. The Bible is clear; Jesus is the Way — the only Way (see John 14:6).

The world says that we are intolerant when we preach the truth. That would be true if our message was, "Jesus is the only Way, and we alone have Him." But it isn't. Our message must always be this: "Jesus is the only Way, and we want to share Him with you. His love for you is great, and He wants to bring you life and purpose."

Does John 3:16 sound intolerant to you? Of course not! Jesus is the means, and the only means by which every person can have an eternal, abundant life with God. No one has been excluded from God's love, grace, and mercy. God chose *all* to be saved, but sadly, not *all* will choose Him. Still, the Church must preach Jesus to everyone everywhere so people can have the opportunity to make that choice.

Being accountable to our Christianity means being absolutely clear about who Jesus Christ is and why He came. After all, how will those around us see who Jesus is and what He came to do if the Church is constantly creating a distorted image? The Church does not provide the proper focus when it tries to minister or to present Christ in ways that are not clear and in line with His Word.

No one can be forced to be accountable; we must enter into accountability of our own will. We have to enter into accountability to Christ and to Christianity. This involves more than merely acting like Jesus would; it envelopes carrying His very Presence within us. We all carry Christ in us as believers. The Church is the multiplied ministry of Jesus as He abides in everyone of us so that *"greater works"* can be accomplished (see John 14:12-14). The Church is the mobilized ministry of Jesus as He strategically places us and determines what we'll do in the Kingdom (see Acts 17:24-28; First Corinthians 12). The Church is the manifested ministry of Jesus as the evidence of Jesus' presence and power are seen and experienced by the world (see Mark 16:15-18).

Being accountable to our Christianity also means doing our jobs as Christ would do them, living our lives as God would live them — because He is doing and being and living in us and through us. What would Jesus do? We really don't need a bracelet on our wrist to remind us. If we carry the Spirit of Christ within us, then we should know what it is He would do.

At the beginning, in Antioch, the word *Christian* carried the connotation of being a "little Christ." The believers there reminded people of Christ. Perhaps it is time to ask how we are representing Christ. Are we accountable to our Christianity? How do our churches represent Christ to the community? While the "churched" population in America is declining, the "unchurched" population is exploding, with many of these people having had a previous church experience. What does this mean? Could it be that the Church is not properly representing Christ? People need to encounter Christ in us and through us by our Christ-like actions. That's being accountable to our Christianity!

Loving in Our Conduct

Even though I am free of the demands and expectations of everyone, I have voluntarily become a servant to any and all in order to reach a wide range of people.　　　First Corinthians 9:19, MES

Finally, if we want our ministry to be real, we must be loving in our conduct toward others. This is the example Christ gave us; there is no other way.

Real love sees the needs of others and will serve those needs. Ultimately, it was love that motivated God's conduct toward the world when He sent His Son Jesus Christ to die for us. Showing love toward others is how we can relate the reality of Jesus in a real way. After all, John the Beloved summarized God in one simple, yet profound, statement: *God is love* (see First John 4:16).

What was Paul talking about to the Corinthian church and to the Church of all times in this scripture passage?

Love is patient, love is kind and is not jealous; love does not brag and is not arrogant, does not act unbecomingly; it does not seek its own, is not provoked, does not take into account a wrong suffered, does not rejoice in unrighteousness, but rejoices with the truth; bears all things, believes all things, hopes all things, endures all things.
　　　First Corinthians 13:4-7

He was explaining that love is what compelled him to reach out to others. Love compelled him to preach the Gospel. He would later write that love is the only way we can really see how to conduct ourselves.

Love is active. Not content to lie hidden within, love seeks expression. We can find our expression of love as we serve the needs of others. A genuine love for God will engender a genuine love for others. As our love for God overflows, it naturally splashes onto those around us. We find ourselves looking for ways to serve others — even people we don't really like very well. We look forward to each expression of love, knowing that as we show love to those around us, we are truly showing God how we love Him.

"This is how much God loved the world: He gave his Son, his one and only Son. And this is why: so that no one need be destroyed; by believing in him, anyone can have a whole and lasting life." John 3:16, MES

Love is the motivation for ministry! Love that embraces people is love that has first of all embraced God. It is difficult to put your arms around God, but not so very hard to hug another human being. The difficulty arises when there are those you cannot seem to embrace. We call them "those people." You know, "those people" who live on the street, or "those people" who commit crimes and are on parole, or "those people" who aren't very clean.

Unfortunately, there are a lot of "those people." But I'll tell you a secret: We are all "those people." We may be "those people" who don't keep a commitment, or "those people" who quickly look the other way when they see a need, or "those people who…"; you can fill in the blank! But God so loved "those people" that He sent His Son for them. How can we love "those people" that God loves? We can do it by realizing that He loves us, and by loving the fact that He does.

When people come to me and say, "I'm having a hard time loving this or that person. What should I do?" I say, "Fall more in love with God!" Because when we fall more in love with God, we fall more in love with what and who God loves! Love acts with acceptance, not on worthiness. None of us deserves God's love, but we all desperately need it.

One of the hallmarks of the second Acts Church will be its loving compassion for the lost, the poor, and the sick. We need the compassion of Christ! Throughout the gospels, we read the accounts of Jesus traveling through the towns and villages teaching and preaching the Good News. Through all of the accounts runs the thread of His compassion.

He healed the people, He fed them, He comforted them, He raised their dead.

We read about Jesus at the height of His ministry in Matthew chapter nine. In this one chapter alone, He healed a paralytic, He called Matthew to be His disciple, and He taught, healed the sick, raised the dead, cast out a demon, and went about the towns proclaiming the Gospel and healing people.

Now, the disciples had seen all of this as they walked with Jesus. One of their primary functions at that point probably was making sure Jesus had some room in which to minister. He was being mobbed! But obviously, Jesus — the God of everywhere and every time confined to a man's body — looked around and was overwhelmed by the magnitude of human need. And so He sat down on a rock in some obscure village and said, "Brothers, don't you see? Can't you see the magnitude of the need of these people? They are lost and without direction. More helpers are needed. Will you help Me?" (See Matthew 9:37-38.) "Will you partner with Me in My ministry?" is still the call of God to His Church!

There is as much human need in the world today as there has ever been. I know. I've seen it, from the United States to India to South America to Africa. God's heart-cry is going out today: "More workers are needed! Who will go and represent the compassion of Jesus in the world?"

As we serve others with a loving heart, we are truly ministering as Christ would have us minister. May we bless the Lord by offering real ministry that draws others close to Him.

A true New Testament church in the twenty-first century will be a REAL church, one that is *relevant* to its culture, *effective* in its commission, *accountable* to its Christianity, and *loving* in its conduct. Is your church a REAL church? If not, begin today to get REAL!

[Chapter Fourteen]
Facilitating Worship Gatherings

But about midnight Paul and Silas were praying and singing hymns of praise to God, and the prisoners were listening to them; and suddenly there came a great earthquake, so that the foundations of the prison house were shaken; and immediately all the doors were opened and everyone's chains were unfastened. Acts 16:25-26

We have looked at the strategic plan the Lord has given us for establishing a second Acts church, including strategic New Testament preaching, prayer, purpose, and people. We have looked at how the church is formed through relationships, through passion, and through recognizing each person's unique FORM for ministry. We've noted the importance of doing ministry in a REAL way. Now we will take a deeper look at the seven foundational pillars and see how to establish the church firmly upon these biblical truths and how to facilitate these ministries.

The first of these foundational pillars is devotion to God. This finds its expression in worship and in worship gatherings as we come together to corporately encounter the Presence of God.

We have been created for worship. We know God's Presence more easily in times of worship. When Paul and Silas worshiped, the chains fell off, the bondage was shattered. You see, something happens when we come together to worship the Lord. The Presence of God is invited into our lives and into the life of the church as we corporately worship our Lord.

Worship is not an event; it is the experience of our lives as believers. Worship is how we relate to God's majesty. *Worship* means "ascribing worth to." So when we worship, we are ascribing worth to God, We are lifting Him up above all other things in our lives; we are giving Him the place of preeminence. When we worship, we see His Kingdom come into our midst (see Psalm 22:3).

The Foundation of Worship

Then God said, "Let Us make man in Our image, according to Our likeness; and let them rule over the fish of the sea and over the birds of the sky and over the cattle and over all the earth, and over every creeping thing that creeps on the earth."   Genesis 1:26

After all had been created, man was given dominion over the planet. Amazingly, Adam and Eve violated God's trust and lost not only that rulership, but also the close relationship with God that they had known. Instead of continuing in their positions as God's kingdom partners, they had bowed before Satan, who cunningly bilked man out of the deed to the planet. Satan became *"the god of this world"* (see Luke 4:5-7; Second Corinthians 4:4, Galatians 1:4) and continues to rob man of God's glory.

Fortunately for us, God was not content to allow man to continue in this state. So He set the stage for redemption, beginning the process of restoration of relationship and, ultimately, rulership. Through the establishment of the Levitical priesthood, a tribe of Israel was set apart to God to usher people into His presence through the offering of the blood of bulls and goats. But man still did not live in obedience to God's Law, leading to even further subjugation.

After a period of slavery to Egypt, the Lord brought His people out of captivity. He led them to Mount Sinai. We think of this as the place where Moses received the Ten Commandments, and so it was. But Israel camped for a year and a half at Mount Sinai, the Mountain of His Holiness. There the people learned to worship.

At Mount Sinai, the Lord instructed Israel in worship: in how to approach Him, in how to come before Him in righteousness and holiness and a right spirit. He taught them through the elements of the Tabernacle and the garments of the priests. Worship was introduced to the people of God. This was God's proclamation to the earth: "I will have a dwelling place!" Wherever people are worshiping God, there He will be. He lives within the praises of His people.

But God knew that man would never be able to walk with Him in his own strength, so He invited man to come into a more intimate relationship with Him.

The kingdom of Israel was established under Saul several centuries later. But under David's leadership, the kingdom reached its largest territorial boundaries. More importantly, David expanded the borders of worship. He began to introduce new elements into Israel's worship. David opened his heart to God. He didn't care what he looked like or

174

what he sounded like. He had a heart after God; his love for the Lord compelled him to lead his people into new realms of worship.

Just as David's intimate relationship with God resulted in expanded boundaries of territory and worship, so the Church's territory expands in direct proportion to its movement and expansion into worship. That's why bringing people together in worship gatherings for the purpose of "offering themselves as living sacrifices" is so important.

As worship was expanded, glory was revealed. In the Old Testament, God's presence filled the Temple. Yet that Temple was later destroyed. In the New Testament, God Himself came to tabernacle with man. The sinless One came and dwelt among us. The planet was penetrated with the sinless Christ, who passed the test Adam failed. As a result, Jesus established another race, a chosen generation that would once again rule and reign with Him over the planet.

Yet just as the Old Testament Temple was destroyed, in the New Testament man tried to destroy Jesus, the heavenly Tabernacle. But He rebuilt the true Temple when He rose from the dead. And glory was released on the face of the earth. That is why all in Heaven fall on their faces before God and before the Lamb, crying, "Worthy, worthy is the Lamb!"

Adam failed. He did not walk in obedience; he could not maintain what God had given him, but yielded it to Satan.

But the sinless One has established a new chosen race, a holy nation, a royal priesthood (see First Peter 2:9). He has created living stones, whom He now brings together to build the House of God. He causes those who have received new life to come together as a dwelling place of God. And when we come together to worship God, the King comes into our midst (see Psalm 22:3), bringing His heavenly Kingdom to earth.

Formation of Worshipers as the House of God

> ... *in whom you also are being built together into a dwelling of God in the Spirit.* Ephesians 2:22

> *Do you not know that you are a temple of God and that the Spirit of God dwells in you?* First Corinthians 3:16

We know that as believers, we are a dwelling place for God. We understand that He lives within us. But have we truly grasped what this means?

If God really lives within us, then we should be radically representing and releasing God's Presence and power on the earth. As "temples of the Holy Spirit," we should be powerhouses filled with God's power to overcome the kingdom of darkness!

The exciting thing about all of this is that ... it's true! God really does live within us! We really are powerhouses in the spirit! But we don't live like that because we do not believe that it is truth. Can we begin to lay hold of this? Can we begin to bring our churches into this truth? Think of it: The Church is not merely a lot of people coming together; it is a group of spiritual powerhouses coming together to worship and to intercede and to overcome the enemy. What a wondrous picture! No wonder Satan tries continually to blind our eyes to this truth. If we step out in this, we can take back lives, take back cities and take back nations because we are moving out in worship and expanding Kingdom boundaries for the glory of God!

Yet we are like Israel in the days of the kings. Israel had a Temple — a wonderful Temple, at that. Yet they came to regard it not as a place of worship and reverence, but as a storehouse. They cluttered it up with so many things that they could no longer even find the Word of God in there. How tragic! They had forgotten what the Temple was meant for.

We need our Josiahs! The Church is crying out for someone with that spirit of renewal. The Church needs a Josiah to come and tell us to clean out the Temple so we can again restore it to its rightful place. As leaders, we must allow the Spirit of God to clean the clutter out of our own lives. Then we can stand before the people and challenge and encourage them to clean up their lives in order to become the Temple of the Holy Spirit. Then we will experience a New Testament Church that God's glory will abide in.

The Facilitation of Worship in the House of God

[Jesus said] *"But an hour is coming, and now is, when the true worshipers will worship the Father in spirit and truth; for such people the Father seeks to be His worshipers. God is spirit, and those who worship Him must worship in spirit and truth."* John 4:23-24

When we come together in worship, God is there. And "God things" happen when God is present. When we come with an attitude of expectancy, God will move among us as He is enthroned on our praises (see Psalm 22:3).

We come together in worship gatherings to worship the Lord together in spirit and in truth. To do this, we must humble ourselves before God and allow Him to lift us up (see First Peter 5:6). We have the responsibility to invite the presence of God into our lives by submitting to Him. And we must be full of the Spirit and not the flesh, by honestly going after God with all that is within us.

Have you ever wondered why Jesus taught His disciples to pray, "Thy Kingdom come. Thy will be done on earth as it is in Heaven"? (See Matthew 6:10.) Is it because it's poetic? Not at all. It's because it is powerful! When we worship the King, this prayer is answered in our lives. The Kingdom of God comes and His will is done. He resides in our praises, bringing His Kingdom into the place of praise.

Yet You are holy, O You who are enthroned upon the praises of Israel.
Psalm 22:3

Wherever there is worship, there is a release of divine power! This creates a place for God's rule to be reinstated and affirmed, releasing the power of the Kingdom of Heaven on earth (Matthew 16:18-20). And then we can expect a shaking, a fresh breeze of the Spirit, and the freeing of those who have been imprisoned.

Worship Reveals Purpose

If we look to the pattern of the New Testament Church, we see that worship gatherings have three key elements: We come together to praise, *"making a joyful noise unto the Lord."* We come together for prayer, to *"make our petitions known to the Lord."* And we come together to hear the Word of the Lord through preaching, *"making God's Word known."* These three elements, praise, prayer, and the preaching of God's Word, are crucial to any worship gathering. In any such meeting, we can expect revelation in each of these three areas.

Worship is not an event; it is an experience. Worship is not a program or a portion of a service; it is about who we are and how we live before the Lord daily. When we worship, we can expect the revelation of God's Presence through praise. This is the Lord among us! He enlightens His Word to us as we are in His Presence. Emmanuel, God is with us, is realized when the spiritually and physically blind receive sight, when the spiritually and physically lame rise up and walk, and when the spiritually and physically oppressed are set free!

We are a worship gathering when we show up expecting God to show up and show us His kingdom. All true ministry flows out of the presence of God, who is the most faithful of all ministers.

The life of a church can rise no higher than the people's worship of God. If the people are limited in their worship, then they will have a limited sense of God. But if they participate in an overwhelming, div-ing-in-with-all-I've-got worship, then God Himself will come diving into their midst in power and will move freely and without hindrance.

Worship Restores People

There is a profound sense of a lack of fulfillment, of purpose in people's lives. Man was created to worship something; he will find some-thing to worship. So we rush back and forth trying to find fulfillment in whatever we can find. We try to fill ourselves with possessions or people or job status, but we are left with an even larger hole inside, a reality of unfulfillment. This is true of everyone; it's true of both the churched population and the unchurched population.

But God wants to bring restoration, to reestablish what sin has ru-ined. He works in us, bringing fulfillment to us. We can see restoration and satisfaction in our lives as we come to Him in worship. It is God who is bringing restoration to our lives. And it is God who is filling us with His Spirit so we can be fulfilled — only then can we be fully satis-fied.

Worship isn't just to bring pleasure to the Lord; there is a reciprocal effect. As we reach up to God in worship, He reaches down to impart His holiness into our lives. He brings completion to the places where we have lacked. When we ascribe all worth to God, we are recognizing that He alone can complete us and restore us to our intended passion, purpose and power for being.

The path into His Presence and the means by which we receive pur-pose, and restoration are described by James:

Submit therefore to God. Resist the devil and he will flee from you.
Draw near to God and He will draw near to you. … Humble yourselves
in the presence of the Lord, and He will exalt you.   James 4:7-8, 10

Have you ever noticed that two people can attend the same meet-ing, yet one will be blessed by God and the other will not? Why is that? The answer is simple: it is because one person has drawn near to God, while the other has not. Sometimes people say, "God never moves in my life." The first thing I wonder is, "Well, have you moved out toward Him lately? Have you humbled yourself before Him?"P Word, when we do these things, He will come to us and will lift us up.

Worship gatherings, regardless of when and what size, are those appointments and places for people to experience revitalization. They may come with broken-down faith and dreams, broken-down marriages and relationships, broken-down finances, and broken-down bodies, but in His Presence, they can find wholeness and hope.

Worship Restricts Pride

We cannot come before God with an arrogant, conceited spirit. The only way to God is to come in surrender of self and in humility.

David, after his sin with Bathsheba, cried out:

Create in me a clean heart, O God,
And renew a steadfast spirit within me.
Do not cast me away from Your presence
And do not take Your Holy Spirit from me.   Psalm 51:10-11

Even after a time of great sin, when David came before the Lord in true humbleness of heart and repentance, God received him and brought restoration to him. Certainly when we sin, there are consequences. We call that the law of sowing and reaping. But God can even take that consequence and use it for good in our lives if we will allow Him to do so.

Often our worship gatherings are not all they could be because we come holding onto our fears, which we then hide behind facades of pride. Fear and pride are closely connected, and they can prevent us from drawing close to God. Why would anyone choose not to draw close to Him? Because of fear and pride: fear of what He might want to do in our lives, and pride in not letting Him do it. Fear and pride are both tools and tactics of the devil, and the only way to overcome them is to first submit to God and then you can resist the devil and he will flee from you (see James 4:7-8).

People are still surprisingly similar to Adam and Eve. Because of our sin nature, we still try to hide from God. Week after week, our churches are full of people trying to hide from God. Worship requires the humbling of self and the exaltation of God — the exact opposite of what the flesh desires.

Where there is an atmosphere of true spiritual worship, there will be submission to the authority of God by leadership and congregation alike, and the Spirit of the Lord will take over. Why is this so? Since worship restricts pride, it develops a people who will submit to divine authority in the church. As we come together in worship gatherings in this way, we become a true dwelling place for God — submitting to God's leading, the leading of the leadership of the church, and to one another.

Worship Releases Power

[Jesus said] *"I also say to you that you are Peter, and upon this rock I will build My church; and the gates of Hades will not overpower it. I will give you the keys of the kingdom of heaven; and whatever you bind on earth shall have been bound in heaven, and whatever you loose on earth shall have been loosed in heaven."*   Matthew 16:18-19

Who will build the Church? *"Unless the* LORD *builds the house, they labor in vain who build it"* (Psalm 127:1, NKJ). Unless Jesus is building the house, it isn't His House. Unless God has taken over the House and He is building it on His power, promises, and purposes for the Church, then it's not His House. If we want our churches to be His House, we had better let Him take over.

I believe that worship is one of the most significant, powerful keys of the Kingdom. Worship gatherings are a point of participation in what God has already accomplished: His rule and reign over all things. Since Jesus already has "all authority," all of God's power has already been released. But there still must be a point of participation on our part to release on earth what has already been released in Heaven. That "point of participation" is the place where we come together in a worship gathering and *"enter into His gates with thanksgiving and His courts with praise."*

The release of God's power is contingent upon a people who will worship. Worshipers make the way for God's Presence and power to be released. And when we come together in worship, we can expect people to be released by God's power, because it facilitates His Presence among us.

Every element of our gatherings, from prayer to praise to preaching, must be facilitated *"in spirit and in truth"* by *"the Spirit of Truth."*

[Chapter Fifteen]
Facilitating LIFE Groups

Now a Jew named Apollos, an Alexandrian by birth, an eloquent man, came to Ephesus; and he was mighty in the Scriptures. This man had been instructed in the way of the Lord; and being fervent in spirit, he was speaking and teaching accurately the things concerning Jesus, being acquainted only with the baptism of John; and he began to speak out boldly in the synagogue. But when Priscilla and Aquila heard him, they took him aside and explained to him the way of God more accurately.
Acts 18:24-26

Spiritual growth involves change. If you're not changing, you're not growing. The second Acts Church is a church that promotes spiritual growth.

We find an example of how change and growth can occur in the second Acts church in chapter eighteen of the book of Acts.

Here we find that Apollos, a Jew from Alexandria in northern Africa, had come to Ephesus. Apollos was a Christian, a devout believer who in his zeal and love for the Lord was teaching the Scriptures. But even though he was *"mighty in the Scriptures,"* he was not yet fully developed in his spiritual life. He was missing some things in his understanding of what God had done and was doing at the time.

Apollos was teaching the baptism of John. This is what he knew at the time. He had not yet heard of the baptism in the Holy Spirit. Now, the New Testament Church was built on the empowerment of the Spirit of God. Yet somehow Apollos was somewhat lacking in his knowledge of what God was doing in the Church at that time. This man undoubtedly loved God. But he lacked something in his knowledge and in his spiritual maturity. The same can be said of many in our churches, as well as in leadership.

Now, Aquila and Priscilla were friends of Paul. They had met Paul in Corinth, when he was there on one of his missionary journeys. We don't know whether they had already become believers when they met Paul, or if Paul had introduced them to the Lord. Either way, they were drawn to this apostle, and they helped to encourage him in his ministry. They had invited Paul to stay with them in their home, as they too were tent-makers. Later, they journeyed with him to Syria.

It's evident that this couple had a heart for the Church. They were probably tremendous prayer warriors. They were people who encouraged others, who came alongside others to help and support them in their ministries and in their spiritual development. They had done this with Paul, and they would do the same for Apollos.

Aquila and Priscilla had moved from Corinth to Ephesus, and were instrumental in the expansion of the Kingdom in Ephesus through Paul's ministry. This is because they continued to do what they had done with Paul. We can consider them as some of the first small group leaders in the New Testament Church. They were obviously in the habit of inviting people into their home so they could mentor them and help them to grow in the Lord.

Now, they were there when Apollos was preaching. How did they respond? Did they jump up in the middle of his teaching and say, "Hey, Apollos! There's more to it than that!" No, they didn't. They waited until an appropriate time. Then they came to him in love. They probably spoke to him with kindness: "Hey, that's a great word. You're doing a great job! It's obvious you love Jesus. But do you realize that there are some other things God is doing? We'd like to share that with you." And in love they showed him a more complete way.

Priscilla and Aquila tended to stay in the background. There is no record of their preaching a sermon, leading worship, or even moving in the prophetic. But I am sure they prayed for Paul and his ministry, and they seem to have had a heart to disciple converts, to fellowship with and to mentor those they could help.

These were people who understood spiritual growth and who weren't afraid to help people. They understood that it was not enough to gain converts — we are called to make disciples. They understood that this was a process that would take time. And they were willing to sacrifice of their time to do the work to which the Lord had called them. These were faithful people.

Jesus gave us the purpose of the Church: *"Go and make disciples of all the nations."* He gave us the process: *"teaching them to observe all that I commanded you."* (See Matthew 28:19-20.) Jesus was speaking this to His disciples, with whom He had spent three intensive years in a teaching environment. He had taught them and mentored them, helping them grow to be mature spiritual leaders. After He had spent so much time with them, watched them minister, poured so much of Himself into their lives, then He said, *"Teach them just as I have taught you."* This describes the process of mentoring. Being a mentor is, simply, the practice of teaching others what you yourself have been taught. From whom did Jesus learn? He learned from the Father:

Therefore Jesus answered and was saying to them, "Truly, truly, I say to you, the Son can do nothing of Himself, unless it is something He sees the Father doing; for whatever the Father does, these things the Son also does in like manner. For the Father loves the Son, and shows Him all things that He Himself is doing; and the Father will show Him greater works than these, so that you will marvel."　　John 5:19-20

Paul wrote of this same principle to Timothy:

The things which you have heard from me in the presence of many witnesses, entrust these to faithful men who will be able to teach others also.　　Second Timothy 2:2

Everyone needs a mentor or those they can learn from. Everyone. If we want to grow spiritually, we need to find someone who has traveled a bit farther down life's road, someone whose life is bearing obvious fruit, and who is learning from others. As we spend time with such people and learn from them, we grow in the things of God that they have learned. And as we grow, we find someone else who isn't as far along as we are and begin to teach him or her the things we have learned. Jesus modeled this process, and so did the New Testament Church. The second Acts Church will do well to follow this pattern.

One of the ways we can encourage Christian witness, fellowship, and the mentoring process is by establishing small groups. Our local church uses LIFE groups. Believing that Christians grow best in the context of strategic associations and relationships, we encourage all members of the body to be involved in a LIFE group. The purpose of the group is explained by its acronym: Living In Focus Everyday. We want to have the proper focus in life and to live in that focus each day. What is our focus? Jesus! We want to keep Him in focus so we can grow to be more like Him every day.

This is best accomplished in a smaller group setting where people are able to interact with and encourage one another. The larger corporate worship gathering does not serve this purpose, as we've already discussed in the previous chapter. The worship gathering is primarily focused on the coming and expansion of God's Kingdom into the community, while LIFE groups prioritize the coming and expansion of God's Kingdom into individual hearts and lives. This is simply because this can be much more focused upon in the smaller setting — much in the model of Jesus and His twelve disciples. The Kingdom came to the crowds through signs, wonders, and miracles, but the Kingdom came to the disciples through personal mentoring by Jesus.

LIFE groups serve to bring people together in a specific, smaller gathering to serve several strategic purposes. LIFE groups serve as teaching centers where people can be taught the truths of God's Word in a practical way as it relates to the dynamics of a particular group. LIFE groups also serve as triage centers where people's needs, whatever they may be, can be sorted out and ministered to by the appropriate ministries. The LIFE groups serve as training centers where people receive training as leaders, or ushers, or deacons, or for whatever purpose a specific group has been formed. They can also serve as a place of support for people with common life situations, such as singles, young parents, married couples, or divorcees. Further, our LIFE groups serve as a testimony center where people can share their stories and faith, inspiring others. Finally, every LIFE group can serve as a "telling others" center where people can hear about Jesus through the hospitality and warmth of true Christians, and perhaps find a door into the church in a neighbor's or coworker's living room.

We were created and designed to grow in the context of relationship. Our relationship with God may be wonderful and exciting; but if we allow ourselves to think it will be just Jesus and us and the Book, we are walking in deception. God designed us for fellowship, both with Him and with other people. In the larger corporate gathering, fellowship is much more difficult, as people can still hide in the crowd. In a much smaller gathering, people cannot go nearly so unnoticed. God is building us into a spiritual house, which is a corporate entity. We grow most effectively and mature most dramatically as believers when we come together in smaller groups of fellowship and relationship with other Christians.

We have a responsibility to continue to grow as Christians. Our prayer each morning should be: "O Lord, please change me and help me to be more like Jesus by the end of this day than I am right now."

Not that I have already obtained it or have already become perfect, but I press on so that I may lay hold of that for which also I was laid hold of by Christ Jesus.   Philippians 3:12

Like Paul, let us press on into the things of God.

Aquila and Priscilla provide an example of how the early Church encouraged spiritual growth in believers and in the church as a whole by coming together in small groups of fellowship and relationship. These small groups played a significant role in the spiritual growth of the church then ... as they will even today.

Spiritual Growth Requires Togetherness

How did Priscilla and Aquila communicate with Apollos? Did they write an anonymous letter? Did they call him? Maybe they sent an e-mail. No. They came together with Apollos and spoke with him personally. They encouraged him and then presented him an opportunity to grow in Christ. According to the Scriptures, they invited Apollos to spend time with them in their home.

We need to consciously create small group opportunities for fellowship and growth. Certainly, Sunday school classes or other ministries can do this. But we also need to purposefully set up small groups, LIFE groups, where people like Priscilla and Aquila can minister. We need to establish ministry and growth outlets for those who say, "Come together with us so that we can all grow and mature in Christ."

My wife and I have been privileged to be in a mentoring relationship with a couple who have gone through things we have not yet gone through. We know that they are there to help us and teach us. And there are those into whose lives we speak.

If we are to grow, we must be in fellowship. We can grow as we come together for corporate meetings on Sunday mornings. But, again, that environment is not really conducive to our being able to ask specific questions or to hone in on specific area of our lives. On the other hand, within a small group of four to eight people, there is a forum in which to speak into one another's lives much more strategically and specifically.

Spiritual Growth Requires Teachability

Apollos was obviously willing to be taught by Aquila and Priscilla. He was willing to speak with them and receive from them as they shared things he had not known. He was willing to learn. Thank God for people like that! This is the only way one can continue to grow and develop into spiritual maturity.

Aquila and Priscilla were qualified to teach Apollos because they, too, were in a position of being taught, as we have seen in their relationship with Paul. The apostle recognized their ministry:

Greet Prisca [Priscilla] *and Aquila, my fellow workers in Christ Jesus, who for my life risked their own necks, to whom not only do I give thanks, but also all the churches of the Gentiles.*   Romans 16:3-4

The churches of Asia greet you. Aquila and Prisca [Priscilla] *greet you heartily in the Lord, with the church that is in their house.*
First Corinthians 16:19

The fact that Apollos' and Aquila and Priscilla's ministries were so effective and so noted in the early Church testifies to the humble and teachable spirit that they obviously maintained. If we want to grow in the Lord, we have to maintain teachable spirits. Yet that is not always what we encounter.

When I was about twenty years old, I went to work for my father-in-law. In order to do the job, I needed to learn how to drive a bull-dozer. My father-in-law tried to teach me. He told me how to run the machine, and what to be careful of. I'm afraid that I wasn't listening too closely. I was thinking, "Come on! How hard can it be? There are only two levers there." So I wasn't paying attention. I had no desire to learn; I already knew it all.

I remember the feeling of getting up into the seat of that bulldozer after he had left. I was in control of that huge machine! It was a guy's dream come true! As I started it up, I paid no attention to one of the last things he had said before he left: "Now, don't forget. This thing weighs about thirty-five tons. Don't get it down into that swampy area over there — bulldozers do sink." So where do you think was the first place I went? Right into that muck and mire. Very shortly it was pulling mud up into the fan, and the motor was locking up. The seat was about six feet off the ground — I'd had to climb up. But when I got off ... well, let's just say I only needed one even step out of the cab to touch the ground. It took three other bulldozers that same size two days to pull that one out. There is a cost to having an unteachable spirit!

Spiritual Growth Requires Truthfulness

Spiritual growth requires truth. We cannot grow if we are walking in falsehood and deception. Part of mentoring others is helping them to walk in truth and uncovering deception wherever the enemy has tried to implant lies.

Aquila and Priscilla knew the truth, for they had been taught by Paul. They passed on what they knew to Apollos so he could become a more effective Christian. The truth that was passed on was the teaching and life of Jesus that was being taught and lived out by people like Paul and Aquila and Priscilla.

Our LIFE groups must be built on the truth of God's Word and on truthfulness in the fellowship and relationships of those who are coming together. In fact, the truth must be the foundation for any fellowship or relationships where Christians come together for the purpose of growing spiritually.

LIFE groups that facilitate spiritual growth can only exist in an atmosphere of transparency, reality, integrity, and honesty. Any lack of truth will hinder, not encourage, growth in the Lord.

Spiritual Growth Requires Trustworthiness

Trustworthiness goes along with truthfulness. We cannot have real trust without truth; we cannot trust someone who is consistently not truthful. Many problems in relationships stem from a breach of trust. Things are kept from one another, and trust is eroded. And when trust is violated, it takes time to heal. Truth builds trust over time.

Apollos needed to be able to trust Aquila and Priscilla in order to submit to their leadership and mentorship. Apparently, Aquila and Priscilla had a proven ministry when they first spoke with Apollos that enabled him to initially trust them. After all, they were close friends and ministry partners with Paul, which certainly contributed considerably to the trust factor.

Unquestionably, as Aquila and Priscilla ministered in truth to Apollos, sharing Jesus' life and words, he grew to trust them even more. An obvious spirit of trustworthiness developed between these three as they continued to come together in fellowship and relationship. This resulted in accelerated spiritual growth in all involved, as it always will when these dynamics are present.

LIFE groups create an environment where people can come together and learn to trust God and one another, because of the truth that is being fostered in the group. Truth is the foundation on which trust is built, and trust forms relationships. LIFE groups built on truth form trustworthy relationships that will soon produce mature believers. These mature believers will then produce mature ministries.

Spiritual Growth Requires Time

The small group dynamic is prevalent throughout the book of Acts. People frequently came together in small groups in each other's homes. They prayed, they shared, they learned. They grew in spirit. I believe this is one of the missing dynamics in the Church today. Too often we don't take the time to come together. We think we're too busy, and then we wonder why we find ourselves growing apart from one another. Separation from worldliness is part of God's sanctification process. But separation from others in this Body of Christ is a scheme of Satan!

Notice how Jesus spent three years investing His time into the lives of His disciples. Then they could invest into others' lives, who could in turn invest into others' lives. This is how the Kingdom is designed to grow. Each one reach one and teach one!

Although the Scriptures do not give a lot of detail concerning the amount of time Apollos spent with Aquila and Priscilla, we do know that they had an established ministry, and a church that met in their home. It is not unreasonable to believe that Apollos did spend time with them more than once.

Obviously, Aquila and Priscilla had been ministered to and taught by someone else who was willing to spend time with them. We know that Paul was one of these people. In turn, they were more than willing to spend time with Apollos and others to help facilitate their spiritual growth. Paul's mention of the couple in subsequent letters is likely a good indication of how Aquila and Priscilla continued to facilitate spiritual growth in believers and churches by taking the time to come together with others to do so.

Natural physical growth occurs over time, and spiritual growth is no different. In order to be successful, LIFE groups must involve individuals who choose to commit their time to coming together with one another to encourage spiritual growth. Group members must be committed to one another and to developing their relationships.

Functioning properly, LIFE groups can help to bring life and maturity to the body of Christ, facilitating spiritual growth.

[Chapter Sixteen]
Facilitating Strategic Prayer and Spiritual Warfare

Even those I will bring to My holy mountain and make them joyful in My house of prayer. Their burnt offerings and their sacrifices will be acceptable on My altar; for My house will be called a house of prayer for all the peoples." Isaiah 56:7

It isn't enough just to talk about the things that are necessary for the second Acts Church to arise. God is calling us to action. He is leading us in ways that are unconventional and unfamiliar. We are coming to a place of total dependency on God. And we are not coming to that place without significant opposition.

These are not ordinary days. I am convinced in my spirit that these are the days of the fulfillment of the Word of God. The Lord is moving through people of His Presence, for we are living in a day when He is separating His true Church unto Himself. These are days when God is uniting the Body of Christ in strategic apostolic networks regardless of denomination. God is concerned with the hearts of men. He is seeking those who will follow after Him, not only with our words, but with the attitudes of our hearts and the actions of our lives.

But that kind of resolve is only found in hearts that are fully committed to God. This kind of dedication and determination is discovered only in those who have developed a warrior mindset. It is found only in those who are committed to walking in daily relationship with the Captain of our Salvation, not in a sterile state that hinges upon intellectual assent to the power of Christ. Lives of this commitment are lives that are steeped in strategic prayer and spiritual warfare.

Jesus clearly said that His House would be a house of prayer (see Luke 19:46). This is still His heart: that His House would be a place of prayer, a place of spirit meeting Spirit.

The early Church recognized some facts that we would do well to acknowledge. First, they realized that their work in advancing the Kingdom of God would be met with strong resistance.

"And from the days of John the Baptist until now the kingdom of heaven suffers violence, and violent men take it by force."   Matthew 11:12

The New Testament believers understood that they were involved in spiritual warfare. Unlike many Christians today, they also seemed to take a long-term view of this warfare. We tend to want to win battles quickly and be done with it; but a battle is not a war. We must understand that it takes more than a day or two of prayer to defeat the enemy in many situations. Oftentimes, victory or defeat hinges on having and securing the right orders for the mission.

I live in the area where the bloodiest battle of the American Civil War occurred — the Battle of Antietam. Over 23,000 men were killed or injured. Interestingly, the outcome of that battle, and perhaps even the outcome of the entire war, could have been significantly different if "Special Order No. 191" had not been lost.

In the annals of military intelligence, there is nothing quite like the "Lost Order." Civil War historians are at a loss to fully explain the significance of this "opportunity of a lifetime" that fell into the hands of the Union Army. Special Order No. 191 was the official designation of General Robert E. Lee's strategic plan for the fall campaign of 1862, and it was key to hastening the defeat of the Union Army. With this particular battle plan, Lee was prepared to finish the fight with a southern victory.

Within Special Order No. 191 were very specific details regarding the movements of six of the nine Confederate divisions under the direction of General Stonewall Jackson. Lee's staff prepared copies of Special Order No. 191 for each of the commanding officers involved, dispatching them by courier. Each copy listed all of the details of Lee's strategy for the final blow, was marked "confidential," and was signed by Lee himself.

All copies of the order were delivered without event except for one. The copy addressed to Major D.H. Hill had been wrapped around three cigars, for Hill was known to enjoy a good smoke. Hill's copy of Special Order No. 191 never arrived. Rather, Hill received a copy of the copy from Stonewall Jackson, from whom he'd been receiving orders all along. As a result, no alarm was ever raised back at headquarters over the lack of a delivery receipt addressed to Hill. Most historians believe that the copy of Special Order No. 191 had simply been dropped by the courier, who contrived an excuse for not having a receipt to verify delivery.

The Union Army under General George McClellan was at a loss as to where to strike the Confederates. Their intelligence was confusing and unreliable. However, two soldiers making camp with their regiments along the Monocacy River chanced upon a bulky envelope containing the document wrapped around the cigars. When the "find" was delivered to McClellan, it changed the course of history! As the two armies engaged on September 17 at the Battle of Antietam, the Confederates were dealt a severe blow that began to turn back the tide of the Confederate victories. Finding the enemy's plans had poured hope and life back into the Union Army, for now they knew where, when, and how to attack to overcome the enemy.[1]

As you know, the Church is involved in a great spiritual war between the Kingdom of God and the kingdom of Hell. The armies of Heaven and Hell are on the move to advance each one's cause. God has written the greatest war strategy for victory of all time, sent by His Son, signed in His blood, and successfully executed when Jesus rose from the dead and empowered His Church. Yet for centuries, the Church has staggered under the blows of the enemy, not knowing where, when and how to attack to bring decisive defeat to the enemy. The world has reviled us because we have appeared pointless and powerless. Sadly, it seems much of the Church has lost her orders by carelessly not holding on to the Great Commission. As a result, there has been too much defeat, too many casualties, and too much wrestling *"against flesh and blood"* (Ephesians 6:12). Many leaders and many churches have lost their way and are losing the fight because they've lost their orders!

Thankfully in these last days, our Superior Officer is reminding us where to find those orders and restoring to us the strategic weapons and tactics He has given us to secure our victory! With special orders and special weapons in hand, the Church embodies the power, authority, and victory of Heaven. As a heavenly army, we must now move out to eradicate the devil and his demonic forces from lives, communities, regions, and nations!

Still, despite having been eternally defeated by Christ, the enemy is developing his own strategic plans every day to hinder the Church in its advancement and expansion into the world. Yes, the war has been won by virtue of Christ's death and resurrection — He has the keys to death, Hell, and the grave (see Revelation 1:18). However, as long as Satan is still legally on the loose, battles over territory for both souls and cities will continue to be fought. We call this spiritual warfare.

In the Old Testament, Elisha had knowledge of the enemy's schemes and was able to warn the people of God and to develop a strategic plan for victory (see Second Kings 6:8-23). So too, the New Testament Church understood the tactics of the devil and was able to overcome him (see Acts 4:23-31). Today, the twenty-first century New Testament Church is able to gain spiritual insight into the enemy's plans and realize spiritual victories because she has secured her Great Order and is carrying it out through SWAT Operations. And the course of history is being changed!

SWAT Operations

In the secular world, SWAT Teams are specialized units of police officers called upon to deal with unusually difficult situations through the use of *Special Weapons And Tactics*. In our church, we also have specialized units. We call our prayer ministries SWAT Operations (Spiritual Warfare Attack Teams and Spiritual Warfare Action Times) because that's the mindset the Church needs to have if we are going to see the expansion of the Kingdom of God. Strategic prayer is a very powerful means by which we wage war *"against the rulers, against the authorities, against the powers of this dark world and against the spiritual forces of evil in the heavenly realms* (Ephesians 6:12, NIV) that desire to not only impede the progress of the Church, but to stop it altogether. The Church is called to be on the offensive, asserting the authority of Jesus Christ, and taking possession of territory in His name. Since this is a spiritual fight, it must be fought through the special weapons and tactics of strategic prayer and spiritual warfare.

So, what are some of these special weapons and tactics necessary to facilitating victory and expanding God's Kingdom?

The Church Prepares for War Through Fasting

But also some of the Jewish exorcists, who went from place to place, attempted to name over those who had the evil spirits the name of the Lord Jesus, saying, "I adjure you by Jesus whom Paul preaches." Seven sons of one Sceva, a Jewish chief priest, were doing this. And the evil spirit answered and said to them, "I recognize Jesus, and I know about Paul, but who are you?"And the man, in whom was the evil spirit, leaped on them and subdued all of them and overpowered them, so that they fled out of that house naked and wounded. Acts 19:13-16

Those sons of Sceva certainly are an example for us! We need to be people of His Presence, walking in the Spirit of God.

You can name the name: "In the name of Jesus." You can speak the formula: "In the name of Jesus whom Paul preaches." And still you can lay hands on people and see no healing. You can speak over people and see no fruit. You can come up against things that you had never expected. And the enemy will laugh as he comes against you.

You see, it's not enough to have a name and a formula. We must be people of His Presence. Jesus Himself told His disciples on more than one occasion that if they expected to see demoniacs delivered and people healed of diseases when they laid their hands on them, then they had to move their prayer to another level: the level of prayer and fasting.

Often when we consider fasting, we think of going without food for a time. Or we may think of giving up only certain foods or activities. But fasting isn't about our sacrifices. It's about His sacrifice. Fasting involves coming closer to Jesus. It isn't about our giving something up; it is about our gaining more of Him. Fasting is coming away to a place where we are willing to do whatever it takes to gain more of Him. This is a vital special weapon and tactic of strategic prayer in our spiritual warfare.

There are several reasons for fasting. First, we fast to humble and chasten our souls. We must walk softly before our God, not being arrogant or full of pride. Sometimes we must fast to place our spirits in a proper posture before God.

But as for me, when they were sick, my clothing was sackcloth; I humbled my soul with fasting; and my prayer kept returning to my bosom.
Psalm 35:13

God gives grace to the humble, and only after we have first submitted ourselves to God can we resist the devil and cause him to flee (see James 4:6-7). That's why fasting is such a powerful special weapon and tactic. It enables spiritual breakthrough and victory.

Fasting brings our minds under the blood of Jesus. It enables us to more clearly see the places where we need the correction of the Lord in our lives. Fasting brings us to a place of humility as we bow at the feet of Jesus, and it places us in a posture of consecration as we separate ourselves unto God.

We also fast when we want to seek God's will on certain matters.

While they were ministering to the Lord and fasting, the Holy Spirit said, "Set apart for Me Barnabas and Saul for the work to which I have called them." Acts 13:2

Perhaps instead of seeking the opinions of all of our friends and relatives, there is only One whose opinion we should seek. There is wisdom in godly counsel, and we should seek the confirmation of what we are hearing from the Lord. But perhaps first we should seek Him, not others' opinions. There are times that we need to be alone with Him and seek His face. After all, God has the strategy we need to facilitate His purposes. Walking in the will and ways of God, so often the result of strategic prayer, is another powerful special weapon and tactic for defeating the enemy.

Another reason to fast is as a point of repentance, an indication of a changed mind. Fasting does not grant us forgiveness; our God does not require acts of contrition before He will forgive. But fasting and prayer can show the seriousness of our intent to change and the depth of our sorrow for our sin.

David therefore inquired of God for the child; and David fasted and went and lay all night on the ground. Second Samuel 12:16

After David's sin with Bathsheba, when the child she bore him lay ill, David fasted before the Lord. Similarly, we can at times fast before the Lord and say, "Lord, I fall short of Your glory. I've failed You. I need to get alone with You so You can know my heart is sincere."

When individual believers and the Church as a corporate entity practice fasting as a point of repentence, we not only experience forgiveness, but we also can receive strategic information from the Lord regarding why we were experiencing defeat. God can then reveal not only the reason for our previous defeat, but also the plan to gain the victory. (See Joshua 7-8.)

The above also provides a final reason to fast: so there can be deliverance from the enemy. Fasting gives us the special weapon and tactic we need to break through spiritual bondages that have held us captive. It enables us to come closer to the Lord, which gives us divine strength.

Finally, be strong in the Lord and in the strength of His might. Put on the full armor of God, so that you will be able to stand firm against the schemes of the devil. Ephesians 6:10-11

Unfortunately, we can also fast for wrong reasons. We can read Jesus' discussion of these in Matthew 6:16-18. We should not fast publicly to impress others with our spirituality. We should not fast to punish ourselves. And we should not fast as a religious exercise to gain God's favor.

Fasting should not be confused with going on a hunger strike. We cannot manipulate God by fasting! Unfortunately, this way of thinking is not unusual in some places. It isn't spoken of in these terms, of course; but beware of people who claim that God "has to" do something because they have fasted, or because fasting has been done in regard to a certain petitioning of the Lord.

Let's be certain that our hearts are right when we fast before the Lord. True fasting is accompanied by a spirit of obedience and prayer. It should always be done with pure motives, that we might separate ourselves to the Lord. If we fast for the wrong reasons, then we have fallen victim to Satan's strategy.

Jesus' Example of Warfare Through Fasting

Jesus emphasized fasting as preparation for spiritual warfare. We see this not only in His instructions to the disciples, but also in His own life. Luke chapter four contains the account of Christ being tempted in the wilderness.

Jesus, full of the Holy Spirit, returned from the Jordan and was led around by the Spirit in the wilderness for forty days, being tempted by the devil. And He ate nothing during those days, and when they had ended, He became hungry. And the devil said to Him, "If You are the Son of God, tell this stone to become bread." And Jesus answered him, "It is written, 'MAN SHALL NOT LIVE ON BREAD ALONE.'" Luke 4:1-4

The first thing we can notice in this passage is that Satan did not begin to tempt Jesus at this point in His fast; he had been tempting Him all along. But as Jesus was coming out of that time of separation to the Father, Satan came to meet Him on the way; he started in again, this time tempting Jesus with food. But fasting put us in a place of humility and trust, releasing God's purposes. Christ placed Himself securely under the protection of the Father as He covered Himself with the Word. In this first temptation, Christ used fasting and God's Word to win His battle with the devil. How powerful the Word of God also is as a special weapon and tactic in gaining victory in spiritual warfare.

And he led Him up and showed Him all the kingdoms of the world in a moment of time. And the devil said to Him, "I will give You all this domain and its glory; for it has been handed over to me, and I give it to whomever I wish. Therefore if You worship before me, it shall all be Yours." Jesus answered him, "It is written, 'You shall worship the Lord your God and serve Him only.'" Luke 4:5-8

Satan tempted a second time regarding just who would serve whom. Ever the liar, he told Jesus that all things were his to give to Jesus, if He would but worship him. However, only the hearts of men can be swayed from kingdom to Kingdom, and these are brought under God's authority as we worship the Lord. Another special weapon and tactic of certain victory in spiritual warfare is to worship and exalt the Lord Jesus Christ as the One and only true King of kings and Lord of lords. Worship of God will be a part of strategic prayer and therefore a powerful special weapon.

And he led Him to Jerusalem and had Him stand on the pinnacle of the temple, and said to Him, "If You are the Son of God, throw Yourself down from here; for it is written, 'He will command His angels concerning You to guard You,' and, 'On their hands they will bear You up, So that You will not strike Your foot against a stone.' "
And Jesus answered and said to him, "It is said, 'You shall not put the Lord your God to the test.' "
When the devil had finished every temptation, he left Him until an opportune time. Luke 4:9-13

This third temptation had to do with attempting to get Jesus to prove Himself. There is a place of presumption in believing that we can make anything happen through prayer. We are given a place in warfare and we are to take it; but at the same time we must understand that God will work things out in His time and according to His will. Our prayer and fasting bring us closer to the Lord, making us stronger in spirit; these things also help us to more clearly hear the special orders that He is speaking to us and to the Church. It is as we pray according to His will that we have the victory, not as we seek to bend Him to our will. Diverting us from doing God's will is Satan's scheme. But doing God's will, realized through strategic prayer, becomes a special weapon and tactic that defeats the devil every time.

God, the Master Strategist, is preparing His Church for battle. There will be warfare in these last days. But we need not fear, for God is calling His Church to preparation. Part of that preparation is in prayer with fasting. There are some battles that will not be won if we neglect this spiritual discipline. For warfare through fasting is indeed a very powerful special weapon and tactic given by God to ensure victory. The second Acts Church will make fasting a priority in the life of the believer and of the local church, preaching and teaching it and, more powerfully — practicing it.

Like the disciples who could not help the demoniac boy, we must listen as Jesus calls us to times of prayer and fasting.

And Jesus rebuked the demon, and it came out of him; and the child was cured from that very hour. Then the disciples came to Jesus privately and said, "Why could we not cast it out?" So Jesus said to them, "Because of your unbelief; for assuredly, I say to you, if you have faith as a mustard seed, you will say to this mountain, 'Move from here to there,' and it will move; and nothing will be impossible for you. However, this kind does not go out except by prayer and fasting."

Matthew 17:18-21, NKJ

Promoting the Intercessors

Are we promoting intercession in our churches? Is the ministry of intercession an established, vital, crucial expression of the body? Or is it left to those who can't really do anything else? How we view intercession is a good gauge of the importance we place on prayer in our lives and in the lives of our churches. Intercession and those who know how to intercede in strategic prayer are other powerful special weapons and tactics of the Church that must be utilized if we are going to expand the Kingdom.

The book of Nehemiah provides an example of the importance of intercession. Nehemiah, cupbearer to the king in the Persian palace, had some visitors. When he had asked about the welfare of the people and of Jerusalem, he found that the people were in great distress. The city wall had been broken down and the gates had been burned. When Nehemiah heard this, he was greatly burdened on behalf of his people.

This servant of the Lord immediately moved into a SWAT mode and turned to prayer. He continued in prayer for four months, interceding before God. He received God's special orders and set out to succeed in them. He also was given the opportunity to intercede before the king. He had such favor with the king that he was allowed to return to Jerusalem to begin to repair and rebuild the wall.

But this idea was not as acceptable to the enemies of Israel as it was to the king. So they came against the work that Nehemiah and the people were doing. Instead of giving up the work, Nehemiah and the builders gave us a beautifully clear picture of intercession. Nehemiah wrote:

> *From that day on, half of my servants carried on the work while half of them held the spears, the shields, the bows and the breastplates; and the captains were behind the whole house of Judah. Those who were rebuilding the wall and those who carried burdens took their load with one hand doing the work and the other holding a weapon. As for the builders, each wore his sword girded at his side as he built, while the trumpeter* [whose job was to sound a warning and rallying call if necessary] *stood near me.*　　　　　　　　　Nehemiah 4:16-18

Nehemiah positioned the builders on the wall, with a sword in one hand for the defense of the Lord's work. Intercessors are those who work to build up the city of God, the Church, by strengthening the walls through their prayer. They also serve as frontline guards to stand in the gap for the Church. Although all can — and should — pray and intercede, there is also a deeper ministry of intercession that is for those who know who they are and the authority they carry in Christ. These are the ones who walk in holiness and purity, careful of what they say and of how they act; in their outward and inner lives, these walk softly before their God.

Thank God for intercessors! Whenever there are those who cannot pray for themselves, or those who are involved in things they should not be, then the intercessors are at work, binding the work of Hell and loosing the work of God in those lives. Intercession … what a powerful special weapon and tactic to send the enemy fleeing in retreat!

Intercession enables us to execute the will of God. Nehemiah received the favor of the king and was able to execute his plan with the king's authority. Even so, we are given authority by our King to execute His plans, His special orders.

The primary purpose of intercession is not blessing God or thanking Him or praising Him, although all of these may enter in. The main objective is to evict evil and to expand the Kingdom. When we intercede, we stand between another person or persons and whatever it is that Satan is trying to work in their lives and circumstances. The intercessor takes the Word of God and brings it against the places where Hell has people under its power. The intercessors smite the enemy and evict the evil, casting it out in Jesus' name. They assault the powers of darkness, going forth with the *"high praises of God in their mouths and a two-edged sword in their hands"* (see Psalm 149:6).

Oh, that God's Church would be a people of intercession! Oh, that our churches would see the need for this special weapon and tactic of strategic prayer. How much would be gained for the Kingdom of God — and lost by the enemy. A second Acts church sees intercession as crucially important to prospering and protecting the work of the church. Intercession is a SWAT operation!

Putting on All of God's Armor

Therefore, take up the full armor of God, so that you will be able to resist in the evil day, and having done everything, to stand firm. Stand firm therefore, HAVING GIRDED YOUR LOINS WITH TRUTH, *and* HAVING PUT ON THE BREASTPLATE OF RIGHTEOUSNESS, *and having shod* YOUR FEET WITH THE PREPARATION OF THE GOSPEL OF PEACE; *in addition to all, taking up the shield of faith with which you will be able to extinguish all the flaming arrows of the evil one. And take* THE HELMET OF SALVATION, *and the sword of the Spirit, which is the word of God.*   Ephesians 6:13-17

How can we expand the power of prayer? We can do it by putting on *"the full armor of God."* This is the only way to remain in readiness for spiritual warfare and to fight to win. The armor of God is another all-powerful special weapon and tactic provided by God, and necessary in strategic prayer to stand against the enemy and bring him down in defeat.

The belt of truth is what secures all the other pieces of our armor. The breastplate, or body armor, of righteousness protects our heart, our most vital area. The feet covered *"with the preparation of the gospel of peace"* speak of a readiness to preach the Good News that keeps us on the right course and keeps our feet away from the land mines the enemy will lay in our path. The helmet of salvation keeps our minds focused on our Hope and Joy of salvation, Jesus Christ. Finally, the sword of the Spirit is the Word of God that stops the enemy in his tracks.

Now we may have put these things on, and we may even think we look pretty good in the outfit. But one thing is lacking. We cannot be warriors if we haven't experienced warfare. What good is armor if we aren't going into battle? We must put on the armor and run to join the fray!

You see, we are called to the battle to enforce the victory of Jesus

Christ. We are prepared through prayer and fasting, which enables us to see the battle from a spiritual perspective. When we have put on the armor of God and have been praying without ceasing, then we will be expanding the Kingdom!

How can we realize the victory in spiritual warfare? We submit to God in prayer, acknowledging our dependence on Him, receiving His special orders and His revelation into the enemy's schemes. When information from God is secured and followed, we will obtain total victory. Then we can resist the devil and watch him flee.

Submit therefore to God. Resist the devil and he will flee from you.   James 4:7

Let us be a people of prayer and of intercession. And let's be those who *"draw near to God."* How can we facilitate victory in spiritual warfare? We can do it through prayer — a powerful weapon and tactic!

---

1 Stephen W. Sears,"Lost and Found: Special Order No. 191," (Prime Media Group: September 2002) pp. 14-20 in *Antietam Commemorative Issue.*

[Chapter Seventeen]
Facilitating the Discipleship Process

And the hand of the Lord was with them, and a large number who believed turned to the Lord. The news about them reached the ears of the church at Jerusalem, and they sent Barnabas off to Antioch. Then when he arrived and witnessed the grace of God, he rejoiced and began to encourage them all with resolute heart to remain true to the Lord; for he was a good man, and full of the Holy Spirit and of faith. And considerable numbers were brought to the Lord. And he left for Tarsus to look for Saul; and when he had found him, he brought him to Antioch. And for an entire year they met with the church and taught considerable numbers; and the disciples were first called Christians in Antioch.

Acts 11:21-26

In the past, the concept of "discipleship" has sometimes garnered negative connotations. There have been times when the idea has been abused, so that discipleship became an excuse on the part of unscrupulous leaders to control people's lives.

Obviously, such was not the biblical model.

A true biblical discipleship process helps to encourage the development of Christian character through the process of changing minds. The believers at Antioch, those newly called "Christians," are part of the pattern God has given for the Church. They had committed themselves to developing godly character through a discipleship process that was changing the way they thought, causing them to act like Christ. They were meeting with Barnabas and Saul for a year, learning and receiving from these godly men. Under this teaching, their minds and characters were being transformed. They no longer acted as they had before. They didn't speak as they used to speak, because they didn't even think as they had previously done. The change was so marked that those around them began, derisively, to call them "little Christs."

Developing Christian Character

Still, there is no point in entering into a discipleship process if we don't know what the result will be. What are we aiming for? What are the hallmarks of Christian character? Paul spoke of these as *"the fruit of the Spirit"* when he wrote to the church at Galatia.

> *But I say, walk by the Spirit, and you will not carry out the desire of the flesh. For the flesh sets its desire against the Spirit, and the Spirit against the flesh; for these are in opposition to one another, so that you may not do the things that you please. But if you are led by the Spirit, you are not under the Law. ... But the fruit of the Spirit is love, joy, peace, patience, kindness, goodness, faithfulness, gentleness, self-control; against such things there is no law. Now those who belong to Christ Jesus have crucified the flesh with its passions and desires.*
> *If we live by the Spirit, let us also walk by the Spirit. Let us not become boastful, challenging one another, envying one another.*
> Galatians 5:16-18, 22-26

According to Paul, Christian character is marked by love that is benevolent and unconditional. This is the love of God as expressed through His people, a love that blesses without holding back or asking for anything in return. Christian character brings a joy that is exceedingly glad. It is not giddy or superficial, but is a gladness of spirit that rejoices in the Lord.

The next quality Paul mentions is a peace that is harmonious. Again, this type of God-peace goes beyond a lack of strife to a place of deep, abiding peace, a sense of well-being that remains regardless of circumstances. The patience that godly character brings is steadfast, and slow to avenge wrongs.

Christian character includes gentleness — not a soft, sugary sweetness, but a true gentleness that is morally good. This type of gentleness covers a strength of spirit and character. Goodness is simply kindness towards others. This is also close to godliness, as "no one is good except God alone" (see Luke 18:19).

Faithfulness is actually a faith that is reliable. This faith remains regardless of circumstance or the whispers of the enemy. It is founded in an abiding relationship with the Lord that produces a faith that is not easily shaken.

Meekness is often misunderstood in our culture. It is seen as weak, as something to be despised. Yet true meekness is a strength, for it takes great determination to yield to the desires of others and to serve as Jesus served, yet without complaining. And temperance is another way of saying "self-control." This can be a difficult trait to maintain, but it yields fruit in its witness to others as well as in preventing so many problems in our own lives.

This fruit of the Spirit is the hallmark of Christian character. It is produced within lives that are filled with the Spirit of God. And although it is planted and imparted by God Himself, it may be cultivated by proper teaching and the discipline of daily living in the Lord.

A Process of Change

Discipleship must be viewed as an ongoing process of placing people's minds in a position to understand so they can change the way they think in order to become more and more like Christ. Paul provides the process for real LIFE (*Living In Focus Everyday*) as a true disciple of Jesus Christ.

Therefore, I urge you, brothers, in view of God's mercy, to offer your bodies as living sacrifices, holy and pleasing to God – this is your spiritual act of worship. Do not conform any longer to the pattern of this world, but be transformed by the renewing of your mind. Then you will be able to test and approve what God's will is – his good, pleasing and perfect will. Romans 12:1-3, NIV

First of all, to be devoted followers of Jesus Christ, people must be encouraged to give themselves to God so they can have abundant LIFE. This is teaching people to *submit* to Jesus Christ as Lord – *"to offer your bodies as living sacrifices."* Many accept Jesus as Savior, but never fully submit to Him as Lord of their lives. Submission, in this regard, is complying with the Word, will and ways of Jesus Christ. The first step every person must make if he or she is going to be a disciple is to submit to the Lord and to the process of discipleship.

The second step in following Jesus as a disciple is to keep stepping away from the pattern of the world and more and more into a new design for LIFE. This is teaching people to *strive* for Christ-likeness – *"this is your spiritual act of worship. Do not conform any longer to the pattern of this world, but be transformed."* Striving to be more like Jesus requires a rigorous, conscientious effort to make the right choices every day. It is choosing to stay steadily up on the "straight and narrow path" rather than travel the "broad way" that the world races down. A disciple must first submit to the Lordship of Jesus Christ and then strive to be daily more like Him in his or her pattern of LIFE.

The third step, as noted by Paul, is to then develop a new process of thinking — thinking like Jesus thinks — *"by the renewing of your mind."* This is teaching people to *study* the Word of God. Study is the application of the mind to the acquisition of knowledge primarily through research and reflection to achieve a new way of thinking and acting. To think and act like God wants us to think and act, we therefore need to study His Word. The Bible is God's principles for LIFE. By ingraining the Word of God in people, they can begin to develop the mindset of Christ. People act like they think. Change on the outside cannot happen until we change the way we think on the inside. The world will be changed by those who are able to change people's minds. That's why the discipleship process is so critical to the church. We are called to make disciples, those who think and therefore act like Christ.

Finally a true disciple of Jesus Christ is someone who has developed the maturity to know the will of God and function in it fully. This is teaching people to *serve* in the ministry that God has for them — *"His good, pleasing, and perfect will."* As people discover and develop their FORM (Focus, Opportunities, Resources, Ministry gifts) for ministry, they can help make the body of Christ a healthy and growing body by doing their part. As people submit to Christ, strive to be more like Him, study His Word so they can think and act like Him, they can then serve His purpose for their lives. This is how the five-fold leadership offices can equip the saints to do the ministry and help the church to grow into maturity.

The discipleship process in the church must be the intentional teaching, training, transitioning and transforming of people through submitting to Jesus Christ as Lord. Only then can the church truly model the concerns, conduct and character of Christ to the world.

There are three phases to the process of developing disciples of Jesus Christ in a second Acts church: commitment, connection, and construction.

A Commitment Process

The commitment process works on two levels: the commitment of the Christian and that of the church. Both of these are crucial if the discipleship process is to be of value.

The process of commitment for the Christian includes three areas. The first of these is the commitment of time. There is no doubt that this is a commitment that gives one pause in today's hurried, harried culture. There are always so many things we need to do, so much that we should be accomplishing. A commitment to come together and to spend time on a regular basis is not something to be taken lightly. For most people, this involves a genuine sacrifice.

But agreeing to come together regularly and spend time together is not enough. If that were all that was needed, we could simply set up basketball leagues and be done with it! No, we need more. We need a commitment to be taught. Believers need to come into the discipleship process with teachable spirits, ready to learn and to grow in God.

Finally, Christians coming into discipleship must commit to staying true. We must walk in truth. There can be no other basis for the sharing of the life of our Lord, who is Truth. We must enter into this process with the intent of honesty and transparency.

On the other hand, the local church also has to make commitments. First, there is the commitment to instruct. It is not enough for people to show up; we must have something substantial to feed them. If they are willing to set aside the time to come, we must make certain that what we have to offer is worth the sacrifice they are making. People who come into the discipleship process may be giving up time at work or time with their families; doubtless they are sacrificing time that could be used elsewhere. Let's be sensitive to that.

Part of the commitment to instruct is preparation. We must be ready ahead of time, we must plan our lessons or topics, we must chart a course. Otherwise, we may meet together week after week and make no progress. We must follow the mandate of scripture:

> *Be diligent* [KJV, study] *to present yourself approved to God as a workman who does not need to be ashamed, accurately handling the word of truth.* Second Timothy 2:15

The second commitment for the church is to invest. If we want to make disciples, we must be ready to make an investment. We are investing time spent in preparation and in spending time with people; we may invest financially in purchasing materials; we will invest in prayer for all who come. There is an emotional investment involved as well. But the investment isn't totally in people; we are investing in the Kingdom of God.

There is also a commitment on the part of the church to involve people. We must involve people who are ready to be discipled. We must also involve those who have gone through the process and are ready to begin to lead others through it.

A Connections Process

The second element of the discipleship process is connecting people in mentoring relationships. We have seen that mentoring is important in shaping the life of the believers, and in passing on the Word of truth. This is a one-on-one relationship, unlike the small groups used in discipling.

In a mentoring situation, it is possible to bring a deeper accountability and also to discuss life areas that may not be mentioned during a small group meeting. Obviously, this requires that only spiritually mature Christians be used as mentors, and that there be oversight of the process.

What is necessary on the part of the believer in entering into the mentoring process? First, the believer must recognize the need to be mentored. He must see that he does have room to grow, and that a mentor can help him, through searching the Word together, through discussion, through prayer, through example. A mentor has been on the path already and so can extend a hand to help. But the believer seeking to grow must still reach out and grasp that outstretched hand.

Second, the believer must understand the importance of being connected and reporting to a mature mentor. Even if a mentor team included Paul, Barnabas, Priscilla, and Aquila, it would not be effective if the younger believer did not show up. He has to take the time to meet together with his mentor. He must be willing to report on how things are going in his life and to do whatever "homework" is required. He must be willing to make changes as needed and to search the Scriptures to encourage his growth in God. If he is not committed to these things, then perhaps he is not a good candidate for the mentorship process.

The final commitment of the believer is to respond honestly to the mentoring situation. Whether things are going well or not, he must share honestly so the mentor can make adjustments, either within the mentoring relationship itself or to the ongoing process.

For the church, the process of mentoring involves making mentoring a priority for Christian development in the church. It is not a program to be started, then dropped, then restarted at will. We are forming relationships, creating connections within the body of Christ. And this is a process that happens over time; mentoring cannot be done within a six-week rotation of teachings. Properly connecting people at the right points is a process that takes time.

In addition, the church must provide a variety of ways for these connections and mentoring to take place. Some mentors will want a book to help direct things; others will simply want to know what topics should be covered. Some may be more comfortable with a Bible study, others with a text, and others with a workbook. And some will simply want to come together to talk and pray. There are as many different styles as there are mentors! After the mentors have been trained, they may be allowed some flexibility to express their ministry. Ideally, mentors will be able to incorporate a variety of teaching methods to best reach those to whom they minister.

Perhaps most crucially, the church has the *responsibility* of connecting and partnering people together in the proper mentoring relationships. A proper mentor must be someone farther along in his or her spiritual journey, able to discern what God is saying and what spiritual forces are at work in various situations. The mentor and the younger believer should, obviously, be of the same sex; however, age similarity is not as crucial. The two must be able to forge a working relationship. There may be some initial awkwardness, but they should be able to come into a genuine friendship. If there is too much of a personality conflict, it may be well to rethink the situation.

A Construction Process

As the Christian is discipled in LIFE groups and mentored on an individual basis by being connected to the right people, he will be developing as a believer. He should be building a life of submission to God's Word, ways, and will in every aspect of living — in family life, in church life and in community life. He should be building a Christ-like life as he strives to become more and more like Jesus in character and conduct. He should be building his life as a servant in the ministry. And he should be developing as a solid, faithful ministry partner of the church. His gifts, his ministry, his role and responsibility — all are facets which need to be constructed and allowed to grow and develop.

What about the church's responsibilities? The leadership team is responsible for constructing the church to be a twenty-first century New Testament church. This will happen through educating the congregation in the Scriptures. They should be equipping the church for ministry. And they should be empowering the church in its mission.

As Christians develop through the commitment, connection, and construction phases of the discipleship process, there are seven pillars that all Christians should be building their life missions on. The church has the role and responsibility of developing and building these seven disciplines in the life of every person God sends to us. These disciplines are: sacrificing to God in worship; fellowship, or surrounding ourselves with other believers; strategic prayer; studying the Word of God; supporting the ministry; serving others' needs; shaping our world for Christ; and sharing the Good News. All of these areas are crucial to building strong, mature believers.

REAL LIFE Commitments Process and the LIFE Institute

We have established in our church the two programs mentioned earlier to ensure that we are truly making disciples, not merely filling pews. These are the REAL LIFE Commitments Process (or RLCP) and the LIFE Institute.

In the RLCP, we teach the vision and mission of the church, the seven foundational pillars of the Christian life and church, the formation of the church through gifted people (which includes the use of a gift assessment to help believers find their places in the body), and the facilitation of the church as people minister in the power of the Holy Spirit in their appointed place.

The LIFE Institute is comprised of classes that cover discipling people from new believers to those in full-time ministry, providing them with the right foundation, formation, and facilitation for LIFE. This process will develop people to be strong Christians in character and conduct.

Throughout all of the training people receive from us, we very intently endeavor to connect people with Christ and with one another, so the church can truly be the multiplied, mobilized, manifested ministry of Jesus in the world!

[Chapter Eighteen]
Facilitating CARE Ministries

"A new commandment I give to you, that you love one another, even as I have loved you, that you also love one another. By this all men will know that you are My disciples, if you have love for one another."
John 13:34-35

The second Acts Church will be a caring Church. Like the early Church, they will be those who express the love of the Father in the things they do as they serve others. Their service springs from the joy and love of the Lord within, not from a sense of duty or compulsion by man.

The early Church exemplified generosity in their caring:

And all those who had believed were together and had all things in common; and they began selling their property and possessions and were sharing them with all, as anyone might have need.
Acts 2:44-45

Now, brethren, we wish to make known to you the grace of God which has been given in the churches of Macedonia, that in a great ordeal of affliction their abundance of joy and their deep poverty overflowed in the wealth of their liberality. For I testify that according to their ability, and beyond their ability, they gave of their own accord.
Second Corinthians 8:1-3

Their generosity did not only show in their financial giving; even when there was no money to share, God was at work to show His love to others through them:

And he began to give them his attention, expecting to receive something from them. But Peter said, "I do not possess silver and gold, but what I do have I give to you: In the name of Jesus Christ the Nazarene – walk!" And seizing him by the right hand, he raised him up; and immediately his feet and his ankles were strengthened. With a leap he stood upright and began to walk; and he entered the temple with them, walking and leaping and praising God. Acts 3:5-8

Goods and finances were shared. Ministry and time were shared. Even in the midst of their own poverty, these early believers gave to help others. Why would they do such a thing? Was this something they had been told to do by man? No. It was prompted by God. As His love overwhelmed them, it overflowed them and poured out to meet the needs of those around them. This is what CARE ministry is all about. CARE ministries are those that serve people's real needs with Compassion, Acceptance, Responsibility, and Excellence.

The Pastor as Caregiver

The pastor and leadership team members must model what it means to live as caregivers. As the shepherding team, the leaders lay down their lives for the sheep. They care for the people's physical needs where warranted, as well as their spiritual needs.

The ministry of the pastor is overwhelmingly one of caring, and churches need leaders who are called and gifted for the pastoral office of Ephesians 4:11. Not every leader fills this office, but there are those who do; such people must be identified so they can step into their proper place in the body. The pastor is the one who gathers the people in and shows them what Jesus is like. He is the person who loves people into the Kingdom. He teaches and shares, helping to train believers. He prays and visits the sick, ministering out of his love for God and for the people He has created. The leadership team, regardless of their individual gifts, support the pastor as he ministers in this way.

There is a great need for the CARE ministries. There are many who feel themselves to be sinking under loads that are too heavy to bear. Because of this, it is important for local churches to spend the necessary time and resources to train those who will serve as pastors or care ministers. These people's gifts can be developed through discipleship training, the connections process, and further training in the Word. The pastor can work closely to help in training those who have pastoral gifts.

Pastors can also model being caregivers as they visit the sick and pray for them, or as they spend time in counseling and prayer with those who are struggling. Providing for the needs of those attending services is another pastoral function, whether that involves overseeing a benevolence fund or setting up a food bank.

Care for the poor needn't be limited to those who are a part of the local church. In fact, as CARE ministries are used to impact the world outside the body, they become a powerful outreach tool. When people see that others really do care for them, that loving one another is not just Christian-speak, then they become willing to develop relationships. Food or clothing banks, crisis pregnancy centers, toy missions, shelters for the homeless, soup kitchens ... ways to serve others are as varied as human needs.

The People as Caregivers

Pastors and leaders are not, however, the only people who are to serve as caregivers within the Body of Christ. They are to serve and to be the models; but they are also responsible to equip the body for service in ministry.

Besides the outreach ministries, there are various ways people can serve within the local church. They can serve as hosts or hostesses and greeters, helping to set the tone of the meeting as they greet people, welcome visitors, and answer questions. Greeters, working with an assimilation pastor, often also help by contacting guests a day or two after a meeting to see if there is any way the church can pray for them or serve them.

People are often needed to help with the giving ministries, both in making the congregation aware of needs and in making sure necessary funds are given to the proper people. They may also oversee the distribution of food or gifts as needed.

Those with servants' hearts will never run out of ways to express their giftings! CARE ministries can help with Sunday school classes; they may assist the worship team by making copies or bringing water; they could be the people who prepare the Communion elements, or shovel the snow, or take meals to those who are ill, or visit the elderly, or drive the church van, or direct parking.

Some of these things may not seem to be very "spiritual." Some may not seem to be very "caring." After all, does it really matter who takes water to the worship team? Well, yes, it does. If the person who does that lowly task has an attitude of love and caring, perhaps he may encourage the team members; perhaps she is praying for the team as she brings the water. It is the same with many of the "small" tasks that need to be done.

But the place where those with caregivers' hearts really shine is in direct interaction with others in ministry that meets their needs.

The Priorities of CARE Ministries

The Brandenburg Gate, a 65 foot high, 213 foot wide and 36 foot thick structure modeled after the Propylaea in Athens, Greece, is located in Berlin, Germany. It was built in 1788 and still stands today, although through the years, it has symbolized several distinct realities. For over a hundred years, it symbolized the status of the esteemed, as only the royal family and their visitors were permitted to use the gate. In the 1930s and 1940s, it became a symbol of frightening demonstrations of Nazi Germany's power. On the night of August 13, 1961, it was closed off by armed forces of the National People's Army and construction of the Berlin Wall began, physically separating East Berlin from West Berlin, but representing the political separation of East Germany from West Germany. The wall was a constant reminder of the division between bondage and freedom. From 1961 to 1989, the Brandenburg Gate remained closed and stood in the "no-man's land" between East Berlin and West Berlin. But in 1989, borders between the two Germanys were opened, and since that time, the Brandenburg Gate has stood at the center and been a symbol of German reunification.

Your church stands as a gate in your community — a gate between the kingdoms of this world and the Kingdom of God. What does it symbolize? Is it a place where only a select few are permitted access? Is it a place where scare tactics are employed to subdue people into submission? Perhaps it is a closed-gate community, keeping in those you want to keep in and keeping out those you want to keep out.

I'll never forget a sign someone told me about one time. It was posted on a wall outside of a convent. It read: "Keep out! No trespassing! Violators wil be prosecuted to the full extent of the law!" But here's the clincher — it was signed, "The Little Sisters of Mercy"! Is your church standing on the issues in no-man's land? Or is it a place that represents reconciliation, restoration, and reformation?

Those at the "gates" of our churches — all of the various ministry partners and ministries that can be encounters with Jesus Christ and entryways into the church — are in reality "gatekeepers." They are those who have the opportunity and responsibility to do good to all people, those in the community, and especially those coming into the family of believers. (See Galatians 6:10.)

Gatekeepers operate their gifts in ministries such as ushers, hostesses, van service, bereavement support, visitation, assimilation, nursery staff, facility care, and community outreach. They are really the "front-line", "first-impression," "face-of-the-church" people who determine whether or not someone's life is going to be opened or closed to the Good News. Their influence is significant. Long before a song has been sung, a Sunday school lesson has been taught, or sermon has been preached, people in your community have already decided whether or not they're coming into your church, or if they're coming back! They have made this decision based on their contact with the people they have encountered first in your church — the gatekeepers!

Compassion

A heart of compassion is essential to anyone, especially a gatekeeper, who desires to be used of the Lord in caring for others. Without that, people will soon become tired and overextended. Caring for people, if not done in love, soon becomes a heavy burden.

> *Jesus was going through all the cities and villages, teaching in their synagogues and proclaiming the gospel of the kingdom, and healing every kind of disease and every kind of sickness.*
> *Seeing the people, He felt compassion for them, because they were distressed and dispirited like sheep without a shepherd. Then He said to His disciples, "The harvest is plentiful, but the workers are few. Therefore beseech the Lord of the harvest to send out workers into His harvest."*
> Matthew 9:35-38

Christ's heart was filled with compassion for the people. As He moved among them, He saw their distress and their hurt. Not only did He minister to them, but He called on others to do so as well. In a real sense, when we are caring for others out of love, compassion, and obedience to what the Lord is asking us to do, then we are colaboring with Christ.

Acceptance

Acceptance is a core part of CARE ministries and the gatekeeper's spirit. When God brings someone to us and says, "Take care of this precious one for Me," we cannot say, "But, Lord! His skin color is different than mine." "She speaks a different language than I do." "He is from a denomination that believes very differently than I do."

He [Jesus] entered Jericho and was passing through. And there was a man called by the name of Zaccheus; he was a chief tax collector and he was rich. Zaccheus was trying to see who Jesus was, and was unable because of the crowd, for he was small in stature. So he ran on ahead and climbed up into a sycamore tree in order to see Him, for He was about to pass through that way. When Jesus came to the place, He looked up and said to him, "Zaccheus, hurry and come down, for today I must stay at your house." And he hurried and came down and received Him gladly. When they saw it, they all began to grumble, saying, "He has gone to be the guest of a man who is a sinner." Luke 19:1-7

How did Jesus respond when He met people who were not the same as He was? He shared a meal with them or visited their homes and offered forgiveness and new life!

Responsibility

A third essential element of CARE ministries and the gatekeeper's mindset is responsibility. Christ spoke of this to Peter after the Resurrection when He met with the disciples, who had been fishing.

So when they had finished breakfast, Jesus said to Simon Peter, "Simon, son of John, do you love Me more than these?" He said to Him, "Yes, Lord; You know that I love You." He said to him, "Tend My lambs." He said to him again a second time, "Simon, son of John, do you love Me?" He said to Him, "Yes, Lord; You know that I love You." He said to him, "Shepherd My sheep." He said to him the third time, "Simon, son of John, do you love Me?" Peter was grieved because He said to him the third time, "Do you love Me?" And he said to Him, "Lord, You know all things; You know that I love You." Jesus said to him, "Tend My sheep. John 21:15-17

Jesus was making sure that Peter understood his responsibility. He was giving Peter a ministry: to feed the sheep. He was to nourish them with the Word, and he was to tend them. Peter was to use his pastoral giftings with the flock Jesus was entrusting to him.

Excellence

The final element of CARE ministry and the gatekeeper's mindset is excellence.

Now at this time while the disciples were increasing in number, a complaint arose on the part of the Hellenistic Jews against the native Hebrews, because their widows were being overlooked in the daily serving of food. So the twelve summoned the congregation of the disciples and said, "It is not desirable for us to neglect the word of God in order to serve tables. Therefore, brethren, select from among you seven men of good reputation, full of the Spirit and of wisdom, whom we may put in charge of this task."   Acts 6:1-3

The leaders here were concerned about the distribution of the food, but they recognized that they were not necessarily the people to oversee the task. So seven men were appointed, people who could do the job, and who would listen to the concerns of the people. These first gatekeepers became an extension of the apostolic leadership. They were definitely a part of CARE ministries, as they served to make sure that all were included and that there was no prejudice or inequity in the distribution. They had to minister with excellence, going beyond what others might do to show the glory of the Lord in the situation. These widows were in need; they had to be treated with equality, regardless of ethnicity. This is what the Lord requires.

CARE ministries and the gatekeepers who implement them play a vital role in the Church. Those who have a heart for the Church are generous, hospitable, mercy-motivated, joyful, and have a passion to reach the lost. They will find many outlets to serve in these kinds of ministries. Their priorities should be to meet people's needs with Compassion, Acceptance, Responsibility and Excellence. As we walk in these things, people's needs are met, and the love of Christ is multiplied, mobilized, and manifested in the earth.

CARE ministries facilitate meeting people's needs by offering a servant's heart. Just as a pastor is an administrator of meeting people's needs, so CARE ministries and gatekeepers administer the compassion, acceptance, responsibility, and excellence of God. A second Acts church will care!

[Chapter Nineteen]
Facilitating Kingdom Expansion

"Go therefore and make disciples of all the nations, baptizing them in the name of the Father and the Son and the Holy Spirit, teaching them to observe all that I commanded you; and lo, I am with you always, even to the end of the age." Matthew 28:19-20

Have you seen any movie trailers lately? You can see them at a theater just before the film you went to watch. Or you can see them on TV or on the Internet. They're the short clips from an upcoming movie — usually the exciting parts — that are designed to make you really want to go see that movie. Trailers are what used to be known as the "preview of coming attractions."

Guess what? You're in a trailer! What is the local church, after all, but a preview of a Coming Attraction? The Attraction! That's right; we are a preview of the coming of Jesus Christ and the setting up of His Kingdom on the earth.

The question is this: How hot are we? Are we capturing the attention of the culture? Will people want to show up early, stand in line at length, and get in on time to experience the "Coming Attraction," the return of Jesus Christ?

But there were some of them, men of Cyprus and Cyrene, who came to Antioch and began speaking to the Greeks also, preaching the Lord Jesus. ... and the disciples were first called Christians in Antioch.
Acts 11:20, 26

Do you recall the beginnings of the church at Antioch? A new move of God had broken out among the Gentiles. Although the leadership of the church at Jerusalem believed it was a move of God, they did not embrace it and continued to minister solely to the Jews.

However, the Word was bearing fruit among the Gentiles in Antioch, and that church was rapidly increasing. Barnabas came from Jerusalem to help with the ministry there. He and Paul began to teach the new converts. As they discipled them, they put them in formation, helping them to find their places in the fulfillment of God's purposes. The church at Antioch was planted; it was a church that would change the world!

A Church of Transformation

A crucial component of facilitating Kingdom expansion is transformation — the process of changing in form, appearance, nature, or character. To expand the Kingdom is to see transformation occurring in people and places.

Do you recall the toys known as "Transformers"? They were very popular a few years ago. The slogan for one of the companies that produced these toys was: "Transformers: More than meets the eye!" Though the toy looked like, say, a truck, it could be changed with a few twists and turns to look like a robot. Well, transformation is like that. It is the process of being changed from one thing to another.

Again, Paul speaks of this transformation in the book of Romans. Here is our foundational scripture for all discipleship:

Therefore I urge you, brethren, by the mercies of God, to present your bodies a living and holy sacrifice, acceptable to God, which is your spiritual service of worship. And do not be conformed to this world, but be transformed by the renewing of your mind, so that you may prove what the will of God is, that which is good and acceptable and perfect.
Romans 12:1-2

We are not to conform or accommodate to the pattern of the age we live in, whose god is the devil (see Second Corinthians 4:4). Instead, we are to enter into a process of change that causes us to become more and more Christ-like in our concerns, character and conduct. For this to happen, our minds must be committed to channels of thinking that are the ideals of the Kingdom of God (see Philippians 4:8).

Transformation — change in people and in places — cannot happen until there is a change in the way people think! When we are endeavoring to expand the Kingdom in people and places, we must realize that all people possess well-rutted roads within their minds, the paths their thoughts travel as they proceed through life.

For some, it may be the path of pain and hurt that their minds constantly travel. For others, it is the street of sexual lust that their minds follow so often. For so many more, it could be the avenue of anger or the boulevard of bitterness, the highway of heartbreak or the freeway of fear. The "god of this age" endeavors to influence people's minds to dwell on that which is ultimately to their destruction. That is the highway that so many are traveling on today.

But that is not the highway to Heaven! Jesus came to show us the way — and He is the Way. His way is to take up residence in a person's life and begin to transform that person by establishing new thoroughfares of thought that lead to abundant life. The expansion of the Kingdom of God begins first in the mind before it results in changed churches and changed communities.

Kingdom expansion means more than merely erecting churches. It encompasses expanding the mind beyond its human liabilities and limits to think of that which is *"exceedingly abundantly above all that we ask or think, according to the power that works in us"* (Ephesians 3:20, NKJ). Kingdom expansion is first and foremost a new way of thinking about oneself, about God, and about the world. We must first allow the Kingdom of God to expand in us personally before we can see God's Kingdom expanded in our communities, cities, and countries.

Kingdom expansion is transformation. The New Testament Church understood the changes that were taking place as God was expanding His Body on the planet through the Church. The Day of Pentecost changed everything! God threw a stick of dynamite into the religious systems and structures of man. And when that dynamite exploded, nothing was the same as it had been!

The distinctive, dynamic purpose of the outpouring of the Spirit in Acts was to empower the Church for ministry. Could it be that God has exploded onto the scene again in this century because everything needs to change? Has our submitted relationship with God become mere selfish religious ritual? Have our churches, once so intense in the Spirit, become institutionalized with the systems of man? Are we more concerned with *Robert's Rules of Order* than with God ordering our steps? Are we forming committees instead of forming Christians? Has prayer been replaced by programs? Are we making disciples or just doing ministry?

Across denominational lines, membership is declining like never before, more churches are closing than ever before, and the number of unchurched people is steadily increasing at an unprecedented rate. There must be a transformation!

God is bursting onto the scene again. This explosion of dynamic proportions is blowing away what has been in the Church to make way for what will be — apostolic people put under apostolic leadership doing five-fold discipleship ministry. The Kingdom of God will expand in people and in places like never before! The case can be made that the Church must recover its New Testament identity and become the people of God pursuing the New Testament pattern and proclaiming the Good News through the power of the Holy Spirit.

As this comes to pass, we shall see that *"all that Jesus began to do and teach"* will again be multiplied, mobilized, and manifested through the Church in every corner of the world (see Acts 1:1). We must move to a new mindset.

A Church of Purpose

The Church that Christ has formed is a Church of purpose. Our vision will determine our actions. Do we have the vision for what He has called us to do? We are to evangelize everyone, everywhere; to empower people; and to expand the Kingdom of God locally, regionally, and globally.

We need to understand that expanding the Kingdom requires apostolic ministry.

> *But I have written very boldly to you on some points so as to remind you again, because of the grace that was given me from God, to be a minister of Christ Jesus to the Gentiles, ministering as a priest the gospel of God, so that my offering of the Gentiles may become acceptable, sanctified by the Holy Spirit. Therefore in Christ Jesus I have found reason for boasting in things pertaining to God. For I will not presume to speak of anything except what Christ has accomplished through me, resulting in the obedience of the Gentiles by word and deed, in the power of signs and wonders, in the power of the Spirit; so that from Jerusalem and round about as far as Illyricum I have fully preached the gospel of Christ. And thus I aspired to preach the gospel, not where Christ was already named, so that I would not build on another man's foundation; but as it is written, "THEY WHO HAD NO NEWS OF HIM SHALL SEE, AND THEY WHO HAVE NOT HEARD SHALL UNDERSTAND."* Romans 15:15-21

I believe *apostolic ministry* may be defined as "taking the responsibility at the local, regional, and global levels of representing Jesus Christ and reproducing Christians who are true disciples." It incorporates recognizing the unique FORM of every person who is converted and releasing them into their predestined places of ministry. Apostolic ministry renews and revitalizes communities through strategic church plants or replants that are founded on the New Testament pattern and power!

When we speak of apostolic ministry, the first person we generally think of is Paul. He was mighty in God and had the office, heart, and spirit of an apostle. He certainly had a heart to teach:

For if I preach the gospel, I have nothing to boast of, for I am under compulsion; for woe is me if I do not preach the gospel.
First Corinthians 9:16

And in his preaching, new works were founded for God throughout the known world.

Paul was highly effective in expanding the Kingdom, for several reasons. First, he *accepted* his apostolic ministry with confident assertion. He was not apologetic about who he was in God or about the ministry with which the Lord had entrusted him.

Second, he *acquitted* his ministry with courageous action. Nowhere in the accounts of the early Church do we see Paul shrinking back from what God allowed him to face.

Third, he *accentuated* his apostolic ministry through strategic apostolic partnerships and networks that rapidly accelerated Kingdom expansion.

Finally, he *accredited* the success of his apostolic ministry to Christ's affirmation. He did not take any credit to himself for all that God accomplished through him.

Once again, we are seeing these same dynamics revisit the Church as God moves expeditiously to expand His Kingdom in this emerging postmodern age.

I believe there are several key elements in expanding the Kingdom through apostolic ministry. We can see these in the lives and ministries of the apostles, particularly Peter and Paul.

We Must Preach Christ

Any other message except the Gospel of Jesus Christ is not "good news!" We can preach good topics with good outlines and good points, but if it isn't all about Jesus Christ the Son of God, Jesus Christ crucified, Jesus Christ risen from the grave, and Jesus Christ Savior and Lord over all, then it's not good enough.

Paul made it clear that his preaching was all about Jesus, as did the other apostles and the New Testament Church. At times, this preaching wasn't popular or politically correct. But it was the only preaching that resulted in redeemed lives. If it is to expand your own kingdom, then preaching what pleases people will serve your purpose. But if it is to expand the Kingdom of God, then preaching Christ is the only message that will have such eternal results. And to preach Christ is to preach truth in the most relevant, effective, accountable, and loving (REAL) manner possible.

But there were some of them, men of Cyprus and Cyrene, who came to Antioch and began speaking to the Greeks also, preaching the Lord Jesus. And the hand of the Lord was with them, and a large number who believed turned to the Lord. Acts 11:20-21

The second Acts Church reaches people by preaching Jesus. The message must be clear: Jesus is our only hope of life! The purpose of discipleship is to change our way of thinking. We must become those who have put on the mind of Christ, that we may share the Gospel of Jesus Christ everywhere, all the time.

Paul's message was consistent:

But we preach Christ crucified, to Jews a stumbling block and to Gentiles foolishness, but to those who are the called, both Jews and Greeks, Christ the power of God and the wisdom of God.
First Corinthians 1:23-24

Paul consistently preached Christ. The Kingdom expands as we exalt the Lord Jesus, and as we bring the good news of the Gospel to the world in a REAL way. Apostolic ministry requires that we first check our message. Are we preaching Christ? Or are we looking to the latest trends, the newest research, the esoteric detail? Our mission is to preach Jesus alone.

The second Acts Church is not about programs, but about promoting Jesus Christ. This Church understands that supernatural power will produce far greater results than natural programs. As believers grow in Christ, they begin to speak as He speaks, think as He thinks, feel as He feels, and act as He acts. As the life of the Lord Jesus is multiplied, mobilized, and manifested in the hearts and lives of those who make up the Church, they will go out to change the world! How will they change it? They'll do it by preaching Jesus in the power and anointing of the Holy Spirit.

We Must Make Converts

The body at Antioch was a church that was converting people to Christ. People were being saved in unprecedented numbers. Evangelism was of utmost concern. (We'll discuss evangelism more in the next chapter.) The church at Antioch was outwardly focused, fixed on bringing their family and friends, as well as so many others, to Jesus for salvation. People were being added to their numbers daily. Can that happen again? It must and it will! As the Church begins to function again in the New Testament pattern and power, we will begin to experience people coming to Christ every day!

Sadly, for many churches and leaders, this is the point where the process ends — having someone repeat the "sinner's" prayer. But if we stop here, we are not fulfilling the purpose of the Church to make disciples. The reason so many see making converts as the climax to their efforts is because it isn't that difficult to lead someone to Jesus. Having that same person become a follower of Jesus is much more difficult because it requires the disciplines of submission to Christ, striving to be like Christ (and unlike the world), studying Christ's life and the Word of God, and serving like Jesus would serve. Evangelism leads people to Jesus, but discipleship is teaching, training, transitioning, and transforming people into followers of Jesus!

We Must Form Christians

As we've noted, it is not enough to make converts; we must also make disciples. We must find each person's unique F.O.R.M (focus, opportunities, resources, and ministry gifts) for ministry.

Since we have gifts that differ according to the grace given to us, each of us is to exercise them accordingly.   Romans 12:6

Part of our task as leaders is to help bring members of the body into formation. We need to teach, disciple, mentor; we are to make disciples who truly yearn to follow in the footsteps of our Lord Jesus. As we minister to others, are they becoming "little Christs"? Are they growing in a vital relationship with the Lord? If so, then we are doing well in bringing them into their proper formation to serve in the body; for it is as we mature and grow in love for the Lord that we become truly effective in ministry.

The example of the church at Antioch is that of a body that was making disciples and helping people discover their giftedness for ministry. This church was filled with gifted people involved in ministry. This is obvious from the kind of impact this church was having. The Kingdom is expanded as people become disciplined to think and act like Christ — and then the world is changed!

We Must Empower the Called

Antioch was releasing people into ministry, especially leadership. Acts 13:1 speaks of the fact that there were *"prophets and teachers"* in the church. I believe there were probably many prophets and teachers, as well as apostles and evangelists and pastors. Based on Paul's pastoral letters, the pattern was that elders were appointed, as were deacons and other leaders. Today, we need to recognize those whom God has anointed for leadership. We must appoint them accordingly. Again, there should be a process of identifying and training leaders to fulfill their roles and responsibilities in the church. Preaching Christ, making converts, and forming Christians will result in the recognition of leaders.

We Must Plant Churches

While they were ministering to the Lord and fasting, the Holy Spirit said, "Set apart for Me Barnabas and Saul for the work to which I have called them." Then, when they had fasted and prayed and laid their hands on them, they sent them away.   Acts 13:2-3

When they had appointed elders for them in every church, having prayed with fasting, they commended them to the Lord in whom they had believed.   Acts 14:23

We cannot simply sit back inside our nice, cozy church buildings and wait for the people to come streaming in. No; that's not the way to reach people. The biblical pattern is for churches to send people out to reach the lost and expand the Kingdom. Why do we gather together on Sunday? I believe it is so that we can send people back out to make disciples. The "called-out ones" are to be transformed into the "sent-out ones."

God's plan is for His Church to grow supernaturally. He wants to replicate the pattern and power of the New Testament Church throughout the world. And He will use apostolic people for that purpose.

In order for second Acts churches to function in this way, they must formulate a plan for sending people out to form the church in other areas. The leadership team must have a Kingdom expansion strategy. This will include such things as investigating a strategic place. Where is God directing and leading? Is this the strategic time for that particular area? We must identify the strategic people to send out to that place. Are the processes in place for making disciples and for beginning a branch church? Are there others with whom we might partner in beginning this new work?

If we are serious about fulfilling the purpose Christ gave us in the Great Commission, then Kingdom expansion and evangelism must drive the Church's agenda.

So then, those who had received his [Peter's] word were baptized; and that day there were added about three thousand souls. They were continually devoting themselves to the apostles' teaching and to fellowship, to the breaking of bread and to prayer.   Acts 2:41-42

As Christ was preached, people came to believe in Him. The early Church continually saw new lives birthed into the Kingdom. I believe this is one of the blessings we will be able to see as the second Acts Church.

Paul planted churches throughout the then-known world as he traveled on his missionary journeys.

Am I not free? Am I not an apostle? Have I not seen Jesus our Lord? Are you not my work in the Lord? If to others I am not an apostle, at least I am to you; for you are the seal of my apostleship in the Lord.
First Corinthians 9:1-2

As far as Paul was concerned, the "seal" of his apostleship was the churches he had planted. This was what validated his apostleship.

Antioch reproduced itself all over Asia by establishing new church plants. They were setting a pattern: first they preached Christ, and then made converts, then formed Christians, then empowered those called to lead, and finally planted new churches. I believe this is a divine order we are to follow and to implement. No new work, whether across town or across the ocean, should be planted unless we are willing and able to follow this divine pattern.

It takes a church with a church-planting passion to plant a church. This may sound obvious, but apparently it isn't. Too often, districts and denominations try to plant new churches with all good intent, only to find that unless a local church takes on the responsibility of parenting that church plant, it will be significantly underdeveloped and stunted in its growth. Somehow, there must be a transformation in our thinking. We need an infusion of the apostolic into the lifeblood of the Church. After all, the very essence of the New Testament Church is apostolic, birthed through the blood of Jesus, the foremost Apostle, to be a Body that is reproductive, multiplying, mobilizing, manifesting, and expanding in the earth!

We Must Impact Cultures

I have become all things to all men, so that I may by all means save some. I do all things for the sake of the gospel, so that I may become a fellow partaker of it.　　　　　　　First Corinthians 9:22-23

There are times when we must echo Paul and *"become all things to all men,"* that we might win some to Christ.

And for an entire year they met with the church and taught considerable numbers; and the disciples were first called Christians in Antioch.
Acts 11:26

The Church at Antioch offers us an example, a pattern for church life. That word *Christian* is important. There is a difference between a believer and a Christian. A believer is someone who believes in the Good News of Jesus Christ. He affirms by faith that it is true. He is walking in relationship with God and is on his way to Heaven. But a Christian is a "little Christ." He is one who daily lives in such a way that others see Jesus through his life.

What happened when the believers in Antioch were living this way? Others around them could see it. These disciples did not call themselves Christians; others did. They could see a difference in the lives of these Christians. As these believers lived lives of obedience and purpose, *"the hand of the Lord was on them."* They were doing the greater things of which Christ spoke! And they changed the world.

Their culture was penetrated and impacted by Jesus working in and through them. Our culture will be penetrated and impacted in exactly the same way ... if we will make the same commitments and live the same level of Christianity as our brothers and sisters at Antioch did. We have all we need to impact our world. You see, the problem is not with what we believe. It is that, too often, we don't live what we believe outside the walls of the church. As the second Acts Church emerges and changes that, our world will again be turned upside down!

Paul and Barnabas are the most noted of those who were sent out from the church at Antioch to change the world. However, we could easily make the case that this church, and the people in it, were focused on making disciples and impacting the culture around them. Certainly Antioch had been impacted; many scholars believe that over 500,000 came to Christ through the ministry of this one church body. We must be relevant to the culture so we can have the most impact possible in fulfilling our purpose of making disciples.

When the local church is functioning properly, the culture around that church will be significantly impacted as the body represents Jesus Christ in a REAL way! Not long ago, I conducted an informal survey of people on the street of my community concerning what they thought about the churches' impact on the city. Although I was prepared for the responses to be somewhat negative, I really wasn't prepared for how irrelevant most felt the church to be.

I was convicted to the core! I have since set out to see this mindset changed. I'm convinced that the culture will be impacted with the reality of Christ when the church becomes the second Acts church she is intended to be. After all, Jesus said we are to be salt and light. If salt isn't salty and light isn't light, what good are they? They are absolutely worthless. Would we be willing to say that many of our ministries and programs are absolutely worthless and need to be thrown out because they don't measure up to God's standard of purpose? Maybe not, but I hope so!

The problem is that there is a lot of salt and light where Christians congregate, while most of the world is a very unsalty and unlit place! Now, I am not opposed to Christian gatherings and fellowships; just the opposite, in fact. However, at some point we've got to spread ourselves out! As someone has said, "Christians are a lot like manure. Pile them all up in one place and they'll really stink. But spread them out all over and they'll be like fertilizer that causes things to grow!"

We Must Transform Communities

As the apostles went forth preaching the Word and the Church grew in numbers, entire communities were transformed. I believe we will see this happening more and more frequently today as God moves in the earth.

A successful community transformation strategy encompasses God's leaders as they come before Him in repentance, come together with one another for reconciliation, and lead His people in restoration. It requires God's leaders and people coming together in right relationship. Then the leaders and the people together must realize revival and reach out to others. Finally, God's leaders and people will cause community revitalization.

The church at Antioch changed its city! Ephesus became another such community. Philippi, Thessalonica, Philadelphia ... all over the world communities were being transformed by the life-changing power of Jesus Christ. Study the great awakenings of history and you will encounter the same thing — community transformation!

Community transformation is, in and of itself, another process. I believe the process we have just seen brings us to this point. But I envision much more for the churches that are willing to embrace this process.

I can see leaders of churches beginning to come before God in repentance for failure to lead in New Testament pattern and power. I can see those leaders then begin to come together in reconciliation and seek to grow in a partnership for reaching the city. Next, these same leaders will lead their churches to come together in right relationship with other churches from which they have been separated through church splits or due to majoring on minor doctrinal differences. I can see revival fire beginning to burn in these leaders, in their churches, and in their communities as these leaders and their churches begin to reach out to the hurting, the lonely, the abused, the neglected, the hated, the despised, the scorned and begin to bring them into an atmosphere of love, health, and belonging. I can see these leaders and these churches revitalizing communities and changing the world.

Can you see it, too? Look! There is a second Acts Church emerging in this twenty-first century! She is preaching Christ, making converts, forming Christians, empowering the called, planting churches, impacting cultures, and transforming communities in the most relevant, effective, accountable, and loving ways possible! I can see my church being a church like that. And I can see yours being a church like that too!

The Expansion Management Team

The second Acts Church is to encourage Kingdom expansion through a process of planting churches. As leaders of local churches with a vision and mission strategy to *"make disciples of all nations,"* it should be our desire to send forth those whom the Lord may call to help lead the church in expanding the Kingdom into all the world.

Our local church uses an Expansion Management Team (EMT) to promote church planting. The duties of this team include the training and equipping of national leaders and pastors; identification of potential church planters; evangelism; exploring other possibilities or strategies for Kingdom expansion; providing resources to plant churches; and providing ministry support for all church plants, branch churches, or network churches.

As the EMT begins a new work, they need to strategically identify what is needed to support that work, that it may flourish as God intends. At our church, we call this our LIFE support strategy. This strategy enables the EMT to identify the vision and mission of the new work. And they need to ask what is working and what isn't and make or suggest changes accordingly.

A Church of Strategic Prayer

Above all, praying for God's direction is one of the most important aspects of the strategic process as second Acts churches work in the area of Kingdom expansion. We are colaboring with Christ, and all that we do should be under His direction.

Unless the LORD builds the house,
They labor in vain who build it;
Unless the LORD guards the city,
The watchman keeps awake in vain. Psalm 127:1

We know that the Lord is building His House; we also need to know that what we are building is part of His House and His plan.

All other aspects of strategic planning in Kingdom expansion — preparing leadership, working with other people or ministries, planting churches, impacting the culture — must flow from a place of prayer if they are to be effective for the Kingdom.

"What are we going to do today?" Expand the Kingdom by transforming people and places through a strategic process of preaching Christ, making converts, forming Christians, empowering the called, planting churches, impacting cultures, and transforming communities!

[Chapter Twenty]
Facilitating Evangelism Efforts

And He said to them, "Go into all the world and preach the gospel to all creation."   Mark 16:15

Evangelism is not what we think it is. It is not an event or a program or even the primary purpose of the Church. Evangelism from the biblical perspective is to preach Jesus to everyone, everywhere (see Mark 16:15, TLB, NLT). We know that making disciples is the utmost purpose and priority of the Church, and everything else, especially evangelism, supports this responsibility.

In a very distinct way, evangelism and discipleship are not two different aspects of the Church's agenda. Instead, they are essential to one another and cannot be separated. To make disciples, you need to evangelize. To evangelize is to lead people to Jesus as Savior so they can follow Him as Lord. The Church can never see salvation as the end result of evangelism, but rather it must be viewed as the first step in the disciple-making purpose and process of the Church.

Evangelism ... making disciples ... expanding the Kingdom. This is what the second Acts Church is all about. This is what motivates us. This is our vision. This is our mission. Discipleship is the agenda of the Church. But evangelism must drive that agenda.

Brethren, my heart's desire and my prayer to God for them is for their salvation.   Romans 10:1

People desperately need God. They just don't realize it. The fact is everyone wants to be loved; they want their lives to count for something significant, and in reality, their lives are empty without Christ. Most people are dealing with some kind of past hurt, some form of bitterness, and some measure of guilt. And even more challenging is the reality that most people also fear death. So, every day people try to deal with their dilemmas in any number of nonproductive ways that only cause further debilitation and duress, not to mention ongoing spiritual deception and defeat.

Thrown into the middle of this morass is the Church, the multiplied, mobilized, manifested ministry of Jesus to the masses, and the only real hope of the world. The evangelistic nature of the Spirit compels us to reach out to the wandering and wondering multitudes and bring them into the Kingdom. This is the Father's heart, and He reveals it to us in His Word:

The Lord is not slow about His promise, as some count slowness, but is patient toward you, not wishing for any to perish but for all to come to repentance.   Second Peter 3:9

Repentance is what New Testament ministry is all about. The evangelistic preaching of the New Testament preachers brought people to repentance,which was a change of beliefs and behavior. People's behavior is based on their beliefs. When people believe in Jesus Christ for salvation, their behavior is one of repentance as the result of a changed mind and heart.

Just as behind every wrong behavior or sin is a wrong belief or lie, so behind every right behavior is right belief. That's what evangelism does. It reaches people with the reality of Jesus Christ, resulting in repentant hearts and renewed minds. After all, people cannot change their behavior until they change what they believe. This is evangelism!

Therefore, evangelism must be the lifestyle of the Church. Reaching out to others by preaching the reality of Jesus Christ through the way we think, live, and act is the responsibility of every Christian. When this becomes the mind, heart, and soul of the people in our churches, we will not only take on the personality of the New Testament Church, but we will also experience the same results. Through "some believers," who are not necessarily apostles, prophets or teachers, but who are ordinary people with extraordinary purpose and power, countless lives can come to repentance and be restored to right relationship with God. (See Acts 8:4; 11:19-21.)

Evangelism is not for the evangelists alone. Yes, some will lead the Church in the capacity of an evangelistic office (Ephesians 4:11). But evangelizing — being a witness for the Lord Jesus Christ — is something every professing Christian does every day, whether by design or by default. And what others see, positively or negatively regarding Jesus

Christ, is projected by the way we're thinking, living, and acting as pro-claimed Christians.

What message do we preach with our lives about Jesus? Are we relating the reality of Jesus or are we falsifying the facts about Him? Are people's postmodern beliefs about the Church being irrelevant, ineffective, non-accountable, and unloving valid or unsubstantiated? Or are they, by virtue of experiencing the grace of God as expressed through relevant, effective, accountable, and loving Christians, being drawn to repentance and a renewed mind and restored life?

Lifestyle Evangelism

To live in focus every day as a Christian is to function in every aspect of life as Jesus would, so others will be able to see Jesus in action and perhaps be compelled to accept Him as the only means of living life to the fullest. This deed will be the result of the good deeds of the Church and will become a means of bringing praise and glory to God. This is exactly what Jesus said lifestyle evangelism would accomplish.

"Let your light shine before men in such a way that they may see your good works, and glorify your Father who is in heaven."
Matthew 5:16

People in the Church must recognize the responsibility of sharing Jesus, the Light of the world, with all those who are in darkness and cannot find their way to the truth. That's why we say the world is lost — because people are not where they're supposed to be, which is in God's house as a member of His Family.

Instead, like the prodigal son, they've taken their inheritance, that which will sustain their lives eternally, and wasted it on loose living. Now they are endeavoring to find sustenance by enslaving themselves to those things that only bring a stench to their lives because what they're doing and how they're living is not in submission to the Father's will and is significantly below the Father's standard. (See Luke 15:11-32.)

So, people grope about trying to find significance and remove the stench. But they only become more lost as they continue to process life according to the pattern of the world. They are lost because they are blind to truth!

And even if our gospel is veiled, it is veiled to those who are perishing, in whose case the god of this world has blinded the minds of the

233

unbelieving so that they might not see the light of the gospel of the glory of Christ, who is the image of God. For we do not preach ourselves but Christ Jesus as Lord, and ourselves as your bond-servants for Jesus' sake. For God, who said, "Light shall shine out of darkness," is the One who has shone in our hearts to give the Light of the knowledge of the glory of God in the face of Christ.   Second Corinthians 4:3-6

This reality, the blindness of the world to truth, can be incredibly frustrating to the Church. But it is the ongoing, persevering effort of evangelism, lived out every day in our attitudes and actions, that causes those in the darkness to see the Light!

A man named Ernest who worked for my father-in-law in the coal fields of western Maryland always seemed to have a smile on his face and something good to say to everyone, no matter the situation or circumstance. He didn't carry a big Bible under his arm to work, nor did he pass out tracts to every person who entered the coal yard where he loaded coal. Instead, he carried Jesus in his heart and shared the love of God through his attitude and actions with his coworkers and with those who came to purchase house coal.

One day as he was loading coal onto a truck with a front-end loader, the driver of the truck stopped him and asked, "Are you a Christian?" "Yes, I am," Ernest replied. "How could you tell?" The driver said, "By the glow on your face!" And then he began to share how he had once attended church years before. He shared all the marital problems he had experienced. He told about his bouts with drinking and about his health problems.

Ernest listened with a gentle, compassionate look on his face and tears in his eyes as that man told his life story there on a cold winter day in a coal yard on the side of a mountain. And when the man finished, Ernest put his hand on his shoulder, smiled, and said, "God loves you and cares about your needs. Would you like to invite Him into your heart right now?"

They both bowed their heads, with the activity of the coal yard going on around them, and prayed. A man who had come to purchase two tons of coal went home that day carrying in his heart the One who had purchased his salvation, his peace, and his joy.

As a young man just getting started in the ministry and working for my father-in-law to help pay the bills, I learned a valuable lesson that day. It was a lesson Saint Francis of Assisi also understood when he once said, "Wherever you go preach Jesus and when necessary use words." I had thought you had to thump a Bible on a pulpit and yell out a message of hellfire and brimstone to see people get saved. That day I realized it was all about preaching Jesus every day in every way to everyone you meet. Evangelism is having so much of Jesus in you that His Light shines through you.

For Christians, discipleship is our strength, but evangelism is our spirit! There must be a spirit of evangelism in our churches. A spirit of evangelism that causes us to want to tell everyone, everywhere about Jesus Christ in the most relevant, effective, accountable, loving ways possible, and when necessary, with words! Every Christian has a circle of influence, and it encompasses all those people they encounter where they live, work, shop, and otherwise go about daily life. We must represent Jesus in a REAL way as we go through daily life in the *"cities and villages,"* seeing the *"multitudes,"* and being *"moved with compassion for them"* (see Matthew 9:35-36, NKJ).

The harvest has never been greater, and the twenty-first century New Testament Church must be a Church of harvesters. Many in our churches want to hang back from evangelism. It sounds scary. It seems overwhelming. Believers may fear being rejected, or saying the wrong thing, or sounding too self-righteous. There are so many reasons — excuses, really — that people give for not wanting to evangelize. Many who would never dream of saying, "I'm not on the worship team; therefore I cannot worship" will nevertheless state, "I am not an evangelist; therefore I cannot evangelize."

How can we help them to do the will of the Father? How can we help them to join in, colaboring with God Himself? How can we help them relate Jesus in a REAL way?

First, the leadership team should model soul-winning. We cannot ask others to do what we ourselves are unwilling to do. Evangelism must be a leader's lifestyle. Our attitude, our actions, and when necessary, our words must reflect and relate Jesus to everyone, everywhere, in every way possible. After all, we reproduce who we are, not what we say. We cannot simply implore people on Sunday to go witness, for they will not unless we are spreading the Good News with the example of our own lives. Let's put ourselves on the front line for the sake of the Gospel and for the salvation of souls!

For I am not ashamed of the gospel, for it is the power of God for salvation to everyone who believes, to the Jew first and also to the Greek.

Romans 1:16

Second, every ministry and ministry partner must have an outreach orientation. There is no ministry or ministry partner that does not have at its or his foundation the commission to win the lost. Let's focus in that direction, allowing the Lord to work through each ministry, each gift, each person to accomplish His will.

Third, we need to develop the evangelists. This means we must identify those who have a heart to reach the lost, who love the Lord, who want to see His Kingdom expanded in the earth. There will be those who are called to the office of evangelist listed in Ephesians 4:11. We must help them develop that ministry and train them in how to effectively communicate the Gospel.

Fourth, we must teach and train every person in our church in the purpose, principles, and priorities of lifestyle evangelism. This can be done through evangelism tracks or classes in the discipleship process.

In our church, our evangelism director has developed highly effective teaching resources to train others. This training is a requirement for every person who desires to be a ministry partner in our church, regardless of whether they are called by God as an evangelist or if they will be involved in specific evangelism efforts within the church.

Christians are witnesses, and every believer must be discipled to be a relevant, effective, accountable, and loving representative of Jesus Christ.

Evangelism should be inclusive. By this I mean that events and strategies should include people of all ages, races, professions, social strata. Jesus came for men and women, for the poor and the rich, for the healthy and the ill. Christ came for all, not just for those to whom we may choose to minister!

For the grace of God has appeared, bringing salvation to all men.

Titus 2:11

REAL Ministry

The second Acts Church preaches the Good News to everyone, everywhere. This Church is more concerned with the salvation of souls than with the status quo. This Bride of Christ is more concerned with people than with programs; she is more concerned with giving than with receiving. she is more concerned with leading people to Christ and then helping them to become followers of Christ than with simply holding services and preaching sermons.

When the second Acts Church arises to claim the lost, she will arise in supernatural power and anointing, for she will be walking in the pattern of the New Testament Church. She will be contemporary without compromise regarding the Good News. Her ministry will be relevant, as she takes on the example of Paul:

For though I am free from all men, I have made myself a slave to all, so that I may win more. To the Jews I became as a Jew, so that I might win Jews; to those who are under the Law, as under the Law though not being myself under the Law, so that I might win those who are under the Law; to those who are without law, as without law, though not being without the law of God but under the law of Christ, so that I might win those who are without law. To the weak I became weak, so that I might win the weak; I have become all things to all men, so that I may by all means save some. I do all things for the sake of the gospel, so that I may become a fellow partaker of it.
First Corinthians 9:19-23

She will be effective in reaching people for Christ, for she will communicate the message in an honest way, empowered by the Holy Spirit. She will use a variety of methods and means that are most effective in reaching others with the Good News because she is sensitive to the fact that people need a Savior.

How then will they call on Him in whom they have not believed? How will they believe in Him whom they have not heard? And how will they hear without a preacher? How will they preach unless they are sent? Just as it is written, "HOW BEAUTIFUL ARE THE FEET OF THOSE WHO BRING GOOD NEWS OF GOOD THINGS!" Romans 10:14-15

The Church will be accountable to Christ and to her Christianity. She will walk in integrity, being as a light in the darkness. The character and conduct of Jesus will be visible in her attitudes and actions.

"Arise, shine; for your light has come,
And the glory of the LORD has risen upon you.
For behold, darkness will cover the earth
And deep darkness the peoples;
But the LORD will rise upon you
And His glory will appear upon you.
Nations will come to your light,
And kings to the brightness of your rising." Isaiah 60:1-3

Finally, the second Acts Church will have the proper motivation. She will not be counting numbers; she will be rejoicing in the hearts and souls that are won to her Lord to be saved, healed, and made whole. She will be filled with the compassion of a loving God.

"For God so loved the world, that He gave His only begotten Son, that whoever believes in Him shall not perish, but have eternal life."

John 3:16

The second Acts Church is arising even now with a spirit of evangelism like never before. God is doing a new thing in the earth and He is sending forth harvesters into the harvest.

The fields are ripe and He is already at work. Are you ready to join Him?

Conclusion

Foundation, Formation, and Facilitation

If we are right in suggesting that the second Acts Church is arising in this twenty-first century, then we may be in the initial stages of the greatest move of God the world has ever witnessed. Locally, regionally and globally, apostolic people are coming together in churches, networks, and partnerships, and the purpose, pattern, and power of the New Testament Church is being restored.

The mindset of the Church is changing from a maintenance mentality to a "mobilized for ministry" mentality. The "sheep" are becoming "soldiers." God's anointed and appointed leaders are emerging and leading the Church in a reformation as they get people in formation to go forth and make disciples of all nations.

The Spirit of God is exploding onto the scene perhaps more powerfully than ever before as a rushing, mighty wind of God is blowing through towns, cities, and nations. Jesus is commissioning His Church again, and a renewed apostolic movement of apostolic ministers functioning in apostolic ministry is arising. The Church is recovering her role and responsibility: preaching Christ, making converts, forming Christians, empowering the called, planting churches, impacting cultures, and transforming communities!

The Church is coming together in worship gatherings, LIFE groups, SWAT operations, CARE ministries, discipleship processes, Kingdom expansion, and evangelism efforts. The foundation for New Testament ministry is being laid. The formation of New Testament ministry partners is taking place. The facilitation of New Testament ministry and ministers is happening — "'not by might nor by power, but by My Spirit,' says the LORD" (see Zechariah 4:6, NKJ).

"What are we going to do today, Lord?"

"The same thing we do every day, Church: *Go and make disciples of all nations!*"